THE GOVERNMENT OF MANKIND

THE GOVERNMENT
OF MANKIND

by

J. A. SPENDER

CASSELL AND COMPANY LTD
London, Toronto, Melbourne and Sydney

First Published - *1938*
Second Edition - *1946*

PRINTED IN GREAT BRITAIN BY
LOWE AND BRYDONE PRINTERS LIMITED, LONDON, N.W.10.

446

PREFACE

A FEW months before he was overtaken by his last illness, I found myself in the company of the late Lord Balfour, and in the course of a talk which went back over old times, he asked me in what respect, if any, after forty years of observation of public affairs, my outlook had changed. I said, after a moment's reflection, that when I started out I thought of government as a comparatively simple thing, requiring only that those who took part in it should have a faculty for public speaking and the kind of intellectual distinction valued by universities, but now I thought of it as the most difficult and complicated of all the human arts.

Lord Balfour flattered me by replying that I had expressed one of his own chief thoughts, and something that he said in the talk that followed put into my head the idea of reading again what had been said about this art by sages and philosophers in past time, and seeing how it looked in the light of modern experience. Such as it is, this book is the result. It covers but a small part of the immense literature of the subject; it passes from point to point with only a glance at the intervening spaces; yet even so it trespasses on ground which is the province of experts in archæology, history, philosophy, and theology, and risks rebuke from those who have made a life's study of these subjects. Its aim is, however, the strictly practical one of fetching from the store-house of past wisdom those deposits which seem to have special value and meaning for the world to-day.

If there is any conclusion to which this study tends, it is that government is an art and not a science, an art of a highly experimental kind, probably in its infancy and proceeding by trial and error to ends which it is impossible to foresee. Belief in the existence of a science from which rules and principles may be deduced for the government of mankind seems to me to be one of the most disastrous of the many political myths that have been current in recent years. If there were such a science, nothing would remain for the rest of us but to discover those who were versed in it and to place ourselves unreservedly in their charge. It would be no more sensible to debate with these experts than for the passengers in a train to argue with the engine-driver or (to use Plato's image) for the crew to usurp the functions of the captain of the ship. It is precisely by appearing as experts who have discovered the science of government that the Dictators in the totalitarian States have been enabled to extinguish liberty and democracy. It needs to be said by all who love liberty that government is not a science but an art in which the co-operation of a free people is essential.

I have been asked more than once in the course of my work as a journalist, "why be so persistent in pursuing the war of ideas on paper, when you object so strongly to the ideological war which would fight them out on the battlefield?" It is precisely because I believe violence to be the worst way of either propagating or suppressing ideas that I feel it to be the more urgent to do battle for them on their own ground of argument and reason. Russia, Germany and Italy whose "ideologies" are examined in this book, will find salvation in their own way, and their neighbours will, I hope, never be guilty of the folly of intervening in their domestic politics. But it is a different matter when they proclaim their own doctrines as infallible and decry all others as antiquated and inferior. Here, if only in self-defence, we must take up their challenge, and they cannot complain if we speak with the same freedom about their institutions as they speak about ours. In this great field of public debate, the pen is the appropriate weapon and the battle will eventually be won or lost "on paper," whatever may be the next phase.

Among the many books to which I am indebted, I should like specially to mention Professor James Breasted's *Dawn of Conscience*; Professor Ernest Barker's *Political Thought of Plato and Aristotle*; Dr. T. R. Glover's *From Pericles to Philip*; Dr. Samuel Dill's studies of Roman Society at different periods; Professor G. H. Sabine's *History of Political Theory* (in the American Political Science series); the recently published *Survey of European Civilisation*, by Professor Ferguson and Professor Bruun (of New York University); Mr.

H. A. L. Fisher's *History of Europe* ; and Professor Trevelyan's *History of England*. To these names, though none of my chapters touch his special subjects, I would add that of Dr. Gilbert Murray, who has been to me, as to so many thousands of others, a constant companion in Greek studies.

I have specially to thank Messrs. Charles Scribner for allowing me to quote from Professor Breasted's *Dawn of Conscience*, and the editors and publishers (Messrs. Heinemann) of the Loeb Classical Library for permitting me to make use of their translations. I was tempted at first to make my own translations, but it is, I am sure, a great advantage to the reader to be referred to a standard translation in which he may see the passage quoted in its context and side by side with the original text. Where there are no such references the translations are my own.

CONTENTS

ix

CONTENTS

CHAPTER VIII

SOCRATES AND PLATO

CHAPTER IX

GLEANINGS FROM THE *REPUBLIC*

CHAPTER X

THE LATER PLATO

CONTENTS

CHAPTER XI

ARISTOTLE

CHAPTER XII

ARISTOTLE ON REVOLUTION

CHAPTER XIII

CICERO

CONTENTS

CHAPTER XIV

THE ROMAN EMPIRE IN ACTION

CHAPTER XV

THE COMING OF CHRISTIANITY

CHAPTER XVI

THE WESTERN EMPIRE — LAST PHASE

CHAPTER XVII

ST. AUGUSTINE

CONTENTS

CHAPTER XVIII

CHURCH AND STATE

CHAPTER XIX

THE PORTRAIT OF CHARLEMAGNE

CHAPTER XX

THE HOLY ROMAN EMPIRE

CHAPTER XXI

THE MIDDLE AGES AND DANTE

CONTENTS

CHAPTER XXII

THE END OF A DREAM

CHAPTER XXIII

MACHIAVELLI

CHAPTER XXIV

THE BIRTH OF PARLIAMENT

CHAPTER XXV

THE PORTRAIT OF AN ENGLISHMAN

CHAPTER XXVI

THE GREAT LEVIATHAN

xv

CONTENTS

xvi

CONTENTS

CHAPTER XXXI

THE AMERICAN CONSTITUTION

CHAPTER XXXII

THE OLD RADICALS

CHAPTER XXXIII

MODERN PARLIAMENTARISM

CHAPTER XXXIV

THE AGE OF THE IDEOLOGUES — HEGEL

xvii

CONTENTS

CHAPTER XXXV

THE AGE OF THE IDEOLOGUES — MARX

CHAPTER XXXVI

THE AGE OF THE IDEOLOGUES — FASCISM AND NAZISM

CHAPTER XXXVII

RETROSPECT AND PROSPECT

CHAPTER I

THE BEGINNINGS

I

THE earliest history of man presents itself as three skulls or bits of skulls labelled respectively *Pithecanthropus* (Ape man or Java man) ; *Sinanthropus* (Pekin man) ; *Eoanthropus* (Piltdown or Sussex man). Recently a fourth has been discovered at Fawkham in Kent which seems to be of approximately the same date, and may be labelled " Kentish man."

In the year 1936 the British Association appointed a committee for the further examination of these remains, and the discovery of the relationship, if any, between them. Pending the result of this inquiry, what can be said is that the earliest seem to go back to the Pleistocene and and may be a million years old ; and that while differing from the skulls of the ape-tribe, all four also differ in important respects from those of man as we know him to-day. They are a hint of something that may be called human in the far backward of time, but what sort of life their owners lived and what qualities, if any, they had in common with *Homo sapiens* is beyond guessing.

Between them and us are several ice ages recurring at intervals during the subsequent 900,000 years, but it is not until the third warm interval—anything between 50,000 and 100,000 years ago—that we come again upon the remains of any creature bearing the marks of humanity. Now we are in the early Stone age, and Mousterian or Neanderthal man, as he is called, the man of this period, has left his tracks all over Europe, but especially in France and Spain. Biologically he shows little advance on Piltdown man or Java man. His jaw is still chinless ; he has a projecting bony ridge over his eyes, and a retreating forehead. But the remains found beside him show that

I

he has some of the attributes of human kind. He is one of a community living in caves, using fire and primitive stone tools, and practising some kind of disciplined life. He traps the great beasts, mammoth and woolly rhinoceros, which were then abundant in Europe, drags their carcases to the mouth of his cave and there cuts them up. He seems to have had some kind of religion and belief in a future existence, for he buries his dead most carefully near the hearth, so as to keep them warm, and provides them with tools and joints of meat. How he came to this relative degree of civilization, and with what sets-back owing to the various ice periods can only be guessed, but the highest point he reached seems to have been little above the level of the lowest kind of savages known in modern times.

Then after a comparatively short interval, some 10,000 or 20,000 years, during which the ice seems to have receded and the climate of Europe to have improved somewhat rapidly, we come upon our own species, known generically as Cromagnon man who differs biologically little if at all from modern man, as he is to-day. There are several varieties of him in Europe, of which the Predmostians of East and Central Europe, the Aurignacians and Magdalenians in France and Spain are the chief. All have tools of different kinds. They work bone and ivory as well as flint ; they employ the bow and arrow and the spear-thrower in their hunting ; they cover large tracts of country in pursuit of the great herds of mammoth, reindeer, bison and wild horse which migrate from their summer pastures in Russia and Siberia to winter grazing in Central Europe.

Man has now become an artist. Working by the light of a little burning fat on a slab of stone he paints pictures of the animals he hunts and of himself with bow and arrow in pursuit—pictures which the modern art critic hails as masterpieces. The vast hairy mammoth and the woolly rhinoceros, both long vanished from the scene, come to life again at his touch. The bison and various kinds of deer are seen in lively motion. He models in clay ; carves the figures of animals out of the hard rock and decorates the ivory handles of his weapons with figures and formal patterns which might belong to the finest periods of later art. It is suspected that some of these pictures had a magical significance, but that the artists took pleasure in doing them for their own sake can scarcely be doubted.

2

By this time the climate of Europe had become what is called temperate and progress quickened its pace. By degrees men came out of their caves and built themselves huts and houses of wattle and daub. The family was their unit and their tribes or communities were groups of families. As they advanced they invented new tools, and to the axe added chisels, knives, drills, saws, and whetstones of flint or other hard stone. They also bored a hole in the axe-head and fitted it with a wooden handle. There are different stages in different countries, but, speaking roughly, the period known as the neolithic age covers the Norse settlement on the Danish shore, the age of the Druids in England and France, and that of the lake-dwellers in Switzerland. The latter appear to have led the advance. Living in communities and being comparatively safe from attack by men or beast they had leisure to develop the arts. Their houses were well provided with furniture and implements, wooden pitchers and spoons, dishes, bowls, and jars of pottery made roughly without the wheel, but serving as kettles in which to cook their food. Beginning with the seeds of wild grasses which the women crushed between stones and made into cakes, they went on to sow and reap barley, wheat, and millet. The women learnt the art of spinning flax and provided garments of woven stuff to replace the skin garments of the former time. Goats, sheep, and cattle were domesticated and bred for food ; the plough replaced the hoe, and in due time the ox was harnessed to it. For long man still continued to hunt while women tended the fields, but as the plough superseded the hoe, agriculture too became a man's job, and he settled down with his family to the life of the farmer. Simultaneously there grew up a class of nomads, shepherds, and cattlemen, living a wandering life with their wives and families, driving sheep and cattle from pasture to pasture and not infrequently raiding and harrying the settled farmers.

Men and women were now living a settled life, building towns and developing some form of government. The stone tombs of this age show the importance of the chieftain. The great stone circle of Stonehenge and the stone avenues at Carnac in Brittany suggest religious and community festivals, with games and chariot races

3

CHAPTER II

EGYPT—THE FIRST STEP

I

NATURE may do nothing by leaps, but in one region of the world we seem to pass at a bound from the wattle and daub huts and little stockaded townships of neolithic man to fully developed states and social organizations. This is the valley of the Nile, which, as a cradle of civilization, had unequalled advantages. It was an enclave surrounded on three sides by an impenetrable barrier of desert created by the gradual desiccation of North Africa. The hunters who settled in it had to defend only the one narrow entry from the south. They had been saved from the rigours and vicissitudes of the ice-ages which had checked the progress of European man and scattered him over wide spaces before the oncoming frost. The desiccation of the surrounding country had concentrated the game in their corridor and made it a hunter's paradise. So far as they practised agriculture, the Nile flood gave the soil a miraculous fertility with the minimum of human labour. If in any part of the world life was easy and man had time to spare from the labour of supporting an animal existence, it was on this favoured spot.

We have only faint tokens of how he advanced into the condition in which we find him about the middle of the fourth millennium B.C. He passed from stone to metals somewhere on the far side of 4000 B.C., and at the beginning of this millennium entered into the recognizable state with a centralized government seated at Heliopolis, embracing several million souls, which Professor Breasted has called the " First Union." This brought under one rule the little kingships scattered about the Nile Delta. After a period of conflict with another group in the valley to the south, this First Union was followed by a Second

6

under King Menes, the first name in history—unless by this time Sir Leonard Woolley has discovered an earlier in the Euphrates valley—who became king of United Egypt in the year 3400 B.C. Progress was now rapid and continuous, and in the subsequent centuries we witness the rise of the great society, with its capital at Memphis, which has left behind it the vast monuments and the sites of its cities, palaces, and country houses, which are seen to this day on the banks of the Nile. Even more eloquent in some ways are the unspoilt relics of arts and crafts, unsurpassed of their kind, which survive from this time. As we look at the specimens of the jeweller's art belonging to the earliest dynasties in the Cairo Museum, they seem suddenly to have reached perfection from nowhere, but behind them is evidently a long story of infinite pains and practice and the refinement of skill and taste in centuries of which we have no record.

What is the characteristic of this civilization ? It is through and through theocratic. The State is protected by the Sun-god, the King is descended from him, rejoins him and becomes his equal, if not his superior, after death. The whole order of things is religious. Pyramids, tombs, and temples bear their own witness, and in addition there is the unique record of the pyramid texts, which hold their place as the first written theology in the history of the world. It is an intricate and difficult theology in which inconsistent ideas are combined in very uncertain balance, and the worship of the Sun-god Re is only with great difficulty reconciled with the cult of Osiris. The details must be left to experts, but one feature is of supreme interest to the student of institutions. This is the absorption of the entire State, rulers and subjects alike, in the contemplation of death and the life beyond it. To keep the King alive even though he dies a bodily death is the concentrated effort of the whole community. To this end a vast monument of imperishable stone must be raised over his embalmed body, and he must be provided with food, furniture, and all else that will enable him to carry on life in a manner becoming to his state until a dimly imagined mystical development enables him to mount to the skies and take his place in the divine hierarchy. In the original thought the King alone seems to have had these privileges ; for the vast majority of his subjects the future life was the dim grey limbo which appears later in Hebrew literature as Sheol. But by degrees the nobles joined the king in the upward ascent, and for them also in their various degrees provision for the after-life became imperative. The whole of this ancient society was in this way dedicated to death, and tomb-building became its national industry and its main object in life.

2

From about 3000 to 2750 B.C. each Pharaoh of the third and fourth dynasties spent a large part of his available resources in erecting one or other of the vast Sakkara pyramid tombs which are now seen on the rim of the Sakkara desert or on the Nile bank at Gizeh a little above Cairo. In his soaring self-assertiveness and his determination to out-build death, the King not infrequently failed to complete his own tomb and handed it on to successors, who had to finish it as well as to build their own. Arrears accumulated and more and more of the labour and wealth of the living was absorbed in an exhausting effort to ensure a continued existence for the dead.

Temples were associated with tombs, and with the temples were endowed priests whose business it was to keep the tombs provided with the provisions and amenities thought necessary to sustain the dead in the afterworld, and to perform the ceremonies ordained on anniversaries and festivals. Within the same group of buildings were the King's central offices, consisting of low, sun-baked-brick buildings housing an army of clerks, who kept accounts in papyrus rolls of the taxes paid in produce—grain, cattle, wine, honey, etc.—and forwarded by the local officials from all over Egypt. Surrounding the pyramids were the tombs of the Queens and the tombs of the great nobles, and extending far southwards from the foot of this cemetery was the royal city of Memphis, containing the palace and its parks and gardens and the villas of the officials and nobles. The sculptures on the walls of the tombs, the statues and the funerary offerings, the models of boats, houses, granaries, and shops contained in them, furnish a unique record of this ancient civilization and enable us to realize it far more vividly than almost any that came after.

What was it like ? It was a highly cultured and extremely agreeable life for the rich and noble. They live in charming villas, surrounded by walled gardens in which are shady avenues, pergolas and pools of running water. The walls and ceilings of their rooms are elaborately painted ; their furniture, their drinking vessels, their knives, their spoons are the work of artists and craftsmen ; their wives are adorned with exquisite jewellery. Grace and beauty surround them ; they picture themselves as fatherly and kind, rejoicing in their children, joining in festivals with the humbler people of their estates. The great river brings everything to their doors, providing one straight, simple line of transport along the whole length of the " elongated market-garden " which is their country. For them are the pleasant things of this world, and such provision as may enable them to share the immortality of the Pharaoh in the afterworld.

What for the remaining multitude ? They have the advantage of some sort of justice, for the officials have to proceed by law, and though the code has not survived, there is evidence that it treated them, in theory at least, as equals. But there is evidence of a large number of slaves, and nearly all the common people seem to have been subject to forced labour, if only during the period of high Nile, when they could not be at work in the fields. It was believed in later times that 100,000 men were engaged for twenty years in building the Great Pyramid and the adjacent buildings. The King could requisition their labour for the building not only of his own tomb but of those of his nobles. With a wave of his hand he assigned the revenues of towns and provinces to the tombs of his favourites. There are records which show the revenues of twelve towns appropriated in perpetuity for the tomb of one prince, and of eleven villages and settlements for the tomb of one baron. Vast stores of food and other offerings were daily brought to the tombs, making a waste so flagrant and impoverishing that priests and nobles and even the Pharaoh began surreptitiously to draw on them for the satisfaction of their own needs and the relief of their friends. Before the twenty-eighth century was out, the royal tombs had so multiplied that their maintenance and administration had become impossible ; and even the wealthiest nobles found it difficult to maintain the tombs of their ancestors. This decay of sepulchral piety may be attributed in part, as Breasted attributes it, to a spiritualising of theology which assigned less importance to the fate of the physical body, but it was also beyond doubt the instinctive rejection of an intolerable burden. Let the

9

dead bury their dead and let Egypt live seems in the closing centuries of this period to have been the subconscious thought of the whole people.

As the archæologist unveils the history of the thousand years of the Pyramid period we may find in it many of the features of Europe before the Protestant Reformation. The mass-priest is pre-figured in the tomb and the temple priest, who battens on the piety and super-stition of the people and gradually converts into saleable magic the genuine and simple mysticism of the old faith. As subsequently in Europe, so in Egypt this is but a temporary shoring up of a decaying structure, and in the last years we see a beggared and mendicant priest-hood driven from their comfortable quarters in the cloisters round the temples and huddling together in hovels which finally share the ruin of the temples. Before the end of the period the sixty-mile rampart of pyramids on the margin of the western desert had already become ancient monuments to the living Egyptians.

So ends the first phase of the history of civilized man.

3

Shall we dismiss it as a survival of barbarism from savage times or interpret it as a necessary phase in the purification of religion and the development of organized government ? Professor Breasted, nearing the end of his devoted labour in the cause of this ancient civilization, pleads eloquently for this interpretation and carries a sympathetic reader far on the road with him. His book, *The Dawn of Conscience*, from which I have already quoted, is indispensable to the student of religious and moral origins. But the student of institutions will, I think, look at it from a slightly different angle.

The cult of death had a pragmatic value of great importance for this ancient society. It is no paradox to say that for the Egyptians of this age death provided an object in life which bound them together as one community acknowledging a common purpose. We may surmise that in neolithic society ancestor-worship and tomb-religion played their part in tribal unity, but in Egypt they are the nucleus around which a whole nation practising the relatively advanced arts of the metal-worker built up an organized life. The Pharaoh whose ambi-tion it was to provide himself with a tomb which should defy time and throw all other human monuments into the shade had to order the life of his subjects accordingly. He could not employ 100,000 men for twenty years without laying elaborate plans for requisitioning labour and supplies, assigning their different functions to builders and craftsmen, arranging for transport and housing, building ships to fetch material from overseas, sending expeditions into Africa and Asia to fetch gold, silver, and precious stones or materials for woven fabrics. Under the pyramid-builders Egypt became a "planned" State devoted to immense public works and public buildings. If too greatly prolonged the process might in the end be ruinous, but for several centuries it gave a unique impetus to engineering and building and to the development of arts and crafts. The group of buildings gathered about the Pyramids of Gizeh, to our knowledge of which archæology every year brings a new contribution, tells its own tale. There was on this site somewhere about the year 2700 B.C. such an aggregation of immense stone buildings, such an assemblage of the combined work of artists and craftsmen as in all probability has never been seen again in a similar space.

But Breasted is undoubtedly right in seeing the purification of religion and new ideas of right and wrong emerging in this period. Out of its cult of the dead there gradually arose the idea of a judgment to come in which even the Pharaoh would need to be justified. In the extraordinary document dating from the First Union, *i.e.* about the year 3400 B.C., which Breasted calls the "Memphite Drama," we find the germs of a monotheism in which the Sun-god is the ruling deity, combined with a philosophical theory which anticipates the neo-Platonic doctrine of the Logos. "All things," says the priestly thinker, "came into being through that which the mind thought and the tongue commanded." It is almost the first verse of the first chapter of the Fourth Gospel : "In the beginning was the Word, and the Word was with God, and the Word was God." More important even than this early metaphysics, religion begins for the first time to be associated with good and bad conduct. "Life is given to the one bearing peace and death to the one bearing guilt. He who bears peace does what is loved ; he who bears guilt does what is hated." The appeal as yet is not to an absolute right and wrong but to the social judgment which approves one kind of action and disapproves of another, in fact to a public opinion forming ethical judgments.

If we turn now to the inscriptions on the tombs of the Pyramid age we find that this judgment is founded primarily on a man's behaviour in his family. The departed noble claims that he was a good son and a good brother (apparently taking for granted that he was a good husband) : " I was one beloved of his father, praised of his mother, whom his brothers and sisters loved." But by degrees these ideas spread out from his family to embrace the neighbourhood and finally the community. A baron of the twenty-seventh century writes on his tomb :

I gave bread to all the hungry in my domain ; I clothed him who was naked therein ; I filled its shores with large cattle and its lowlands with small cattle. I satisfied the wolves of the mountain and the fowl of the sky with the flesh of small cattle. . . . I never oppressed one in possession of his property so that he complained of me because of it to the God of my city ; I spake and told that which was good. . . . I speak no lie, for I was one beloved of his father, praised of his mother, excellent in character to his brother and amiable to his sister.

4

As the years go on, these moral mandates become binding on the State officials and even on the Pharaoh. The just vizier is one who never lets his judgment be warped by partiality for his family and friends. Subsequently viziers have even to be warned against the excessive scrupulosity of a certain Kheti, who decided against his kin without considering the merits of the case lest he should be suspected of partiality. In the twenty-eighth century King Userkaf is described as a " doer of Maat "—a word signifying righteousness and truth ; and the same King's vizier claims to have " done righteousness for the King even unto the grave."

This vizier, the great Ptahhotep, has left a series of maxims addressed to his son, which combine worldly wisdom with an almost Hebraic fervour for righteousness and righteous government. I am permitted to draw on Professor Breasted's translation of this document :

Established is the man whose standard is righteousness, who walketh according to its way.

Behold a worthy son whom the God gives renders more than his lord says to him. He does righteousness : his heart acts according to his way.

A hearkener is one whom the God loves, one whom the God hates is one who hearkens not. . . . The wise man rises early to establish himself, but the fool is in trouble. As for the fool who hearkens not, there is none who has done anything for him. He regards wisdom as ignorance, and what is profitable as useless.

If thou art an administrator, be gracious when thou hearest the speech of the petitioner. Do not assail him until he has swept out of his belly what he ought to say to thee. He who is suffering wrong desires that his heart be cheered to accomplish that on account of which he has come. . . . It is an ornament of the heart to hear kindly.

If thou art an administrator issuing ordinances for the multitude, seek for thee every excellent precedent, that the ordinance may endure without error therein. Great is righteousness ; its dispensation endures, nor has it been overthrown since the time of its maker ; for punishment is inflicted on the transgression of its law. . . . Although misfortune may carry away wealth, the power of righteousness is that it endures.

Attain character, make righteousness to flourish and thy children shall live. . . . Precious to a man is the virtue of his son, and good character is a thing remembered.

If thou hast become great after thou wert little, and hast gained possession after thou wert formerly in want, be not unmindful of how it was with thee before. Be not boastful of thy wealth, which has come to thee as a gift of the God. Thou art not greater than another like thee to whom the same has happened. . . . Beware of the days that may come after.

If thou art a successful man establish thy house and take to thyself a wife as the heart's mistress. . . . Fill her body, clothe her back.

Have no knowledge of the former low estate of thy Chief . . . be respectful towards him because of what he has achieved ; for substance cometh not of itself.

Be silent (from untimely speech), for silence is better than teftef flowers. Speak thou when thou knowest that thou solvest difficulties. It is a craftsman who speaks in council and speech is more difficult than any craft.

Be not proud because of thy learning. Take counsel with the unlearned as with the learned, for the limit of a craft is not fixed and there is no craftsman whose work is perfect. Worthy speech is more hidden than greenstone, being found even among slave women at the millstone.

Let thy face be cheerful as long as thou livest. . . . Follow thy desire as long as thou livest. Do not more than is told thee. Shorten not the time of following desire. It is an abomination to encroach upon the time thereof. Take no care daily beyond the maintenance of thy house. When possessions come, follow desire, for possessions are not complete when the owner is harassed.[1]

Thus in the twenty-seventh century B.C. does this ancient Lord Chesterfield instruct his son, combining a mellow and tolerant worldly wisdom with an ethical fervour which will scarcely be found in his eighteenth-century successor. The document is of the highest importance in the history of morals, but its relevance for my present purpose is in the light that it throws on government at this remote age. The writer is the chief official of the Pharaoh, and he assumes that his son too will be an official. He is instructing him not only in the art of living, but in the art of governing, and he bears witness that righteousness, justice, discretion, modesty, and kindness are the qualities to be cultivated by the ruler and official. " Established is the man whose standard is righteousness and who walketh on the way." There is another side to the story, as we shall see presently, but the appearance thus early of an inner witness qualifying and correcting the absolute claims of rulers to the submission of subjects marks a profoundly important stage in the history of what in later times came to be known as the " social contract."

---

[1] Breasted, *op. cit.*, pp. 129–32.

CHAPTER III

EGYPT—EMPIRE AND DOWNFALL

I

THE fall of the "Old Kingdom" about the year 2500 B.C. brought the Pyramid period to an end. Side by side with the civilizing process which had purified men's thoughts, humanized their conduct, and given a moral content to their religion, an inner decay had been at work which seems gradually to have undermined and broken up the central government. Weakened by the monstrous load which its cult of the dead and the necessity of maintaining their tombs had placed upon it and by the perversion and corruption of the swollen priestly and official classes, it seems to have fallen an easy prey to ambitious barons and nobles, who rejected its authority and were presently fighting among themselves for the succession. It had lasted for a thousand years and done a unique work for the world, but the impulse which carried it forward from barbarism appears to have been exhausted for the time being, and the elements which had coalesced in the Second Union fell back into a confusion of warring units.

Followed five hundred years in which we have only a few flashes of light, such as the instructions to his son Merikere from a nameless wise King in Heracleopolis ; the beautiful and haunting "song of the harp-player," with its anticipation of the "preacher" of the Old Testament ; the grim lament of an Egyptian Job ("Lo, my name is abhorred ") ; the story of the "eloquent peasant " and his impassioned appeal for social justice ; the appearance of sages and prophets denouncing the corruptions of the times and looking forward to the appearance of a Messianic King who shall do justice and restore the fortunes of the country. There are astonishing resemblances in

15

2

The restoration seems to have lasted about 200 years ; then decay set in again and Egypt fell a prey to the nomad invaders who established themselves as the Hyksos dynasty (Shepherd Kings) and ruled her for the next 200 years. Next came the line of patriot kings who drove out the usurpers and established the new empire with its centre at Thebes. These warring monarchs not only reunited Upper and Lower Egypt, but extended their sway to the adjacent territories of Africa and Asia and even to the Greek Islands, the coasts of Asia Minor, and the highlands of the Upper Euphrates. They stamped out feudal separatism and internal disaffection and turned the government into a military despotism. They were ruthless men who spared neither defeated enemies nor rebellious subjects. Immense booty, armies of slaves, kings in chains graced or defaced their triumphal return from their foreign wars. Amenophis II brought seven captive kings to Thebes from his expedition to Syria (c. 1480 B.C.). The kings he sacrificed to Amon, and hanged six bodies on the walls ; the seventh he carried south to Napata and there exposed it as a terror to the Ethiopians.

There was, nevertheless, one power to which even these conquerors had to defer, that of the priestly caste which established itself in the new capital of Thebes, as their predecessors had done in the old capital of Memphis, and began once more to drain the resources of the country. The tyranny of the tombs and of the mass priests who gathered about them and worked on that extraordinary obsession with death which haunts Egyptian history is written as clearly on the records of this new age as on those of the Pyramid age. The traveller who visits Luxor, the modern town on the site of the ancient Thebes, crosses the river to a vast city of the dead, with an inexhaustible series of rock tombs in which kings and nobles lie buried and the wealth of the country was sealed up generation after generation for the benefit of rascally priests or sacrilegious plunderers. Nearby on the hither side of the river is the colossal Temple of Karnak, even in its ruins putting in a claim to have been the greatest shrine ever erected by human hands to deities known or unknown. Tombs and temples bear their own witness to the wealth of plunder and human capital in slave labour which the kings of this period brought back from their wars and poured out upon these amazing monuments.

But suddenly breaking the line of these kings there appears the great religious zealot and reformer, Ikhnaton, protesting against the perversion by the priests of Thebes of the worship of the old sun-god Aton, and its corruption in the cult of the local deity, whom they named Amon. There followed a struggle to the death between King and priests. The King, thinking it impossible to purify the priest-ridden city of Thebes, turned his back on it and founded a new capital at Amarna to be " the seat of truth and righteousness." He was followed by a party of nobles, who built their homes there, and for the next fifteen years he and his supporters worked with feverish energy to make it the permanent centre of religion and government in the country.

Ikhnaton is the first great monotheist and, as such, a figure of supreme importance in the history of religion. His sun-god is no local deity, but " the father and the mother of all that he has made." In the great hymns which are inscribed on the tombs of Amarna we have, as Breasted says, a glimpse of a new world of thought in which the King and his associates " discern God in the illimitable sweep of his power—God no longer of the Nile Valley only, but of all men and of all the world." That passages from these hymns passed into the Hebrew psalms seems highly probable ; the thought of both is often the same, the words are astonishingly similar. They reveal the unspoken thoughts which were stirring in the Eastern world and are to this day its mystical background. It is to be observed that through it all Ikhnaton holds to the traditional idea of a special relation between the King and the God. The sunbeams enfold him and only him and his Queen and the royal children on the surviving monuments. He prays " May my eyes be satisfied daily with beholding him, when he dawns in this house of Aton and fills it with his own self by his beams, beauteous in love, and lays them upon me in satisfying life for ever and ever." Religion is purified, but the divine attributes of kingship remain as before.

3

In the Egypt of the fourteenth century B.C., these ideas were before their time. Ikhnaton was not only the mystic of the gentle face and dreaming eyes of his portraits ; he was also a fanatical zealot and iconoclast. He sought to sweep away at a stroke traditions, customs, and superstitions which had grown up over centuries. He banished Osiris, forbade his name to be mentioned, shut and desecrated his temples, cut the name of Amon from all inscriptions, waged ruthless war upon priests,[1] exorcisers, and all the vested interests which had battened on the old religion. But he could not stamp them out in the twenty years of his reign. His opponents remained festering and groaning at Thebes, working on the multitude, which the departure of the King and the Puritanism of the purified religion had deprived of their music and their festivals and innumerable little diversions and consolations in a hard and drab life. There is no passage in ancient history which would be more enlightening than the story of the counter-reformation which followed on the death or downfall of Ikhnaton, whichever it was, and the short reign of his son-in-law and successor, Tutenkhamen. Unfortunately it is lost to us. The foundations of Amarna, that " lonely outpost of idealism," remain to show the extraordinary energy of the reformer during his short life, and the ambitious scope of his plan, but all that we know of the sequel is that his successor came back or was brought back to Thebes and there re-established the old religion. His tomb in the ancient resting-place of the Kings, with its piled-up treasures from the palace and the offerings, as they seem to be, of his mourning subjects, suggest that he had won their affection in his still shorter reign, but how he came by his death and whether he was more than a puppet in the hands of the priests is unknown to us.

The counter-reformation was as ruthless as the reformation. After twenty years Thebes was reinstated, the new capital destroyed and deserted, the worship of Amon restored as the orthodox religion, that of Aton denounced as heresy and treason, and all traces of it removed

---

[1] It is tempting to compare Ikhnaton's failure to banish the images of Amon with that of Leo the Isaurian to enforce his edicts against images in Italy and his excommunication by the Pope A.D. 731.

from monuments and inscriptions. Tutenkhamen is represented as claiming that he had restored righteousness and expelled iniquity. Nevertheless, though the old gods returned and monotheism fell into the background, Ikhnaton's movement had profound and lasting results on the religious life of the country. The extraordinary treatise called the " Wisdom of Amenemope," belonging to the tenth century B.C., glows with a sense of the consciousness of God as the ruling factor in all life and behaviour. The humble votive tablets found in the Theban tombs of the same period point to a simple personal piety among the Egyptian masses which persisted in spite of the official priestcraft. But the general judgment appears to have been that the pursuit of religious and ethical ideals was too expensive for the rulers of a great empire. Events, indeed, had played into the hands of Ikhnaton's enemies, for while he lay dreaming at Amarna and his opponents and supporters were fighting about the true faith, the Hittites had made large inroads into Egypt's Asiatic empire, and it could plausibly be said that the outraged God Amon was showing his displeasure.

4

In a tomb of the eighteenth dynasty (about 1300 B.C.) we have a list of the duties of the vizier, or chief official of the Pharaoh, which enables us to reconstruct the methods of the central government at this period. Egypt is conceived as the estate of the Pharaoh and the vizier is his chief steward. The vizier is Chief Justice, Chief of the Police, Minister for War, Secretary of the Interior, and Secretary of Agriculture. The only check upon him seems to be that he has to make a daily report to the Chief Treasurer, who requires to know that all is well with the great royal estate. But he himself also reports daily to the Pharaoh, taking precedence of the Chief Treasurer. (" He shall go in to Pharaoh before the Chief Treasurer ; he shall wait at the northern flagstaff. . . . Then the vizier shall come, proceeding from the gate of the great double façade.") He works through an army of officials, mayors and sheiks, all of whom have definite duties assigned to them. The local officials make periodic reports and come to Thebes and pay in the dues in gold or in kind they have collected in their districts. Everything is recorded and checked. There are precise directions for the hearing of petitions and the conduct of trials, both civil and criminal. The vizier is described as

Chief of the six courts of justice, a mouth giving satisfaction in the whole land . . . judging justly, not showing partiality, sending two men forth satisfied, judging the weak and the powerful, not bringing sorrow to the one who petitioned him ; satisfying the heart of the King before the Two Lands, prince before the people, companion approaching the sovereign, favourite of him who is in the palace.

The inscription above his portrait describes him as

going forth over the land every morning to do the daily favours, to hear the matters of the people, the petitions of the South and the North ; not preferring the great above the humble, rewarding the oppressed, bringing the evil to him who committed it.

Again and again, as in the Pyramid age, the stress is on the vizier being a " good hearkener."

The description of the vizier's duties in this inscription is evidently based on law, and we know from other sources that there was a codified law, though none of it has survived. There was also, and even in the earliest times, something corresponding to our common law based on decisions of viziers and judges, for the greatest importance is attached to the faithful keeping and guarding of the records of the courts.[1] It is part of the duties of the vizier to enter the judgments of the criminal court in the " criminal docket." Wherever we examine the record scrupulous regard for method and order is an unfailing characteristic. To the pessimist of the feudal age there is no more horrifying sign of the demoralization of the time than that the records of the judgment hall are scattered, and that men are walking upon them and the poor breaking them open in the midst of the streets.

5

The restoration of the god Amon was finally accomplished by a soldier, one Harmahib, who had the good sense to keep extortionate

---

[1] *Records of Ancient Egypt*, II, p. 276.

priests and officials in their place while he brought order into the chaos that now ruled at Thebes. The way was now clear for the great line of war-like kings, Seti, Rameses I, and Rameses II, who marched through Palestine and defeated the Hittites, and restored the glories of the Empire of Libya and Nubia. Flaunting of power, terrorism, self-assertion, grandiosity were now the characteristics of the Egyptian monarchy. We see it all in the great Temple of Abu Simbel, on the Upper Nile, where something like a cathedral with nave and side aisles, 180 feet long, 61 feet broad, and 50 feet high, has been scooped out of the solid rock for the glorification of Rameses II. We look in vain for any trace of spiritual religion here ; it is all grossly barbaric and intimidating. Rameses is everywhere ; the great seated Colossi which flank the door are all portraits of him ; he stands thirty feet high against each of the pillars that support the roof ; he appears again and again in the series of sculptured pictures that depict his wars with the Hittites ; we see him doing heroic deeds in all postures— shooting arrows in his chariots, standing haughtily over prostrate captives, smiting his enemies with a club, hacking at them with a curved sword. He is god and man alternately, and Rameses the man makes offerings to Rameses the god. The whole company of heaven—Amon, Mat, Re, Herakte, Astarte—is depicted on these walls, and Rameses is familiarly at home with all of them. He is a god among the gods and they are all in league with him. Any Nubian invader tempted to try his fortunes in Egypt would have looked up from the river to see the frowning Colossi keeping guard over the doors of this temple, and if he had gone within would have learnt of the terrible prowess and ruthless character of the great sovereign who ruled over all Egypt and had made footstools of his enemies north, south, east, and west.

History repeated itself in the subsequent reigns. Under Rameses III the priests recovered their power and once more the wealth of the country flowed into tombs and temples, to the impoverishment of the multitude, which retaliated with strikes and plots that were ruth- lessly suppressed. But at this point the interest of Egypt for the student of institutions rapidly evaporates. There is nothing for him to learn from the grandiose monuments of military sovereigns. As time goes on we see them in conflict with all the other fighting

23

murabi ruled over the whole region and introduced the reign of law. Babylon remained all-powerful for between 700 and 800 years and achieved great commercial prosperity, developing a system of banking, organizing posts and transports, and providing systematically for the education of children, whom it would need in the future as clerks and officials. By this time the tiny city of Assur in the north-west had produced an ambitious race who were passing west towards the Mediterranean. In this region they were held up for a long period by a combination of Aramæans, Phœnicians, and Hebrews. These they gradually crushed under Sargon II, whose son Sennacherib made himself master of Babylonia, destroyed the ancient city of Babylon (745 B.C.), and founded a new capital at Nineveh. In the next twenty-five years Sennacherib's son and grandson conquered Egypt (680 B.C.) and established the greatest empire the world had seen up to that time. After another hundred years this empire too began to crumble, and eventually went down before another incursion of hardy mountaineers from the north-east, men of the Indo-European race, Medes and Persians, probably part of the great Aryan migration and the forerunners of what we now regard as European civilization. By this time the rule of Nineveh had been successfully challenged by the Chaldeans and Medes, who had conquered Babylonia and under Nebuchadnezzar rebuilt Babylon and restored its splendours (604 B.C.). This was the biblical monarch who destroyed Jerusalem and took Judah into captivity, as in the previous century the Assyrians had taken Israel. But compared with their predecessors both Nineveh and the restored Chaldean Babylon were short-lived, and both surrendered to the Persians (539 B.C.).

2

There is a friendly controversy between the Egyptologists and Assyriologists as to the priority of the civilizations they are respectively bringing to light. Were the Sumerians, whose remains Sir Leonard Woolley has unearthed at Ur of the Chaldees, or the Egyptians first in the field, or did both draw on a still earlier people who possibly started on the race in the region between the Euphrates and the Indus? The rapidity and novelty of the discoveries of the last few years warn the non-expert against trespassing on this ground. Anything he may say or accept on the present evidence is liable to be superseded by some later discovery before the ink is dry on his pen.

But the priorities are immaterial to the study of institutions. The interest from that point of view lies in the appearance of certain ideas of the nature of government, whether simultaneously or successively, in both regions in the earliest times. In Ur, as in Memphis, religion is supreme. The State is under the protection of the gods or the prevailing god ; the King is descended from the gods and has a special felicity preparing for him in the after-world. " Then came the Flood, and after the Flood kingship again descended from the gods," [1] says the Sumerian chronicler. In Ur, as in Memphis, we draw a large part of our evidence from the tombs of the Kings. Sir Leonard Woolley argues very persuasively that those extraordinary sepulchral chambers in which scores of the corpses of gentlemen and ladies of the court and of soldiers and horses have been found beside the coffins of king and queen are not, as might be supposed, evidence of the practice of human sacrifice, but rather of a special privilege granted to these favoured victims. " If the king was a god, he did not die as men die, but was translated ; and it might therefore be not a hardship but a privilege for those of his court to accompany their master and continue in his service." Possibly they met a painless death by drugs and narcotics.

When as many years have been spent on excavation in the valley of the Euphrates as have been devoted to the Nile valley, it may be possible to speak positively on this and other problems presented by these discoveries. It may be observed in passing that the part played by human beings in the royal tomb at Ur was played by statuettes and figurines in Egyptian tombs of approximately the same date. Whether or not human sacrifice was practised in pre-dynastic Egypt, the substitution of symbols for living victims when we get to the historic age is, I think, a point in favour of the Egyptians. For most practical purposes the common life seems to have been very much the same in both regions. Both depended on their rivers for irrigation and transport ; both developed the art of writing, the Sumerians by cuneiform inscriptions on clay tablets, the Egyptians

---

[1] Woolley, *Ur of the Chaldees*, p. 65.

by picture scripts which presently served the purpose of an alphabet, and being written on papyrus lent themselves more easily to literary form. Both had music and musical instruments and bards or court minstrels who made history in song. But as founders and originators of written literature the Egyptians were undoubtedly far ahead of all the primitive peoples. There is nothing in the Sumerian record so far which is at all comparable to the fervent and eloquent moral maxims with their aspirations towards truth and justice which have survived from the Pyramid age in Egypt.

3

Since the Egyptian code has not survived, priority in the institution of law has generally been conceded to the code of laws promulgated by Hammurabi, King of Babylon, some time between 2280 and 2100 B.C. This is a combination of civil and criminal law, providing penalties for crime and laying down rules for the holding of landed and other property, and its disposal at death ; for the conduct of commerce, the relations of merchant and agents, master and slave, the rights, duties, and wages of different kinds of workmen, including gardeners and cultivators. It deals with marriage, divorce, and the custody of children, the penalties for adultery, the position of concubines and maid-servants who have borne children to their masters, and so on through all the activities of life, down to the hiring of boats and the building of houses.

It is not socialistic or communistic, for its main concern is the guarding of private property, but it lays down rigid rules for the conduct of individuals. The society to which it applies seems to be extremely methodical and greatly concerned with trading and money-making. It has careful rules for banking on deposit, for the recovery of debts, and for distraint on defaulters ; for the maintenance of irrigation, and the punishment of those who neglect to strengthen the parts of the banks for which they are responsible or open their tunnels inadvisedly and cause their neighbours' lands to be flooded. In all these respects it is almost modern, but behind is a latent savagery, which suggests that to keep order by terrorism rather than by justice is its main object. The penalties are death, maiming and branding ; the *lex talionis*, an eye for an eye, a tooth for a tooth, is the governing principle ; the penalty may fall upon the innocent, so long as the principle is maintained. One law for the rich and another for the poor is an openly avowed principle of this code :

> If a man has caused the loss of a gentleman's eye, his eye one shall cause to be lost.
> If he has shattered a gentleman's limb, one shall shatter his limb.
> If he has caused a poor man to lose his eye or shattered a poor man's limb, he shall pay one mina of silver.
> If he has caused the loss of the eye of a gentleman's servant or has shattered the limb of a gentleman's servant, he shall pay half his price.
> If a man has made the tooth of a man that is his equal to fall out, one shall make his tooth fall out.
> If he has made the tooth of a poor man to fall out, he shall pay one-third of a mina of silver.[1]

Severe penalties attend the practice of the professions. The doctors whose surgery in dealing with a severe wound has " caused a gentleman to die " or to lose his eye shall have his hands cut off. The judge who alters a sealed sentence after it has been delivered shall pay twelve-fold the penalty which was in the sentence and be deprived of his judgeship. If a builder has built a house and that house has fallen and caused the death of the owner, that builder shall be put to death ; and if he has caused the son of the owner to die, his son shall be put to death. The boatman or pilot who undertakes to navigate a ship and causes her to be lost or injured has an unlimited liability for ship and cargo. Reading this code we may wonder how life was carried on at all in a community in which these fearful liabilities attached to every profession or calling.

No doubt it was mitigated in practice, but Professor Breasted is clearly justified in saying that the maxims of the Egyptian sages and such indications as we have of Egyptian law are on a higher plane of justice and humanity than this Babylonian law. Hymns to the Sun-god and the Moon-god have survived among the Babylonian records which suggest that there were among the priests of the temples men who were rising to the conception of a universal god, judge of all the earth, who frowned on injustice and evil-doing and rewarded the

---

[1] Johns, *The Oldest Code of Laws*, p. 43.

just judge. Some of these appear to have passed into Hebrew literature, but there is little trace of the sentiments embodied in them in the common life of the Babylonian peoples so far as it can be reconstructed from monuments and inscriptions. They seem to have been a hard, realistic, business-like people who did not let their ideals conflict with their interests.

4

I am looking among the records only for indications of the art of government and its development. Innumerable questions arise about the comings and goings of the various races—Sumerians, Akkadians, Amorites, Babylonians, Assyrians, Hittites—which chase each other over the scene, about their wars with each other and with the Egyptians ; about the life of the sea-faring Phœnicians and the development of trade under their lead ; about the coming of the Aryans and its effect upon the other races ; and so forth. Much of it is treacherous ground better avoided by the non-expert, who finds that almost any statement by one authority is liable to be challenged by another, and indeed to be superseded by explorations which are now for the first time being undertaken systematically under the supervision of universities and learned bodies. But no further discoveries are likely to efface the impression left by monuments and records that certain thoughts and ideas were common in all the early civilizations.

These were few and simple. In the beginning religion was everything. The community was under the protection of its god or gods ; the king, or chief, was a god or descended from the gods. He was also chief priest and his ministers were priests. But there was no necessary connection between religion and morals ; the king being a god could do as he chose, and was answerable to no one else. His principal duties were to defeat his enemies, to discipline his subjects, to prevent them from rebelling, to see that certain rites were performed which propitiated the gods and ensured their good-will. He governed by decrees which had the force of divine commands and could not be disobeyed without impiety. These were the assumptions of kingship all over the Eastern world in early times, and they were judged by their results. The ruler who suffered defeat in war or was overthrown by his rebellious subjects was *ipso facto* convicted of having lost the favour of the gods, and few or none gave him sympathy or pity when he was slain or driven into exile. So long as he remained on his throne, the king could, quite literally, do no wrong. He alone was the law-giver and all things were lawful which he deemed necessary for his own honour and glory—an object assumed to be identical with the welfare and interests of his country. For his enemies to attack him was arrogance, and for his subjects to disobey him was impiety.

5

Efforts have been made to deduce formulas for the rise and fall of empires from the experience of these west-Asian kingdoms, but it is impossible to discover any ruling principle which can be said to have decided their fate. Some are short-lived and others long-lived ; the methods which suited the bronze age became inadequate when iron was discovered ; the warrior on foot lost his ascendency when the horse was brought down from the mountains and chariots were invented. The silting of rivers, the desiccation of land areas, the changing of trade routes through the activities of Phœnicians at sea or of the ubiquitous cosmopolitan Aramean merchants on land, and numerous other factors to which we have no clue may have profoundly affected the destinies of empires whose prosperity and ability to make war depended in large measure on the success of their trade. As compared with the Egyptians, all these west-Asiatic peoples seem to have been matter-of-fact and business-like, and their chief occupation in the years of peace to have been the spread of commerce and the making of wealth. The organization of trade-routes and transport, the use of silver by weight for measuring value, the development of banking and credit were their chief contributions to civilization, and in later days they developed the art of governing provinces and collecting taxes through officials, which made it possible for the city-state to become an empire. The Babylonian Empire could scarcely have survived for so many centuries if it had not provided a tolerable life for its citizens in the long periods of which we have no record, but when we come to the last millennium B.C. the record is mainly of warrior kings who waged ruthless and destructive war, destroying the cities of the vanquished, ravaging their country and carrying into exile

been invented by the Persians, but they survived in many a modern embassy, where the part was played by subordinate officials who corresponded behind the backs of their chiefs with foreign secretaries and even with Emperors before the great European war. The tyrant, whether ancient or modern, must have secret information by which he can check the activities of his officials, and he must be perpetually on guard to break up any nucleus which might develop into a rival power to himself. In this and other respects the Persians were Oriental despots, but Herodotus and Xenophon bear witness to many admirable qualities which distinguished them from previous conquerors. They were great gentlemen ; they taught their boys to ride the horse, to shoot with the bow, and to speak the truth ; their nobles had beautiful houses and parks, full of trees and wild animals ; they were well-read and lively in talk. Their men were handsome and their women beautiful ; they tried to do justice according to their lights—witness the story of the judge whom Cambyses deposed and whose skin covered the cushion on which his son and successor sat to administer the law. Thanks to their prophet, Zoroaster, they had a religion which approached the sun-worship of the Egyptians at its purest and best. But their best period was short and after Darius their rulers rapidly deteriorated. They overreached themselves and suffered a disastrous blow to their prestige in their effort to conquer the Greeks, and though the fall of the Athenian Empire at the hands of Sparta gave them back something of what they had lost, they were on the downgrade from this time. " It is not in their institutions," said the Greek orator, Isocrates, " to make a great general or a good soldier—how could a man be either who is better trained to slavery than our houseservants ? " Cyrus, Cambyses, or Darius might plausibly pose as gods, require their subjects to prostrate themselves in their presence, claim all power and all responsibility, live in unparalleled splendour and multiply their wives and concubines, but when it came to Darius II, Artixerxes II, and the other weaklings who succeeded them, the barbaric ritual and the accompanying luxury and depravity hastened their ruin. Persian luxury became a proverb with both Greeks and Romans ; and that their Empire was crumbling from within, a prey to the fierce intrigues of queens, courtiers, and satraps, had become an open secret in its last years. It was Cyrus, Dr. Glover says acutely—

the Cyrus of Xenophon's *Anabasis*—who dealt the final blow to the empire of his fathers.

It was not that he intrigued or rebelled, but that he marched a body of 13,000 Greeks right into the heart of the kingdom and ignominiously defeated the King in battle.   Cyrus fell, but his Greek troops fought their way to the sea and got back to Greece.   They brought with them a new knowledge of what the Persian Empire had become—and the knowledge was fatal. [1]

---

[1] T. R. Glover, *From Pericles to Philip*, p. 231.

CHAPTER V

THE IMPORTANCE OF THE JEWS

I

UNTIL quite recent times it was part of the tenets of orthodox religion that the Jews were from the days of Abraham a " chosen people," who after various trials and vicissitudes, due largely to their own sins and backslidings, were destined to enter into and possess the promised land of Palestine. This in their later years was their own belief about their own history, and it may be seen briefly stated in the 78th Psalm. A somewhat different story is told by the higher critics of the Old Testament and by the archæologist-historians of recent times. According to these, the Jews were originally a nomad Semitic tribe which, like most nomads in primitive times, threatened the cities in the regions in which they moved, and under exceptionally able and ruthless warrior chiefs raided and captured a good many of these. They were not, according to this version, the superiors of the Canaanites whom they displaced, but a rough and aggressive people, with the manners of desert tribes, and it was from their sojourn in Egypt and afterwards from the Canaanites that they learnt the art of dwelling in cities and whatever other culture they acquired as a settled people. Where they differed from other peoples was in a passionate attachment to their tribal god and their belief that he was a " jealous god." This gradually developed into the faith that he was the one and only God, ruler of all the earth, who was just and merciful as well as " jealous."

Important as they may be in the history of religion, these origins have no great significance for the student of institutions. The belief, in which most of us were brought up, that the Jewish state was marked off from all others in being what is called a " theocracy " can clearly

36

not be sustained, if by that is meant that the Jews alone believed themselves to be under the special protection of their God and associated
priests with rulers. It would be truer to say that in this respect they
merely conformed to the prevailing types of ancient governments,
in nearly all of which the king was a god or descended from gods and
a leading part in the administration was played by priests.

Nor, in view of the Egyptian records and the importance of the
idea of " Maat " from the Pyramid age onwards, would it be true to
say that the Jews were first to associate religion with morality and to
regard justice and mercy as attributes of the ruler. The Egyptian
records give us glimpses of piety and humanity which are on a higher
plane than many phases of the much later Hebrew history. The
Jewish scriptures bear traces of Egyptian and Babylonian influences ;
Jewish cosmogony and Jewish law drew freely on Babylonian sources.
The Jews were not a politically gifted people ; they failed to keep their
tribes united in their little country, and by their division into two
groups greatly complicated their internal problems and weakened
their resistance to their powerful neighbours. They suffered all the
troubles and anxieties of a little people holding what their great
neighbours considered to be a key position, and were in perpetual
difficulties about the right policy to pursue under pressure from these
neighbours.

2

How then have they come to hold their unique place in the history
of religion and of law and institutions ? The answer, broadly speaking,
is in virtue of their Bible, which for the first time presents us with the
continuous history of a people and their religion and institutions. In
this book we can trace the life of this people from their beginnings as
a nomad folk living in tents, grazing their flocks and herds, ruled by
patriarchs, worshipping their tribal god, suffering captivity and slavery
at the hands of the Egyptians, wandering in the wilderness, learning
the art of war, conquering the land they coveted, expelling or sub-
jugating its original inhabitants and establishing themselves as a
fighting and trading Power, with which the surrounding great Powers
had to reckon. The documents, a blend of history and legend, which
tell this story, are so selected and edited as to be not merely a narrative

of external events, but the witness of an inward and spiritual process whereby the tribal god becomes the God of all the earth with a special concern for His chosen people, the Jews, whom He rewards if they conform to His laws, and punishes if they fall away from them. There is nothing like this Bible in the history of any other nation, and the judgment of the world which regards it as the greatest contribution to the advance of human morals before the Christian era stands secure. We see the same vision intermittently in the records of other nations, but only in the Jewish record do we see it as a flame which burns steadily and continuously and will not be extinguished by any calamity or any defection on the part of those who are appointed to guard it. The Jewish prophets of the one God have the same struggle to make their worship prevail as the Egyptian Ikhnaton, and their peoples were subject to the same relapses as the Egyptians from the ascetic and puritan ideals of monotheism ; but whereas Ikhnaton's effort is a solitary incident in Egyptian history, in Jewish the corresponding effort is the continuous theme of a movement which in due time was to be the greatest religious influence in the world.

Under this influence the Jewish theocracy became a religious form of government differing in essentials from anything resembling it in the adjacent civilizations. In the Jewish state the identification of politics and religion is complete. Throughout the Old Testament narrative, political error is constantly presented as a falling away from Jehovah, and its consequences as His judgments upon a faithless people. This is no vague and generalized belief ; it is definitely asserted as fact, and the prophets and sages who fill the part of political reformers claim boldly to be the spokesmen of God. " Thus saith the Lord " is their constant refrain, and it was so far believed that the kings and the opposing parties very seldom ventured to lay hands on any of them, exasperating though it may have been for them that these leaders of opposition, as they would be called in modern times, should claim to be divinely inspired. Though in all other respects the king was an absolute monarch, the existence of prophets who appealed over his head to the multitude and who might at any moment rise and denounce him was a salutary check to his rule.

3

This characteristic of Jewish prophecy is nowhere more evident than in the prophecies of Isaiah. These are, in effect, eloquent protests against the foreign policies first of Ahaz and eventually of Hezekiah, Kings of Judah. Judah, at the moment when the prophet appears on the scene, is called upon to take a political decision of the highest importance. The Syrians are attacking her on the east and it is rumoured that the Northern Kingdom (Ephraim, or Israel) is in league with Syria to invade Judah and destroy the House of David. Already, it was said, a certain " son of Tabeel " had been chosen to supplant Ahaz, whose " heart is moved and the heart of his people as the trees of the wood are moved with the wind." Filled with panic, Ahaz throws himself on the protection of Assyria, and dispatches an embassy to that country laden with treasures of the palace and the temple to announce that the King of Judah regards himself as " the servant and the son " of Tiglath-Pileser. Seeing his chance that monarch sets his army in motion, defeats the Syrians, disperses the anti-Judah coalition, captures Damascus, and, as a reward for these services, receives the homage of Ahaz in that city. I have examined this passage of Jewish history in another book, and may repeat here what I wrote in that.[1]

To Isaiah the whole transaction was humiliating folly. In order to escape the lesser danger of the Northern Confederacy Ahaz had thrown himself into the jaws of the devouring Assyrian and reduced his people to an ignominious servitude, whereas he had only to stand firm and Tiglath-Pileser must in his own interests have dealt with Pekah and Rezin and saved Judah without exacting submission or any other price for that service. Between the lines of his prophecy we may trace a political thesis such as a modern statesman might have developed from his place in Parliament in secular language. But to Isaiah it is charged through and through with religious issues. Where the modern statesman would impute weakness and lack of patriotism, he finds a betrayal of Jehovah by his chosen people. The defection is not merely the surrender of the abject king ; it is also the climax of the corruption, the evil living, the oppression of the poor, which have brought judgment in their wake.

---

[1] *Public Life*, II, pp. 147–8.

All through this tremendous book we see politics and religion blended in a chain of imperatives which are self-evident and compelling to the prophet. Isaiah is not solitary among politicians or prophets in his absolute conviction that he is right, but his appeal to the inner witness lends power and terror to his words. When his counsel is rejected, he is unmoved and passes into opposition—as a modern politician might say—with a magnificent gesture of defiance and contempt :

For the Lord spake thus to me with a strong hand, and instructed me that I should not walk in the way of this people, saying, Say ye not, A confederacy to all them to whom this people shall say, A confederacy ; neither fear ye their fear, nor be afraid. Sanctify the Lord of Hosts himself ; and let him be your fear, and let him be your dread. And he shall be for a sanctuary ; but for a stone of stumbling and for a rock of offence to both houses of Israel, for a gin and for a snare to the inhabitants of Jerusalem. . . . Bind up the testimony, seal the law among my disciples. And I will wait upon the Lord that hideth his face from the house of Jacob, and I will look for him.

The same issue arose thirty years later when Merodach Baladan, the Chaldean usurper, was seeking support from the western vassals of Assyria and had sent an embassy to Hezekiah, who was now King of Judah. Hezekiah wavers, but is inclined to join the Philistines in a rally to Merodach Baladan, if he gets a promise of support from Egypt. At this point Isaiah (or a successor) breaks in again and says to Hezekiah, as he said formerly to Ahaz, " Have none of these alliances, confederacies, and foreign entanglements. Stand alone in your strength and trust in Jehovah." To this he adds a shrewd worldly warning not to assume that the power of Assyria is broken because Sargon is dead. Sennacherib may be worse than his father :

Rejoice not thou, whole Palestina, because the rod of him that smote thee is broken ; for out of the serpent's root shall come forth a cockatrice, and his fruit shall be a fiery flying serpent. Let then the answer to the ambassadors from Nineveh be that the Lord hath founded Zion and the poor of His people shall trust in it.

Thus Isaiah in his zeal for " splendid isolation." The Assyrian yoke is bad, but to attempt to throw it off by an alliance with Egypt would be worse. It is impossible not to feel some sympathy with Hezekiah in the very difficult choice he had to make. Ephraim had gone down because she had supported Egypt against Assyria, but what will happen to Judah if Merodach Baladan makes himself master of Babylon and she has refused to support him ? Between Egypt and Assyria there is safety nowhere, and the prospect of maintaining independence without obtaining the support of one or the other and paying the price for it may well have seemed remote to a practical statesman at this period. On the other side was nothing but the sublime confidence of the prophet in the help of Jehovah and his concern for his chosen people. To go unarmed and in quietness and in confidence to await the result—this was his advice, the advice given in modern times by the extreme pacifist.

Nevertheless the prophet prevailed. Hezekiah rejected all alliances, gathered his people within their fortress and awaited the result, which in the Bible narrative more than justified Isaiah's prediction and his faith. A sudden pestilence fell on the army of Sennacherib just at the moment when it seemed about to sweep Judah out of existence and the survivors fled in panic to their own country. It is surmised that the part played by Hezekiah was not quite so passive as would appear from this version of it. Military historians hold Sennacherib to have been a blundering soldier who contributed to his own undoing. It was nevertheless a triumph for the prophet and confirmed the belief of which he was the fervent apostle that statesmanship consisted in discovering and doing the will of Jehovah.

Justification by results was by no means a necessary part of Hebrew prophecy. To Isaiah in Jerusalem as to Amos and Hosea previously in Samaria, the Assyrians were the instruments of Jehovah's wrath and if they prevailed, as they had done, over Israel, and might again over Judah, it was a just retribution for sin and backsliding. These prophets were also social reformers and denouncers of oppression, extortion, and ungodly living, and their chief weapon was the threat of disaster at the hands of a foreign enemy if the wicked persisted in their wickedness. " What mean ye that ye beat my people to pieces and grind the faces of the poor ? said the Lord God of hosts. . . . Thy men shall fall by the sword and thy mighty in the war." Hosea was as fully justified when Israel was destroyed as Isaiah when Sennacherib's army was smitten with pestilence. Nor was faith in

Isaiah dimmed in the heart of any pious Jew when eventually Judah suffered the same fate as Israel and was carried captive into Babylonia by Nebuchadnezzar. These prophets had the great advantage that, whatever the event, they could not be wrong.

4

The Messianic idea which runs through Hebrew prophecy is not original to it. It appears far back in the Egyptian feudal age in the utterances of the sage Ipuwer and in the predictions of the priest Neferrohu.[1] Both turn from the picture of corruption and desolation that they see around them to the coming of a saviour-king who shall cast out unrighteousness and restore the kingdom, at whose coming " the people shall rejoice and he shall make his name for ever and ever." Jeremiah, indeed, seems to borrow the images and even the words of the Egyptian Amenemope in his likening of the man that trusteth in Jehovah to a tree planted by the waters. But if in this sense they stood, as Breasted puts it, on Egyptian shoulders, the Hebrew prophets gave the idea exalted and mystical extensions far beyond the thought of the Egyptians. Whatever exactly was in their minds, whether they were thinking of a just king or a reign of justice, it was the dawn of the belief in what moderns call progress. By comparing the evil that was with the good that might be, and giving their dream the setting of reality, they set men's faces towards the light and led them on to the thought that what might be must be. The gloomiest prophet—even Jeremiah—was in this sense an optimist. Not to believe, even in the darkest hour, that right would triumph would for him have been unfaithfulness to the God who watched over Israel and who neither slumbered nor slept.

The special contribution of Judaism to political thought is that it conceives of the whole nation in its national organization as the religious unit and requires us to think not of the faith and obedience of individuals but of the faith and obedience of a nation as expressed in the functions of national life. Righteousness exalteth a nation. This doctrine brings all public affairs to the test of an absolute right and wrong and excludes all theories which make the State an object

---

[1] See *supra*, p. 16.

in itself, seeking its own glorification or the expansion of its power. The State, in the Jewish theory, exists for the service of God, and it is justly visited with His wrath if it refuses to do His will. It is in that sense " totalitarian ", but what it has in mind is a total dedication to the service of God.

This thought has had great power and value in subsequent history, and it stands to-day in striking contrast with the idolatry of the State as its own supreme object and self-justification which marks the European reaction in the twentieth century. But it is impossible to deny that the Old Testament has often in the same history lent itself to a cruel and gloomy fanaticism. The self-righteousness of the Hebrew and his belief that his God was a jealous God, who rejoiced in the slaughter of idolatrous priests and required that his enemies should be hewn in pieces, are reflected in the conduct of persecutors and zealots in the story of most nations ; the sword of the Lord and of Gideon has swung unmercifully in the religious wars of Christian times. Modern criticism distinguishes between the earlier and the later ideas of the Hebrews, but no such distinction could be drawn by those who believed in the verbal inspiration of the Scriptures—a long-lasting, politically calamitous belief from which the world only gradually and painfully released itself.

CHAPTER VI

THE COMING OF THE GREEKS

I

DARKNESS only partially dispelled by the labours of archæologists hangs over the early history of Mediterranean civilization. A high-light falls upon Crete, which bears all the signs of a highly civilized, gay, and prosperous life lasting in all probability from about 3000 B.C. to 1400 B.C. But it is light without sound. The Cretan script is, so far, undecipherable, and we can only guess who these people were, whence they came, how they were governed, and why they were suddenly blotted out. The same darkness surrounds the early history of the Greeks on the mainland, and the stages by which they passed from the primitive, heroic life suggested by their great epics, the Iliad and the Odyssey, to the highly civilized city-states which were their special contribution to the art of government. For any clear light we have to wait until the fifth century, when the great Greek writers take us at a bound out of the twilight of ancient and Eastern history into a vivid, living world of men like ourselves, recognizable personalities engaged in actual affairs, illustrating in their conduct the great dilemmas which present themselves to ancient and modern statesmen, winning triumphs, suffering adversity, lashed by the blows of circumstances and fate. The historians display them in action ; the philosophers ask what are the principles which would show them the way to act wisely and justly, and enable the citizens of their States to attain the good life under just government. It is scarcely an exaggeration to say that the Greek writers of these years were the inventors and discoverers of what the modern world calls politics.

44

2

Fortunately for political philosophy the Greeks never succeeded in establishing—or even had any ambition to establish—an empire on the Assyrian or Persian model. Only once, and then under the extreme pressure of the threatened Persian invasion, were they able to form a fighting alliance among themselves, and that fell apart as soon as the danger was over. The Greek made his city the object of his pride and affection and sought to reproduce its character and institutions in any colony that he founded. The Greek world was thus furnished with a great variety of governments and constitutions, and comparisons between them with a view to discovering which was best or in what respect one was superior or inferior to another became quite early in the day one of the chief subjects that the Greek thinker turned over in his eager and restless mind. Hence the richness and variety of his contribution to political thought.

In the great Oriental monarchies dictation and submission exhausted the rights and duties of rulers and subjects. The cry of the poor was heard occasionally, and the more advanced, like the Hebrews and Persians, conceived the process of history as a conflict between the powers of light and darkness, between Jehovah and his enemies, between Ormuzd and Ahriman. In the typical Oriental empire it was expected of the king that he should do justice, but the great majority accepted his rule and that of his viziers or agents as rooted in the nature of things and beyond challenge or argument by subjects. A great silence envelops the common folk. They are literally the " dumb masses " and their fate is absolutely bound up with that of their masters. When these were defeated, they might be slaughtered by the million, sold into slavery, and whole cities and tribes of them swept as captives into the cities and countries of their conquerors. Even in peace thousands of them might be uprooted and conveyed to another city or locality at the whim of their rulers. That they could have any voice in their own destiny or that there was any possible way of governing the world except that of which they were the subjects or victims seems seldom or never to have occurred to them.

All this is changed when we come to the Greeks. The city-state is now the unit ; in it are no " masses," but only moderate numbers

45

of citizens, every one of whom is interested in the way he is governed. The great Greek historians and philosophers, Thucydides, Plato, Aristotle, bring everything into question. They look back over history and mark the rise and fall of the different types of constitution : the rule of aristocracy or king in the early city-states in the eighth and seventh centuries ; the age of tyranny in the subsequent 150 years ; the different kinds of democracy, of which the supreme type is the Athenian of the fifth century ; the oligarchies or authoritarian States, of which the supreme type is Sparta. For these writers the subject is not merely what we should call politics in the secular sense ; it is the foundation study of the whole moral and religious life of man. The constitution of the city-state is the frame of reference within which man lives, moves, and has his being. Only if it corresponds to his inner nature will he be able to realize his true self and live the good life.

3

The debt of the moderns to Greek political thought is immense, but before we generalize from Greek to modern times it is essential to be clear about the particular chapter of history and the contemporary conditions which the Greek writers have in mind, and which they bring into judgment in their writings. These writings have the universal character of all great literature, but they are at the same time intensely topical and are only rightly understood if read in their context of contemporary history. Let me try briefly to indicate the main characteristics of the political life which is, so to speak, the subject-matter of these writers.

In the fifth century B.C. neither Athens nor Sparta nor any Greek city-state had a population exceeding that of an average English county-borough. In the Periclean age the total population of Athens of both sexes and all ages appears to have been about 140,000 and of these one eighth, or approximately 17,000, were enfranchised, *i.e.* qualified to sit and vote in the Assembly. A normal meeting of the Assembly would scarcely have filled the Albert Hall, and the democratic leaders or demagogues who are described or pilloried by the Greek writers were platform orators in direct contact with this number and able to guide or mislead it by the art of rhetoric.

Athens in her own estimation and that of her neighbours was a
" democracy," and this meant that all the skilled craftsmen and artisans,
merchants, manufacturers, landowners, and farmers possessed the right
of sitting and voting in the Assembly (ἐκκλησία), which, though
permitting itself to be guided and advised by a Council of 500 elected
by lot from the whole body of citizens, kept the final power in its
own hands. There were certain paid magistrates, archons, and
generals, also elective, carrying on the day-to-day administration,
but the Assembly, *i.e.* the whole body of citizens, decided all the major
issues including the making of war and peace, and, when it decided
on a military or naval expedition, appointed one of the generals or
admirals to conduct it. For the administration of justice every citizen
who wished could place his name on a panel from which the judges
were elected by lot, and the courts were empanelled from this list.
Since the judges were paid and no qualification of experience or
knowledge of the law was required, this judicial service was specially
attractive to the poor and idle. The boundaries of politics and justice
were nearly as vague as in modern Russia, and justice was so dispensed as to keep it in line with state policy or state necessity. Except
so far as the archons and the generals served the purpose, there was
nothing corresponding to the executive in a modern government.

Greatly different was the constitution of Sparta, the opposite type,
which was determined by the fact that a comparatively small privileged
population was living in the midst of a conquered people, superior in
number, whom it had reduced to the condition of serfs and whose
rebellion was always a dangerous possibility. But even in Sparta
there was a substantial measure of popular control. In the fifth
century all the Greek States professed to abhor tyranny, and a Spartan
would have denied indignantly that his Government could be justly
so described. In fact, he could point to numerous checks and balances
to prevent tyranny arising. There were two kings who watched one
another, and five ephors, elected annually by lot from the whole
population above thirty years of age, who watched them both.
Every month there was an exchange of oaths between kings and
ephors, in which the king swore that he would observe the laws of
the State, and the ephors swore that they would uphold him so long
as he did so. There was a Council of Elders (Gerusia) consisting of

47

thirty elected by the whole people, but subject to the double qualification that all but the two kings, who were *ex officio* members of it should be over sixty years of age and of noble birth. Finally there was the Assembly of all the citizens (Apella) which met once a month, elected the Council and the ephors, and was in theory supreme, but in practice was liable to be overruled by the Council " if it made a crooked decree." The Council—like the corresponding body in Athens—prepared the agenda for the Assembly and acted as a court of justice for criminal offences. Civil jurisdiction fell to the ephors, who in most respects performed the duties of the executive.

The reality in Sparta beneath these forms was an iron discipline directed to the single object of efficiency in war. The Spartan people, the original conquerors, lived on the labour of the helot or conquered people, who tilled their lands for them and set them free to fit themselves for war and so to fortify their position against internal rebellion and outside aggression. From time to time there were serious revolts of the helots, who lived in a state of chronic discontent, and a special secret police was appointed to watch and report upon their activities. When rebellion was feared, young Spartans were sent into the country and empowered to kill any helot whom they had reason to regard with suspicion.[1] Romantic militarists have painted the education of these young Spartans in glowing colours, but in reality it was hard and prosaic. Every citizen was to be a soldier and the discipline began from birth. A new-born child was submitted to the inspection of the head of its tribe, and if judged to be unhealthy was exposed to die on the slopes of Mount Taygetos. Boys at the age of seven were handed over to State officials, who submitted them to a rigorous hardening, saturated them with the Spartan spirit, and brought them up in great schools conducted on military principles. Not till the age of thirty were they supposed to have completed their training and to be qualified for the full rights of citizenship. Thereafter they kept intimate touch by dining together in public messes, to which the members of each mess made monthly contributions of barley, cheese, wine, and figs. So far as was possible, the individual was to have no life except in, through, and for the State. Helots saved him from the

---

[1] Bury, *History of Greece*, p. 131.

business of earning his living, as in other cities or states ; his education was of a kind to discourage all independent thinking ; he was a member of a privileged military caste—to maintain its authority and replenish its ranks were the objects of his existence.

Women, too, came of necessity into this scheme. Their business was to produce children who would be suitable material for a military career. Girls in common with boys went through an arduous gymnastic training, and it was thought quite becoming for them to practise their exercises almost nude. They had a high reputation for chastity, but placed themselves at the disposal of the State, irrespective of the marriage tie, when it directed them to bear children. Compared with other Greek women, they were independent and free ; but the marriage relationship was severely matter-of-fact and governed by its object—the procreation of children. Romance was between the boys and their instructors, the latter of whom were between the ages of twenty and thirty, *i.e.* in the intermediate period before they qualified to be full citizens.

4

These two actually existing societies in Athens and Sparta fixed the points of departure for Greek political theory and made it in the eyes of contemporaries a criticism of current politics. It is tempting and in some respects legitimate to treat them as prototypes of the modern democratic and totalitarian states, and they do undoubtedly represent highly simplified solutions of the problems presented by man in his relation to the State in modern as in ancient times. But the differences between the ancient and the modern types are seen at once in any detailed comparison.

Athens claimed to be a democracy, and her claim was generally admitted by her neighbours ; but large qualifications are necessary before the word is used in the modern sense. Her enfranchised citizens were in one very important respect a privileged caste, for behind them were at least 115,000 slaves imported from Asia Minor, Thrace, and the coasts of the Black Sea, who provided a large part of the labour required by industry and did the menial work of the free household. No doubt these slaves depressed the wages and standard of life of the poorer and less skilled artisans, but they enabled the great majority of free citizens to live a life of relative ease and comfort. In Sparta it was the positive aim of the ruling caste to release its members from the necessity of earning their livelihood through the labour of the helots. In Athens the same purpose was to a large extent achieved by slaves.

One of the chief difficulties—perhaps the greatest of all—in attempting to realize the conditions of ancient life is to get back into an atmosphere in which slavery was taken for granted as a necessary basic institution and to trace its ramifying consequences in life and thought. The slave is everywhere, in the home, in the workshop, in the fields, even in the army and navy and the police. The police of Athens consisted of 1,200 slave Scythian archers. If the landowners were able to reside in Athens, it was because they could safely leave their estates to be cultivated by slaves, who in the same way enabled the gentry to live at ease without soiling their hands with menial or *banausic* occupations. When, therefore, we begin to talk of the Athenian democracy—the relatively small number of privileged free citizens—as if they corresponded to the "proletariat" of a modern State, we are in danger of going very much astray. We shall be nearer the truth if we think of them as the favoured, highly educated class to whom could appropriately be addressed such speeches as Thucydides puts into the mouth of Pericles.

There is yet another great difference when we try to compare Greek society with modern, and that is the all-pervading atmosphere of religion. The Athenians were both sceptical and superstitious. Their advanced thinkers questioned the popular mythology, but the mystery religions, Orphic and Eleusinian, had a strong hold over them, and even the most enlightened believed in oracles and omens. The horror and anger aroused by the mutilation of the Hermæ on the eve of the sailing of the Sicilian expedition in the Peloponnesian War tell their own tale of the feelings of the multitude. Divination and soothsaying made large inroads upon both policy and strategy. An eclipse of the moon caused Nicias to delay his withdrawal from Syracuse, and so sealed the doom of the Athenian army. Any considerable enterprise might be delayed or abandoned if the omens were unfavourable. Religious ceremonies attended the departure of fleets and armies, witness Thucydides' account of the sailing of the Sicilian expedition.

When the ships were manned and everything required for the voyage had been placed on board, silence was proclaimed by the sound of a trumpet, and all with one voice before setting sail offered up the customary prayers ; these were recited not in each ship but by a single herald, the whole fleet accompanying him.   On every deck officers and men, mingling wine in bowls, made libations from vessels of gold and silver.   The multitude of citizens and other well-wishers who were looking on from the land joined in the prayers.   The crews raised the pæan, and when the libations were completed, put to sea.

In fact, there existed in Athens a powerful apparatus of priests and oracles—as powerful in its way as the mediæval Church.   Even the choice of officials by lot, which is often quoted as one of the marks of extreme democracy, had a mystical aspect in the eyes of Athenians for it was thus that the gods were given their opportunity of intervening in the affairs of mortals.   In all these respects the Greek mind is almost as difficult to interpret as the mediæval.

Finally, we have to remember that the great Greek writers Thucydides, Plato, and Aristotle came late into the field, when the great struggle between Athens and Sparta had shattered Greek institutions, and good and bad alike had been swamped in the tide of war, and its inevitable sequel, the revival of tyranny to combat anarchy.   It may be debated whether a democracy can govern an empire ; but it is very unlikely to survive the loss of an empire in an unsuccessful war. Coming after the event, the Greek writers seem to be holding a grand inquest on the decay of Greek institutions, and always with an eye to the part played by individuals.   All their reflections on the past, all their debates on constitutional forms bring them back ultimately to the question of the behaviour of men like ourselves in the difficult business of governing their fellow-beings.   No institutions, they seem to say, will work unless the citizens of a State have the capacity to make them work ; the best may be wrecked by the follies, corruptions, over-reaching ambitions, and jealousies of those who are in charge of them.   It is not the resemblance of institutions but the astonishing similarity in ancient and modern times of the qualities and defects of those who are appointed, or appoint themselves, to the business of government which gives their writings inexhaustible interest for the modern reader.

CHAPTER VII

THUCYDIDES

I

IT may help at this stage to glance briefly at the principal events of the great fifth century of Greek history. After the repulse of the Persian invaders (479 B.C.) the Greeks continued the war in an effort to liberate their brethren in Asia from the Persian yoke, and the Athenians organized a maritime confederation with its centre and treasury at Delos. At the same time the Peloponnesian Confederation was prolonged under Spartan headship nominally for the same purpose, but in a state of veiled and growing antagonism to the Athenian group. The latter in the next twenty years were suspected, rightly or wrongly, of bidding for the supremacy of Greece, and it conducted a running warfare with varying fortunes, but on the whole with success, against the islands and cities which resisted them. In 454 B.C. the custody of the common funds of the Athenian Confederation was moved from Delos to Athens—a decisive step which converted the Confederation from an alliance of free States into an empire which more and more tended to be taxed and governed from Athens. Reversing the process whereby the communities of the British Empire were released from Downing Street government to become self-governing nations, Athens brought her partners more and more under her control.

Her case was that this imperialism if it is rightly so called, was forced upon her, since the other Greek States could not be relied upon to defend the common cause of Hellas against the barbarians. It was true, but it aroused the jealousy of the Spartans and divided the Greek world into two camps, according as they sympathized with the democratic institutions of Athens or the oligarchic institutions of

Sparta, or as they were dominated by the sea-power of the one or the land-power of the other. From 431 to 404 B.C. the two parties were engaged in the ruthless struggle of the Peloponnesian war, which added the ferocities of civil war to the horrors of external war. The Athenians brought many of their troubles upon themselves by the stubbornness with which they rejected all opportunities of a moderate peace and the recklessness with which they engaged in ambitious efforts at oversea conquests which culminated in the disastrous Sicilian expedition. This, however, has not exonerated the Spartans in the eye of history from the shame of the disgraceful bargain with Persia, the traditional common enemy of Greece, whereby they gained the final victory.

2

Our main authority for this period is Thucydides, the historian of genius whose narrative, though severely anchored to fact, is in effect a searching commentary on political institutions and the behaviour of politicians in war and peace. At his touch the struggle of these little Greek States takes on a universal significance, well justifying his claim that his account of it will be a possession for ever.

A question arises at the outset. Is Thucydides an impartial witness telling, as he claims, with scrupulous accuracy the march of events, of which the judgment is left to his reader, or is he taking his revenge on men at whose hands he had suffered injustice and the bitterness of exile? The question is asked of Dante, as of Thucydides, and there is no positive answer to it in either case. "It befell me to be in exile from my country for twenty years after the generalship at Amphipolis "[1] is all that Thucydides himself has to say about it. He, appointed general in 424 B.C., lost the commanding position of Amphipolis after a brief campaign and was banished from the city by the unforgiving Athenians. Was it a "verdict of guilty fully merited," as Grote says, or was he, as others hold, a victim of misfortune who had done all that human prudence and activity could have done to avert disaster? He does not tell us, he merely records the fact; but his silence is that of a man into whose soul the iron has entered. With all his claim to be objective, he often seems to be struggling with an

---

[1] His own version of this affair is given in IV, 108.

emotion too deep for words. No writer reminds us so often of the essential difficulty of writing to the man who thinks, the difficulty of expressing in words the tumult and agitation of thought. He struggles and agonizes and carries his readers out of their depths, but precisely in this way conveys the sense of destiny moving below the surface of things. The gnarled and twisted sentences in which he seems for ever to be trying to pack the swirl of his thoughts into a minimum of words have a magic which is not easily translated. In what follows I am allowed to quote from the admirable translations of the Loeb Classical Library in which the reader may see the English version side by side with the Greek text.

If there is any one theme in Thucydides, it is not, as is sometimes said, the failure of democracy, but the disaster of *hubris*—an untranslatable Greek word which signifies pride, overbearing and overreaching, a thing fatal to wisdom and balance. The picture which he paints of Athens in her great days through the speeches that he puts into the mouth of Pericles is unforgettable in its beauty. Athens in these great days is entirely free from ὕβρις. She is modest, helpful, hospitable, ready to share all her good things with the whole Greek world.

" We do not copy our neighbours," says Pericles, " but are an example to them. Though we are called a democracy, for the government is in the hands of the many, the law secures equal justice to all alike and the claim of excellence is recognized, and when a citizen is in any way distinguished, he is preferred to the public service not as a matter of privilege, but as the reward of merit. There is no exclusiveness in our public life, and in our private life we are not suspicious of one another, nor angry with our neighbour if he does what he likes. For our weary spirits we provide many relaxations from toil ; we have regular games and sacrifices throughout the year ; at home the style of our life is refined ; and the delight which we daily feel in these things helps to banish melancholy. Because of the greatness of our city the fruits of the whole earth flow in upon us, so that we enjoy the goods of other countries as freely as our own."

In contrast with the secrecy and suspiciousness of Sparta, Athens, according to the orator, opens her doors to the whole world and never expels a foreigner or prevents him from learning anything of which the secret, if revealed to an enemy, might profit him. Her people rely not upon management or trickery, but upon their own hearts and hands. Equally contrasted are the two kinds of education, the hard, concentrated military training of Sparta, the free discursive life of the Athenian youth, who are equally ready to face danger when the call comes. "If then we prefer to meet danger with a light heart rather than by laborious training and with a courage which springs more from our manner of life than from the compulsion of law, are we not greatly the gainers?"

The speaker glows with his theme. Our city is equally admirable in peace and in war.

"We are lovers of the beautiful, yet simple in our tastes; lovers of wisdom without loss of manliness. Wealth we employ not for vulgar boasting, but as a means of action; we consider it no disgrace to acknowledge ourselves to be poor; what is disgraceful is to have taken no steps to avoid it. We alone regard the man who takes no part in public affairs not as one who minds his own business but as good for nothing. Instead of regarding debate as a hindrance to action, we consider it wrong not to have informed ourselves fully by debate before we come to action. For we differ from other men in being most daring in action and yet at the same time most given to reflection upon what we undertake. With others, on the contrary, boldness is founded on ignorance and reflection brings hesitation. They, surely, are rightly thought to be most courageous who, recognizing most clearly both the pains as well as the pleasures involved, do not on that account shrink back from danger.

"I claim finally," says the orator, "that our city as a whole is the school of Hellas, and that, as it seems to me, each individual amongst us could in his own person, with the utmost grace and versatility, prove himself self-sufficient in the most varied forms of activity. And that this is no mere boast inspired by the occasion, but an actual truth, is attested by the very power of our city, a power which we have acquired in consequence of these qualities. For Athens alone among her contemporaries, when put to the test, is superior to the report of her, and she alone neither affords to the enemy who comes against her cause for irritation at the character of the foe by whom he is defeated, nor to her subject cause for complaint that his masters are unworthy. Many are the proofs which we have given of our power and assuredly it does not lack witnesses, and therefore we shall be the wonder not only of the men of to-day but of after times; we shall need no Homer to sing our praises, nor any other poet whose verses may perhaps delight for the moment, but whose presentation of the facts will be discredited by the truth. Nay, we have compelled every sea and every land to grant access to our daring, and have everywhere planted everlasting memorials both of evil to foes and of good to friends. Such, then, is the city for which these men nobly fought and died, deeming it their duty not to let her be taken from them ; and it is fitting that every man who is left behind should suffer willingly for her sake." [1]

The great panegyric is familiar, yet it is difficult to resist the temptation of repeating at least these parts of it. As the description of a refined and exalted patriotism it is still without equal in any subsequent literature. Through it there runs the note of what in modern language we should call liberalism and even internationalism. Athens is the beautiful city with which her own citizens fall in love ; but she is more than that ; she is an education for all Greece ; she has no secrets which she will not share ; she welcomes all-comers. " Because of the greatness of her city " the fruits of the whole earth flow in upon her, so that she enjoys the goods of other countries as freely as her own. Only after considering the institutions of other cities does she conclude that her own way of life is the best. The devotion of her people is no impetuous fancy ; nor is it imposed upon them by law and discipline. It is the deliberate choice of men who reflect and debate, who believe that wisdom comes from the expression of many thoughts.

Is it fanciful to think that the placing of this speech with its glowing description of Athens in her prime in the forefront of his narrative is the clue to the historian's thought ? Behold this beautiful city, he seems to say, as she was, in the guiding hands of a great statesman— see what happened to her when he departed and was followed by men who had none of his sense of the limits of power, his moderation and sanity, his large-minded feeling for what was due to all Greece ! Contrast with this man his successors, the vulgar and blatant Cleon ; the upright and well-meaning but dilatory and incompetent Nicias ; Alcibiades, the young genius with his inherent falsity and aptitude for intrigue ; his youthful supporters with their exuberant thoughtlessness who, as Nicias pathetically said, " rather alarm me." Against all these who by their folly and disunion and overreaching involved

---

[1] *Thucydides*, II, 41, trans. by C. Forster Smith, Loeb Classical Library.

Athens in the catastrophe of the Sicilian expedition and brought ruin on her free institutions, the figure of Pericles seems to rise up in judgment, contrasting the vision of Athens as he meant her to be with the tragic picture of the plight to which his successors had reduced her.

There are some grounds for thinking that Thucydides before his banishment was of the moderate party which looked with some alarm upon the imperialism of Pericles, but as he looks back his judgment is explicit about the comparison between him and his successors :

For so long as he presided over the affairs of the State in time of peace he pursued a moderate policy and kept the city in safety, and it was under him that Athens reached the height of her greatness ; and, after the war began, here too he appears to have made a far-sighted estimate of her strength.

Pericles lived two years and six months beyond the beginning of the war ; and after his death his foresight as to the war was still more fully recognized. For he had told the Athenians that if they would maintain a defensive policy, attend to their navy, and not seek to extend their sway during the war or do anything to imperil the existence of the State, they would prove superior. But they not only acted contrary to his advice in all these things, but also in matters that apparently had no connection with the war they were led by private ambition and private greed to adopt policies which proved injurious both as to themselves and their allies ; for these policies, so long as they were successful, merely brought honour or profit to individual citizens, but when they failed proved detrimental to the State in the conduct of the war. And the reason for this was that Pericles, who owed his influence to his recognized standing and ability,[1] and had proved himself clearly incorruptible in the highest degree, restrained the multitude while respecting their liberties, and led them rather than was led by them, because he did not resort to flattery, seeking power by dishonest means, but was able on the strength of his high reputation to oppose them and even provoke their wrath. At any rate, whenever he saw them unwarrantably confident and arrogant his words would cow them into fear ; and, on the other hand, when he saw them unreasonably afraid he would restore them to confidence again. And so Athens, though in name a democracy, gradually became in fact a government ruled by its foremost citizen. But the successors of Pericles, being more on an equality with one another and yet striving each to be first, were ready to surrender to the people

---

[1] Pericles had been an admiral and his chief title to fame in war was as a leader of several successful naval expeditions.

even the conduct of public affairs to suit their whims. And from this, since it happened in a great and imperial state, there resulted many blunders. [1]

It is this picture of wise and humane statesmanship embodied in Pericles which again and again comes back to us as we read on. What would he have said to Cleon, " the most violent of the citizens," clamouring for the death-sentence against the Mitylenæans, " nobles and common people alike," insisting on impossible terms when the Spartans are willing to make a tolerable peace, dragging the Athenian Assembly step by step from ground on which he had made her safe ? Or again when we come to the terrible Melian dialogue, with its cynical avowal that self-interest and not justice or mercy is the religion of the Athenian people and its grim conclusion—" the Athenians thereupon put to death all who were of military age and made slaves of the women and children "—how does this sound against the claim of Pericles that Athens was an education for all Greece, and willing to share with all her Greek neighbours the treasures for body and soul which she had laid up for herself ?

And then finally in the contrasted figures of Nicias and Alcibiades we see again the ghosts of the past, Alcibiades out-Cleoning the demagogue Cleon ; Nicias, with the wisdom of Pericles but without his character, seeing, as Pericles did, the limits of the power of Athens, but failing to convince others, and in the long run consenting to execute a policy which he believed to be fraught with ruin. The debate has now by the lapse of time become one between age and youth, age pleading for the caution of the old Athens, youth impetuously rushing ahead and seeking to brand as cowards those who declined to follow.

Hear Nicias :

The matter is one of great seriousness, and not such as a youth may decide and rashly take in hand.

It is of such youths, when I see them sitting here in answer to the appeal of this same man, that I am afraid ; and I make a counter-appeal to the older men, if any of you sit by one of these, not to be shamed into fear lest he may seem to be a coward if he do not vote for war, and not, though that may be *their* feeling, to have a morbid craving for what is out of reach, knowing that

---

[1] *Op. cit.*, II, 65.

few successes are won by greed, but very many by foresight ; on the contrary, on behalf of our country, which is now running the greatest risk it has ever run, hold up your hands in opposition. [1]

" Mankind," retorts Alcibiades, " does not await the attack of a superior power, they anticipate it. We cannot cut down an empire as we might a household ; but having once gained our present position, we must keep a firm hold upon some and contrive occasion against others ; for if we are not rulers we shall be subjects." So the Empire, which by the law of its being must keep attacking, goes to its ruin. Between Nicias and Alcibiades, the Athenians, say the historians " were in a state of incessant fear and suspicion," and presently they sent a ship to recall Alcibiades and put him on trial for his life for his supposed part in the affair of the mutilated Hermæ. The story of that extraordinary adventurer—his escape, his intrigues with Spartans and Persians, his readiness to go anywhere and do anything which would enable him to be avenged on his enemies and eventually to return as master to Athens—cannot be pursued here, but it shows the amazing confusion of purposes and causes in which the Greek world and the Greek city-states had become involved as the struggle between Athens and Sparta proceeded.

3

Thucydides presents this struggle as what in modern phraseology would be called an ideological war, and in a masterly way he traces its gradual degradation until the original causes were swamped in a blind struggle to win victory or escape defeat. Athens tried to form a " popular front," arming the other cities and states of Greece for the defence of liberty and democracy, as she understood it, against oligarchy of which Sparta was the model. There is no reason to suppose that she was other than sincere in the early days, but she found herself against two principal obstacles when the war was prolonged : first that in nearly all these cities there was an oligarchical party which intrigued with the enemy ; second that she was driven by military necessity (or what she thought to be such) to behave brutally and ruthlessly to many of those whom she desired to make her friends.

---

[1] *Op. cit.*, VI, 12–13.

Neither side could afford the defection or even the neutrality of the neighbouring states. "Be my brother or I will slay thee" was the formula of both. Even before the death of Pericles, Athens, as he acknowledged, had come to be known as the "tyrant city" in spite of her claim to be the champion of liberty against the Spartan oligarchy.

The "ideological" war thus became for most of the belligerents a combination of internal revolution with external war, bringing down on them horrors of both. In one of the few long digressions that he permits himself—that suggested by the terrible events which followed the sedition in Corcyra—Thucydides describes the situation thus created. The revolution in Corcyra, he says, seemed at the time to be worst, but only because it was the first :

Afterwards practically the whole Hellenic world was convulsed, since in each state the leaders of the democratic factions were at variance with the oligarchs, the former seeking to bring in the Athenians, the latter the Lacedæmonians. And while in time of peace they would have had no pretext for asking their intervention, nor any inclination to do so, yet now that these two states were at war, either faction in the various cities, if it desired a revolution, found it easy to bring in allies also, for the discomfiture at one stroke of its opponents and the strengthening of its own cause. And so there fell upon the cities on account of revolutions many grievous calamities, such as happen and always will happen while human nature is the same, but which are severer or milder and different in their manifestations according as the variations in circumstances present themselves in each case. For in peace and prosperity both states and individuals have gentler feelings, because men are not then forced to face conditions of dire necessity ; but war, which robs men of the easy supply of their daily wants, is a rough schoolmaster and creates in most people a temper that matches their condition. . . . Those who came later into revolution carried to still more extravagant lengths the invention of new devices, both by the extreme ingenuity of their attacks and the monstrousness of their revenges. The ordinary acceptation of words in their relation to things was changed as men thought fit. Reckless audacity came to be regarded as courageous loyalty to party, prudent hesitation as specious cowardice, moderation as a cloak for unmanly weakness, and to be clever in everything was to do naught in anything. Frantic impulsiveness was accounted a true man's part, but caution in deliberation a specious pretext for shirking. The hot-headed man was always trusted, his opponent suspected. He who succeeded in a plot was clever, and he who had detected one was still shrewder ; on the other hand, he who made it his aim to have no need of such things was a disrupter of party and scared of his opponents. . . . Citizens who belonged to neither party were continually destroyed by both, either because they would not make common cause with them or through mere jealousy that they should survive.

So it was that every form of depravity showed itself in Hellas in consequence of its revolutions, and that simplicity, which is the chief element of a noble nature, was laughed to scorn and disappeared, while mutual antagonism of feeling, combined with mistrust, prevailed far and wide.[1]

4

In this way the Athens of Pericles passes step by step to her doom. In the end it is no longer democrats and oligarchs warring for principles, but desperate men pursuing the fight to a finish in fear and wrath.

So far as it reflects on institutions, the judgment of Thucydides is by no means the whole-hearted condemnation of democracy that it is sometimes represented as being. He has no love for the Spartan oligarchy ; the picture which he paints of Athens in her prime is as much a tribute to her institutions as his story of her decline and fall is a judgment on those who misused them. No city could even have resembled the description of Athens which he puts into the mouth of Pericles if there had not been great virtues in its citizens and in its methods of government. The verdict of Thucydides is not so much that democracy is a bad method of government as that demagogues are fatal to it. Had he continued his story to the end he might equally have discovered the vices of oligarchy, as illustrated in the final chapters. The demagogues whom he paints are not left-wing extremists, but insatiable militarists who again and again reject the opportunities of a moderate peace. In the one passage in which he passes beyond the bounds of his narrative he pays a notable tribute to the Athenian people :

And yet, after they had met with disaster in Sicily, where they lost not only their army but also the greater part of their fleet, and by this time had come to be in a state of sedition at home, they nevertheless held out ten years not only against the enemies they had before, but also against the Sicilians, who were now combined with them ; and, besides, against most of their allies, who were

---

1 *Op. cit.*, III, 81–82.

now in revolt, and later on, against Cyrus, son of the King, who joined the Peloponnesians and furnished them with money for their fleet ; and they did not finally succumb until they had in their private quarrels fallen upon one another and been brought to ruin." [1]

This was the cry of the defeated at the end of·an even greater war.

The term democracy, as understood in modern times, is far too big for comparison with the government of any Greek city-state. The warmest friend of modern democracy would admit that Athenian methods of government courted disaster. Athens was still in the primitive stage in which the necessity of acting through an executive and seeking the specialized services of competent officials was not yet thought of. It is to us an absurdity that the appointments of generals and admirals and the power of instructing them should have been in the hands of a town's meeting. The Athenian Assembly, to whom finally all decisions were submitted, was not, in the pictures of it presented to us by the historians, presumptuous or interfering ; it was the easy victim of any glib politicians who knew how to make what we should call a platform speech. In time of war the greater number of its members were serving with army or navy, and even in peace it was difficult to procure the quorum of 6000 needed for such functions as the ostracism. It is often suggested to us that those who attended did so in order to earn the day's pay, and that among them were a great many idlers and triflers. They were in any case a very small number to bear on their backs all the stripes which the theorists of later times have laid on democracy. It is as though large political inferences were drawn from the behaviour of a mass meeting in an English county-borough.

The mental processes of the Athenian crowd appear to have been a mixture of high culture and extreme simplicity. The Athenians were men to whom the great funeral oration of Pericles could appropriately be addressed ; and to understand what that means we have only to imagine the corresponding oration being delivered to an unassorted gathering of 10,000 Englishmen. Yet the same Athenian crowd appears to have been governed by an almost childish belief that something which it conceived as virtue ($\dot{\alpha}\rho\dot{\epsilon}\tau\eta$) would yield equally

---

[1] *Op. cit.*, II, 65.

good results in all spheres. Thus the poets who had won its applause in the great dramatic competitions found themselves in extreme danger of being appointed generals or admirals. Sophocles actually was appointed admiral, and it is perhaps not quite fanciful to suppose that Thucydides himself owed the disastrous appointment as general which brought ruin upon his head to his striking literary ability. Again, the Athenian Assembly has at times a touching and dangerous fidelity to men whom it likes. It insists that Nicias should remain at his post though he warns them that he disapproves of the policy which they are pursuing and is a sick man whose usefulness is exhausted. As between him and Alcibiades there is no doubt which has character and which is to be trusted, but there is equally no doubt that for the particular purpose in hand Alcibiades has the requisite drive and strategical ability and Nicias has not. So between the two the Sicilian expedition passes to its disaster and Nicias to his death. These are not specifically democratic failings—we should rather look for them in a weak and benevolent aristocracy—but they have all been set down to the account of democratic Athens.

All this must be borne in mind when we come to the criticism of the Greek philosophers. Looking back on this story when it has come to its final and melancholy conclusion, they see a confusion of ideas about the nature of government and its aims and conditions, and seek to clear it up. They use the terms current in their time— democracy, oligarchy, aristocracy—and conceive of the problem in the terms and under the conditions which alone were within their experience. The interest of their inquiry for us is rather, as I have already suggested, in its analysis of human conduct in collective action than in any judgment that it passes on forms of government which have no analogy in the modern world. As that inquiry goes forward, it takes us into deep waters and raises questions about the nature of man and his purpose and destiny in life which have a never-failing interest for the modern as for the ancient world.

CHAPTER VIII

SOCRATES AND PLATO

I

IN 404 B.C. Athens acknowledged defeat and was compelled by her enemies to demolish her walls and surrender her fleet. There followed a succession of revolutions which put at first " the thirty " and then " the ten " in power, and in 401 restored democracy. In 399 Socrates, the persistent " gad-fly to the Athenians," was tried and executed. The story of his end is sometimes compared with that of the trial and crucifixion of Jesus Christ, but except in the one respect that both deliberately chose their fate and declined to parley with their accusers, there is little resemblance between the two events. The death of Socrates was merciful ; his enemies would probably have much preferred that he should have walked out of the prison door which they left open than that they should be under the necessity of putting him to death ; they wished only to be rid of a man who, from their point of view, was a formidable centre of opposition. But what could they do when he quietly insisted that he greatly preferred death to the alternatives of submission and flight that they offered him ? Such a man could only crown his life by being steadfast unto death.

Yet up to this point his life had been witness to the tolerance of the Athenians. All through the stormy years of the war he had gone about the city pursuing what beyond doubt he considered to be his divine vocation, questioning, rebuking, using just those methods of irony and cool scrutiny which most exasperate when men are swept by passion. But now at the end the democracy which should have been his friend suddenly turned upon him and accused him of corrupting youth. Who, they asked, were his favourite pupils—who but the clever and faithless Alcibiades, who but Critias, who had brought in the thirty tyrants? Having desperately got back to power, were they to stand by and see this aged sophist gather about him another group of clever young men to encompass their downfall? Socrates would certainly have had short shrift from any modern dictator, and for the Athenian leaders at this moment their own safety was the first thought. Burke more than 2000 years later thundered against the clever intellectuals grubbing away the foundations of the accepted morality whom he had met on a visit to Paris, and the verdict of the Athenian jury was that Socrates had done the same dangerous thing with disastrous results on youthful minds.

But, again, words will deceive us if we think of the leaders of any party in ancient times as concerned for liberty of thought, as moderns understand that expression. The executioners of Socrates were deeply concerned for what they held to be right opinions on questions of faith and moral; the first charge of their indictment against him was that he denied the gods recognized by the State and sought to introduce new and strange divinities (δαιμόνια). Was not his pupil Alcibiades suspected of the outrage on the Hermæ? Had he not questioned the credibility of the orthodox faith and suggested human standards for divine beings, for example when he said that nothing was to be believed of the gods which would be disgraceful if applied to men? What was this strange δαίμων to whom he referred as possessing an authority overriding that of the whole Pantheon?

Undoubtedly from their point of view Socrates was a most dangerous man. He questions a host of things commonly taken for granted, the current phrases about religion and politics, the slogans of parties, the rhetoric of politicians, the meaning of quite ordinary words, such as justice and injustice, knowledge and ignorance. He left not a few of his own questions unanswered, but he had an extraordinary faculty of kindling thought and doubt. He was in his own phrase the midwife of ideas, but, since he never put pen to paper, we have to piece him together from the memories of his contemporaries, whose portraits of him remain still as that of the world's greatest "character." Outwardly he was everything that was unprepossessing, and his ugly face and pot-bellied figure and homely manners made him an easy butt for the comic poets. But this did not prevent him from being the beloved master of choice spirits ; and the greatest of the benefits conferred upon the world by his martyrdom and death was that they inspired a supreme man of genius to enshrine his memory in the noblest body of philosophic writing that ever came from the pen of one man.

It is no disrespect to Xenophon, whose homelier record in the *Memorabilia* may in some ways bring us nearer the real Socrates, if Plato is taken as the great evangelist of this beloved man. In the *Republic*, written about 370 B.C., we see him taking the Socratic questions and suggesting answers to them by imagining an ideal State in which man might realize himself and pursue the good life as the sage desired it to be. Politics and philosophy thus join hands. The *Republic*, in Nettleship's words, is in reality a dramatized philosophy of human life. It shows us in a series of logically connected pictures

the nature, nurture, and development of the soul ; the life which it makes for itself in religion, art, politics, science, philosophy ; its rise to the height at which it is almost one with the divine, its fall to the depth at which it almost ceases to be human ; what it is and what it is capable of being upon earth, what it may hope and what it may fear to be after death.[1]

Or again, to quote the same writer,

as we follow Plato in his delineation of an ideal society we see that he has only begun on the outside and is working inwards, tracing the external organization of the community back to its hidden source in human nature, and showing ultimately how the principles which regulate industry, war, and government are only the more superficial expression of those which regulate the moral life of man. Thus the question, How does justice work for good in the soul independently of visible results ? is answered by showing that the whole visible structure of civic life depends upon invisible forces and principles, and that what is called justice, so far from being an arbitrary convention, is that condition of the soul itself without which society would dissolve.[2]

To treat this great allegory of the soul as though it were a manual of practical politics is to lay a very heavy hand on it. In order to understand what was in Plato's mind, we have to think, if we can, of

---

[1] Nettleship, *Philosophical Lectures and Remains*, I, p. 337.
[2] *Ibid.,* p. 349.

a world which was without the Christian or any other ethical tradition carrying either general acceptability or the sanction of religion, in fact without any categorical imperatives, whether of the ten commandments or of the practical reason. In Greek society what was believed of the gods and their dealings with one another had little or no bearing on human conduct, and much of it, as Socrates insisted, was in flagrant contradiction with decent human instincts about right and wrong, justice and mercy. The thought of a morality superior to that of the gods was by no means absent from earlier Greek thought. But the pre-Socratic philosophers, being mainly engaged in speculation about the physical nature of things, had not given it form or precision ; and large numbers of sophists and cynics were at large questioning whether there was any settled code of conduct or, if there was, whether there was room for it in public affairs and the dealings of States with one another. The *Republic* of Plato is the first great effort to supply the moral and religious background for the pagan world which the Hebrew prophets had provided for the Jewish tribes. Looking back on the confusion of the past years—the lack of standards in private and public life, the incompetency and inefficiency of statesmen and soldiers, the absence of any rational division of labour in the governments of States, Plato is moved to ask through the mouth of Socrates, Is there a real distinction between right and wrong, justice and injustice, are there any discoverable rules for the governments of States and cities ?

2

The popular idea of the *Republic* of Plato is that it prescribes Communism and the abolition of the family as the acceptable way of life. Undoubtedly the association of Communism with the loosening of family ties owes something to the supposed authority of Plato, but if he is to be invoked at all, it must be for something widely different from what moderns understand by either Communism or sexual freedom. He is thinking of a small Greek city-state and prescribing for its governing class a discipline which shall secure its complete dedication to the public interest. The members of this class must not be concerned with private property or the care of wives and children ; they must live in common ; the State must provide for their needs and take charge of their children. The same line of thought may be traced in the Christian gospels[1] and has led to the foundation of religious orders and a celibate priesthood. It is, as far as it goes, an ascetic idea and certainly lends no support to indiscriminate sexuality. Nor has this kind of Communism anything to do with what moderns call the problem of poverty.

But again and again Plato warns us that his thoughts belong to the world of ideas and must not be taken as counsels of practical politics. In the world of ideas you follow your thought wherever it leads and are not under the necessity of adjusting it to the exigencies of practical politics. Perhaps, he says, the pattern is laid up in heaven and will never be realized on earth, but even to present a shadow of it may be serviceable to the earth-bound. So let the philosopher go his way undeterred by the scoffs of those who will tell him that his ideas will not work in the actual world. His duty is to go all lengths with his thought, leaving the practical politicians to apply what parts of it they can or will.

But Plato's thoughts were not so remote to his generation as they may seem to the modern reader. He had before him the actual example of Sparta, where boys were taken from their parents at the age of seven and where the ruling class had their meals in common and to a certain extent led the common life. That the small number which constituted this class should go the whole length of pooling their families and their private property might well seem to be carrying the Spartan idea to its logical conclusion. Similarly with the idea of breeding for various functions which is the foundation of the caste system of the *Republic* (the men of gold, the men of silver, the men of copper and iron). The Spartans deliberately bred for military efficiency, practising infanticide to weed out the inferior stock. This led to consequences, dullness, uniformity, lack of culture, which Plato himself criticizes with much severity. But these consequences, he seems to think, would be avoided if the breeding were for various functions, so as to provide the State with the different kinds of aptitude and intelligence which a well-balanced community should have. Again, no doubt, an impracticable idea, but it provided the philosopher

---

[1] Matt. x. 37 ; xii. 46–50.

with just the framework he needed to develop his vision of the perfect State.

As we read on into the *Republic* we more and more relegate these fantasies into the background. What projects itself as the overwhelming dominant thought is that good politics must correspond to the moral and religious nature of man. The object of the perfect State is the good life, and in his effort to define the good, the philosopher again pursues his thought to its utmost limits, even in the end beyond time and space to the vision of reality which may not be in this world. *Ex umbris et imaginibus in veritatem.* Almost in certain passages he seems to anticipate the mediæval thought that the life of this world is only a passage to the world hereafter. That, indeed, is explicitly stated in the *Phædo*, where the life of the true philosopher is presented as a dying to the body that he may live to the soul, a foretaste of that freedom to which he looks forward after death when he hopes to see the truth in its purity with purified eyes.

3

It would nevertheless be a great mistake to suppose that Plato is other-worldly in the sense that his interest is transferred from this world to another. All through he is asking what is the meaning of life here and now, how should a rational man live, why has he failed, why is there so much confusion, discord, cruelty, and suffering in life as we know it? The answer is that man is at war with himself internally and in his relations with other men, that his higher nature is in subordination to his lower, his reason to his irascible and concupiscent qualities, and that States as they exist reflect this conflict and confusion ; whereas he is so constituted that he can only have happiness and the good life as a man among men, if he is at peace with himself and in the society of like-minded men. The last condition is all-important, for it is only in such a society that man can lead the good life. Here we touch a fundamental difference between Plato's idea of the State and all modern ideas which make the State an object in itself to which the individual owes unconditional obedience. The State, in Plato's scheme, provides the frame within which the individual lives the good life. The good man can only find perfection in the good State. But the State is not something outside the individual which should dictate his way of life and command his allegiance for its own ends. It is or should be the voluntary expression of a man's best self, the result of his willing co-operation with his fellows. Dictation, compulsion, regimentation play a very small part in Plato's scheme. If the citizens of his State are divided into philosophers, rulers, administrators, and common citizens, it is because the division corresponds to their nature and character. They are born with gold, silver, iron, and copper in their constitution and will be so educated and brought up as not to wish to play parts for which they are unfitted. The rulers will be on the look-out for the child born of iron and copper parents who may have gold in him, or the child of gold parents who may have iron and copper in him, and the one will be promoted to the ruling class and the other reduced to the ranks. There will thus be equality of opportunity and fitness will be the only test. But prior to everything is the right education, which will dispose the citizen to accept this constitution as commending itself by its self-evident rightness. If it issues in aristocracy understood as the rule of the fittest, it will be because a right-thinking democracy so decides.

Philosophy and politics are so mingled in Plato's thought that we are often in doubt whether he is developing a philosophic theme in the guise of politics or a political one in the guise of philosophy. To find the points of juncture between the ideal State and the theory of ideas, the parable of the Cave, the vision of Er the Son of Armenius about the future life, the discussions on poetry and music, and the numerous other digressions which enrich this amazing book is not easy for the modern reader. At first sight the dialogue which follows " wherever the argument leads " and carries the reader from point to point, with sometimes only a gossamer bridge over the precipices that divide them, mystifies and even irritates the modern mind, accustomed to formal arrangement and careful classifications of subjects that Plato lumps together. But throughout we have to bear in mind that his theme is far wider than anything that we understand by politics ; it is not merely the city built with hands but the city of man's soul that he is exploring. To discover what the good policy is we must have some clear idea of the meaning of life, the nature of man, and the working of his various faculties. Ethics, psychology, and religion join hands in this inquiry, and if we could imagine Plato criticizing modern theories of government, he might consider it a disaster that they have so often parted company in the subsequent years. There are many passages in the *Republic*, specially those that dwell on the importance of the unconscious and the subconscious in education and even on the significance of dreams in unveiling the lower nature, which anticipate the most modern psychology. Many later studies in what moderns call political science are a return to the ideas of Plato.

4

But his great significance for his time and generation lay in his bold affirmation that the object of government was the good life and the happiness of the individual. It would be an exaggeration to say that this thought was unknown to the ancient world. We have found traces in the Egyptian Pyramid age of an unspoken contract between the Pharaoh and his people by which the former was bound to do justice ; the Hebrew prophets had preached that the select circle of the chosen people were dedicated to the service of a righteous and jealous God. But looking backwards on history as he knew it, a Greek of the fourth century would see it taken for granted all over the barbarian world and over a large part of the Greek world that the first duty of a ruler was to keep himself in power and be strong against internal or external enemies who would deprive him of power. It is not mere cynicism which makes the sophists in the *Gorgias* and the *Republic* argue that justice is the interest of the stronger ; they do but reflect the common opinion about the purpose of government. The argument which goes on perpetually in Thucydides about the treatment of prisoners and which assumes that whether they are killed or spared or sold into slavery is not a question of mercy or humanity, but a pure question of expediency, is sometimes attributed to the irony of the historian ; but it is repeated too often and is too seldom challenged to make it seem other than a reflection of common opinion. True that the Greeks had shown themselves in advance of other peoples in their detestation of " tyranny " and in the means they had taken to rid themselves of tyrants, but few of them in Plato's age would have questioned the assertion that the first duty of the rulers of a State, whether they called themselves democrats, oligarchs, or aristocrats, was to maintain themselves in power.

Nor in fact does Plato question it. He says a State will only be strong and able ultimately to defend itself if it is governed by reason and justice and makes the well-being of its citizens its first object ; otherwise it will be the victim of disharmony which will end in revolution and defeat. But how is this state of harmony to be produced ? In answering these questions Plato brings us to what he calls his " waves." The first is that women shall have the same education and the same status and liabilities as men, and share in the toils of war and in the defence of their country.[1] The second is the community of wives and children for the guardian class. The third (" the great wave, as I call it, at which I expect your laughter to be as the letting out of water ") is that

" Unless either philosophers become kings in our States or those whom we now call kings and rulers take to the pursuit of philosophy seriously and adequately, and there is a conjunction of these two things, political power and philosophic intelligence, while the motley horde of the natures who at present pursue either apart from the other are compulsorily excluded, there can be no cessation of troubles, dear Glaucon, for our States, nor, I fancy, for the human race either. Nor, until this happens, will this constitution which we have been expounding in theory ever be put into practice within the limits of possibility and see the light of the sun. But this is the thing that has made me so long shrink from speaking out, because I saw that it would be a very paradoxical saying. For it is not easy to see that there is no other way of happiness either for private or public life." " O Socrates," said Glaucon, " after hurling at us such an utterance and statement as that, you must expect to be attacked by a great multitude of our men of light and leading, who forthwith will, so to speak, cast off their garments and strip and, snatching the first weapon that comes to hand, rush at you with might and main, prepared to do dreadful deeds. And if you don't find words to defend yourself against them, and escape their assault then to be scorned and flouted will in very truth be the penalty you will have to pay." [2]

In the development of this thought Plato poses most of the questions which were in debate in mediæval times and are still at the heart of the controversies about the nature of government in Europe to-day.

---

[1] This appears to apply only to the picked women who are to be the help-meets of the guardian.

[2] *Republic*, V, 473. Trans. Prof. Paul Shorey, Loeb Classical Library.

What manner of men are these philosophers ? They participate in a divine wisdom which makes them the natural guardians of justice and truth ; they have the practical good sense and the fund of knowledge which make in combination the perfect administrator ; they are not empiricists, but, as a modern would say, men of science applying scientific principles to the business of government. The functions which the mediæval world divided between Church and State are united in them. They are both popes and civil ministers, as popes asserting the mystical and transcendental purpose of the State, as ministers conducting its mundane affairs. In both capacities the argument tends to the conclusion that they are infallible. They know ; the others know only in part or do not know at all.

More ingratiating and persuasive descriptions of the qualities that make the ideal public man could scarcely be found than in the sections that develop this theme. But a modern has the uneasy feeling that behind them there is looming up the ugly apparition of the totalitarian States, with their domineering experts and dictators. These States would assuredly be classed by Plato among the tyrannies which he regarded as corruptions of his ideal, but in so far as he encourages the idea that there is a precise kind of knowledge which can be attained by experts and applied by them to the business of government—in the same way as the engineer applies his mathematical formulas to the building of a bridge or a breakwater—he lends himself to their pretensions. If there is such knowledge and they are in possession of it, it is absurd that it should be questioned and that they should be tripped up by an inexpert mob. Plato's parable of the navigator who is deposed by the ignorant and unruly crew exactly fits the case.

Fundamentally the question is whether politics is a science or an art, a science in which humanity can be treated as fixed material, subject to discoverable rules and principles, or an art requiring constant adjustments to the undiscoverable and unknowable, the infinite varieties and free movements of the human spirit. It would be absurd to charge Plato with ignoring the element of change and variety in the human character. In the last books of the *Republic* he gives us incomparable pictures of the virtues and corruptions, the flowering and the decay of the principal types. Other dialogues show a lively and humorous appreciation of the varieties and whimsicalities of different types. But in certain parts of the *Republic* they seem to be thrown into the mould of fixed castes where most of them remain crystallized and frozen—passive material for handling by the philosophers and experts, but not intelligent beings with a voice in their own destiny, or even with the modest right to complain. When these castes are fixed, all but the highest pass out of political existence.

This is the logical result of criticizing the existing State with its inefficiency and disorderliness by setting against it an imaginary perfect State from which human ignorance and fallibility and human waywardness and sinfulness have been eliminated. It is a method which enables the philosopher to range at large over the whole field of religion and politics, but is full of pitfalls if selected parts of it are applied to the actual world of erring mortals. A form of government which would be justified in the hands of angels and demigods may be a detestable tyranny in the hands of ambitious and ignorant men.

5

Even on his own ground Plato the politician seems often to be lost in Plato the philosopher. We ask what is the specifically political wisdom which his philosopher kings—" spectators of all time and all existence "—bring to bear upon the government of the State, and the answer eludes us. When we seem to be near it, he escapes into allegory or employs words and images which cloud his meaning. He apparently assumes that with their knowledge of the good in itself attained by profound study of the principles of morality in their youth and early life, his rulers will know intuitively what is the wise course in public affairs. They are to be tested until the age of thirty to see if they have the power of seeing things together (*synopsis*), and whether they are steadfast ; they are then to have a five years' course of dialectics, which seems to mean a study of the principles of conduct and human life ; they are next to have fifteen years of experience through actual contact with the forms of good and evil about which they have been taught ; and only then, at the age of fifty, when they have been continually tested to see if they stand being " pulled about in all directions by the circumstances with which they have to contend " are they to be permitted to govern and organize the State. In all this the gap between the ideal good and what is good here and now in the conduct of affairs seems never to be bridged, and there are passages in which Plato himself seems to be in extreme doubt whether, after all this training, the philosopher-kings might not be extremely impracticable and inefficient rulers, if not actually dangerous and fanatical cranks. No one is better aware of the perils of false dogmas when asserted as truth. In some passages he seems to say that the philosopher will be of no use unless he finds a city fit for him—in which case he would presumably not be needed.

Plato, in fact, is in so much difficulty with his endeavour to treat politics as a science that he is constantly thrown back on his reminder that after all the " pattern may be laid up in heaven." Nevertheless, what most strikes one on returning to the *Republic* is that it raises with uncanny foresight one of the fundamental questions about the nature of government which is still at issue in Europe to-day. Is there a body of knowledge, existing or ascertainable, in virtue of which a select few may claim absolute control over their fellow-men ? The Christian Catholic Church decided that in the sphere of religion and morals there was such a body, and for centuries endeavoured to enforce it by methods which, given that assumption, seemed to be logically justified. The Church still maintains this theory, but has abandoned the attempt to impose it on the unwilling. Coercion is now the weapon of secular popes, who claim for their political dogmas the same infallibility as the Church for its spiritual doctrines, and who denounce criticism or dissent as treasonable and criminal. To discover the proper spheres of science and opinion respectively and to prevent either from becoming a tyranny is still the main problem of States desiring to be free.

CHAPTER IX

GLEANINGS FROM THE "REPUBLIC"

I

LET me try in this chapter to bring together certain ideas taken from the *Republic* which, apart from Plato's theory of the State or his general philosophy, have a special interest for the modern world.

It is impossible to read the second and third books, dealing with the early education of the rulers, without being struck by their anticipation of modern theories. We have here a large part of the modern philosophy of the subconscious, but without the additions which in recent years have given it a morbid twist in a sexual direction. Education in early years is to be largely indirect. The soul, which is by nature imitative, is to absorb its surroundings without being aware that it is doing so. Children, therefore, especially in their early years, are to be protected from contact with corruption and depravity. The poets whom they read must be compelled to embody in their poems the image of the good character or else take their poetry elsewhere ; the artists and craftsmen who furnish their surroundings must love the beautiful :

" Our guardians may not be bred among symbols of evil, as it were in a pasturage of poisonous herbs, lest grazing freely and cropping from many such day by day they little by little and all unawares accumulate and build up a huge mass of evil in their own souls. But we must look for those craftsmen who by the happy gift of nature are capable of following the trail of true beauty and grace, that our young men, dwelling as it were in a salubrious region, may receive benefit from all things about them, whence the influence that emanates from works of beauty may waft itself to eye or ear like a breeze that brings from wholesome places health, and so from earliest childhood insensibly guide them to likeness, to friendship, to harmony with beautiful reason."

" Yes," he said, " that would be far the best education for them." " And is it not for this reason, Glaucon," said I, " that education in music is most sovereign, because more than anything else rhythm and harmony find their way to the inmost soul and take strongest hold upon it, bringing with them and imparting grace, if one is rightly trained, and otherwise the contrary ? And further, because omissions and the failure of beauty in things badly made or grown would be most quickly perceived by one who was properly educated in music, and so, feeling distaste rightly, he would praise beautiful things and take delight in them and receive them into his soul to foster its growth and become himself beautiful and good. The ugly he would rightly disapprove of and hate while still young and yet unable to apprehend the reason, but when reason came, the man thus nurtured would be the first to give her welcome, for by this affinity he would know her." [1]

One thinks of Wordsworth's " Beauty born of murmuring sound shall pass into her face." Education going forward in these surroundings is to consist of two parts, " music " and gymnastics, music covering all that we should call literature in addition to the songs and sounds to which the word is limited in modern times. Music takes precedence of gymnastic or physical culture in the early years and must begin with the telling of stories which, " though not wholly destitute of truth, are in the main fictitious." Parents must " fashion the mind with these tales even more fondly than they form the body with their hands ; and most of those which are now in use must be discarded."

This brings us to what a modern would call religious education, which in Plato's time consisted mainly of tales taken from Homer, Hesiod, and other poets, " who have ever been the great story-tellers of mankind." These are either to be disallowed altogether or to be severely censored before they are permitted in Plato's nursery. His general rule is that nothing is to be imputed to God which would be thought disgraceful if imputed to men. " God is always to be represented as he truly is, and since he is truly good, he must be represented as such." This standard would disallow large parts of the Old Testament and not a little of what in past times has been taught as Christian doctrine.

Associated with this part of the argument is the profound suspicion

---

[1] *Republic*, III, 401. Trans. Prof. Paul Shorey, Loeb Classical Library.

with which Plato regards poetry and music and the plastic arts. Being himself an artist and poet, he is haunted by a doubt of the effects of the arts on the emotionally susceptible. Certain kinds of music are enervating and demoralizing ; their effect on the character is like dram-drinking.[1] The poets use their art as a means of tickling the palate of demos. In another dialogue (the *Gorgias*) poetry, especially tragic poetry, is classed with rhetoric as a branch of art appealing to and pleasing the crowd, and it is associated with the arts of the confectioner and the perfumer. In the old days, says Plato, the audience was swayed by people who knew bettter than they ; at present there is a theatrocracy on a low level of taste and the dramatist plays down to it.

This is an odd inversion of the modern view that poetry is a luxury of high-brows. It is difficult to think of Æschylus, Sophocles, and Euripides tickling the ears of the groundlings. That such a thought could cross the mind of Plato throws a sudden shaft of light on the state of culture of the Athenian demos. But the artist, whether poet or painter, is represented as in a chronic state of conflict with reality. He is an imitator who puts before us not the purpose and meaning of life, but certain appearances only, who distracts the mind and keeps it playing on the gaudy surface of things. I can imagine a modernist painter or poet finding appropriate passages in Plato in defence of his efforts to dive below the surface and express something that is in his mind about them, but Plato, I think, would have answered that it was the nature of the plastic arts to express the outward aspect of things, and that in attempting to go behind it the artist was exceeding his part and trespassing on the ground of the philosopher. The artist can only deal with appearances, but he must do so quietly and soberly.

Plato is divided between his love of the arts and his fear of what moderns call the artistic temperament. He will praise the poet, tell him what a beautiful creature he is, and then put a garland round his neck and conduct him to the frontier. Having witnessed the downfall of Athens, he seems to be oppressed by the thought that the city beautiful, so thrillingly described in the great Funeral Oration of

---

[1] Nettleship, *op. cit.*, p. 342. An old music-master used to speak of " slarney-blarney, backbone-rotting tunes."

Pericles, was over-æstheticized, and owed some of her disasters to the diversity of her interests and the preoccupation of her gifted and versatile citizens with the glitter and gaiety of their surroundings. In his ideal state he tries to get the best of both worlds. The young, as we have seen, are to grow up amidst fair sights and sounds—one thinks of the view of Athens from the groves of Academe and the sound of the shepherd's pipe coming in from the fields—but the poet and the artist are to play a carefully limited part in their subsequent education or in the life of the adult citizen. It seems ungrateful to the artist, whose services must, one would suppose, have been enlisted to provide the fair sights surrounding the cradle of youth, but in all this and especially in his suspicion of the theatre and the actor, Plato anticipates seventeenth-century Puritans. Actors and public entertainers are in the same disgrace with him as with them. Imitation kindles his wrath : " The man who has no self-respect will imitate anybody and anything ; sounds of nature, cries of animals ; he will whistle like the wind, rattle like hail, growl like thunder, play on any instrument ; also he will bark like a dog, baa like a sheep, and crow like a cock." Acting is a violation of character which should be kept one and whole. What Plato would have said to modern " variety " dispensed by wireless to a million homes is beyond thinking. But while he moralizes, his touch is so light and gay that we can never think of him as a kill-joy.

2

Gymnastic or physical culture follows music in education, with the proviso that since the soul is related to body as cause to effect, if we educate the soul, we can safely leave the body in its charge. But there are certain hints. The ordinary gymnastic of the wrestling ground is a sleepy, heavy sort of thing, and apt to be dangerous when left off suddenly. But diet is important. Sicilian cookery and Attic confections are to be avoided like Corinthian courtesans. It is disgraceful to employ a physician not for the cure of wounds or epidemics but because a man has blown himself out like a bladder and has more diseases than he knows the names of, or than existed in the days of Asclepius. The system of nursing disease is a modern invention introduced by a fashionable trainer who by a combination of medicine and training tortured first himself and then a good many other people and died a long time after he ought to have died.

Asclepius, who was a statesman, refused to practise this art because he knew that the citizens of a well-ordered State had no leisure to be ill. That is the luxury of men who can afford it. The rest must be at their business ; if they recover, well and good ; if not, there is an end of them. Asclepius and his sons did not wish to preserve useless lives or raise up puny offspring to wretched parents. They would, therefore, have nothing to do with persons whose lives were of no use either to themselves or to others, even though they might have made large fortunes out of them. Harley Street would have been ruthlessly cut down and its practice limited to the deserving and curable sick, useful and busy people of moderate means who could not afford to be ill for more than the briefest space of time or to pay more than the most moderate fees. A further discouragement to the practice of medicine is that the physician is required to have had experience of disease in his own body. Plato stops short of Samuel Butler's *Erewhon*, in which sickness is a crime for which a sick person is liable to find himself in the dock, but he has no mercy on invalidism.

In gymnastic the mean must be found between the athleticism which makes men stupid and the culture which makes them soft. But the end in view is military service, and children are to be habituated to it from early years. Plato goes the length of saying that their parents should take them to look on at a battle just as potters' boys are taken to look on at the wheel. To the parents themselves, he says, as to other animals, the sight of the young ones will prove a great incentive to bravery, but the young ones must not run into any serious danger, though some risk may be taken for the sake of the training. They should be placed in the hands of veterans and provided with swift horses to enable them to escape. For that reason one of the first things to be done is to teach the young to ride.

Plato is evidently no pacifist. The most warlike of moderns may well find something repulsive in his idea of taking children to witness scenes of wounds and slaughter. Yet there are the germs of internationalism in his ideal. He draws a clear distinction between wars between Greeks, which are civil wars and ought to be avoided, and wars between Greeks and barbarians, which are necessary for the defence of their liberty. Greeks should not enslave Greeks or devastate one another's territory. They should be "lovers of Hellas and think of Hellas as their own land and share in the common temples." Differences between them should be regarded not as war but as quarrels between friends who intend some day to be reconciled. They will be correctors, not enemies. At the end of the Peloponnesian war, with all that Greek had suffered at the hands of Greek in vivid and bitter memory, this idea may well have seemed as remote and Utopian as that of European nations living in peace with the League of Nations playing the part of "corrector." To Plato, as to all Greeks, the "barbarian" remains outside the pale, but it was something in his day to dream of peace within the pale.

3

Plato observes that since States are made of flesh and blood and not of "oak and rock," there must be five human natures in individuals which correspond to the five States into which he divides the possible constitutions : the ideal, the timocratic, the oligarchical, the democratic, and the tyrannical. This is in strict accord with his governing idea that the constitution of States should correspond to the inner nature of man, but when worked out in detail it seems strained and far-fetched to the modern reader (and extremely exasperating to the student who is—or was—expected to memorize it). Nevertheless, it gives him an opportunity of introducing the brilliant sketches of human types which fill the eighth and ninth books of the *Republic*, and have a real, even if they have lost their symbolical, significance. His contemporaries would probably have recognized these as portraits of men they knew, and thus have gained a clear idea of what he meant by his classifications and have related them to Greek history. There is, I think, a cryptic element in these books which is beyond recovery, but this does not affect what is mainly of interest to the modern reader, namely his criticism of democracy and the steps by which he supposes it to pass over into tyranny.

By democracy Plato means the civic condition in which everybody is at liberty to do what he chooses and to consider himself the equal of everybody else. It "assigns equality alike to the equal and unequal." Such a constitution is the exact opposite of the ideal Republic, in which all the citizens have their work and their stations in life assigned to them according to their capacity and upbringing, and government is by general consent delegated to a class of experts bred and trained for the purpose.

The first count against democracy, then, is that it is disorderly. It is full of busybodies who are perpetually encroaching on the spheres of the experts, playing many parts, being everything by starts and nothing long. It is " a charming form of government, full of variety and disorder, and dispensing equality to equals and unequals alike." The democratic city is frank and free and " spangled with the manners and characters of mankind like an embroidered robe which is spangled with every sort of flower." And " just as women and children think variety charming, so there are many men who will deem this to be the fairest of States." In a democracy " the master fears and flatters his scholars, and the scholars despise their masters and tutors ; and in general young and old are alike ; the young man is on a level with the old and is ready to compete with him in word or deed ; and old men condescend to the young and are full of pleasantry and gaiety ; they do not like to be thought morose and authoritative and therefore they adopt the manners of the young." Even the animals catch the infection and get out of control. In such an atmosphere drones, who produce nothing, multiply and live on politics. " They are almost the entire ruling power, and the keener sort speak and act, while the rest sit buzzing about the rostrum and will not permit a word to be said on the other side."

It is useful to turn back from these passages, which are culled from the eighth book, to the seventh, in which Plato arraigns the democratic society—obviously that of Athens—which he sees around him. He is asking why the philosophic soul is so easily corrupted and its narrow path is so difficult to follow. The answer is that it is born into an atmosphere which is largely fatal to it, that of the public opinion which envelops it in the Assembly, the law-courts, the theatre, the army, everywhere where men are gathered together. This public opinion is invincible and irresponsible ; it is the source of law and the principal educator. It is " the one great sophist " ; the men who are called by that name and who are supposed to be corrupting youth do but repeat and formulate the dictates of the society which blames them for its own shortcomings.[1] Sophists and politicians are curiously identified in these passages, and we are often in doubt whether Plato means to place the blame upon the sophist-politicians or upon the society which is both the great sophist and the "great beast" who needs to be fed by political sophistry. Several of the passages most often quoted as in dispraise of politicians seem to be addressed not to those whom a modern would call by that name, but to all sorts of performers and mountebanks whom he saw trying to catch the fancy of the multitude. Best-selling novelists, greatly circulating newspapers, popular painters and film-stars would certainly not have escaped Plato's scrutiny if he had been living in these times.

4

It was evidently a very special kind of democracy in which the popular leaders could be depicted as perverted philosophers. It is as though a modern critic of institutions were to trace in the careers of Asquith, Balfour, or Curzon the corruption, in their contact with the great beast, of the principles they had learnt or ought to have learnt in the philosophy schools of Oxford and Cambridge. It is possible that even in these august quarters Plato would have discovered some sophists.

But this, too, is the logical result of the equation between philosophy, understood as knowledge of the good and the expert knowledge supposed to be needed for government, which runs through the whole of Plato's criticism of institutions. This knowledge requires the supremacy of the philosopher or, as we should say, the expert. So far from realizing this ideal, the actual State, as he sees it, is infested with amateurs who pretend to know everything and in fact know nothing, and who prevent the experts doing their proper business by railing at them and invading their territory. Justice and good government depend upon every man remaining within his own territory and doing the work for which he is competent, whereas in a democracy the ignorant and incompetent are running about all over the ground and preventing those who know from using their knowledge. It seems highly probable that, if he were living in these times,

---

[1] Nettleship, *op. cit.*, II, p. 206.

6

Plato's criticism of democracy is much more often quoted than his denunciations of tyranny, and his idea that the one must pass over into the other is commonly accepted as a generalization which has been justified by history. But it really amounts to little more than this, that where there is disorder in a State the tyrant gets his opportunity. He has got it indubitably in recent years in European States, in which dictators have come on the scene to clear up disorder caused by the failure not of established democracies but of inexperienced or fanatical partisans to combine sufficiently to keep order and carry on administration. Mankind will accept anything rather than anarchy.

Plato's Tyrant is one of the subtlest of his portraits. He is the man who offers himself as a protector of the people, and getting the mob behind him, kills or banishes his opponents, or " by the favourite method of false accusation brings them into court and murders them." After this " what can be his destiny but either to perish at the hands of his enemies or from being a man to become a wolf—that is, a tyrant ? "

" At the start and in the first days does he not smile upon all men and greet everybody he meets and deny that he is a tyrant, and promise many things in private and public, and having freed men from debts and distributed lands to the people and his own associates, he affects a gracious and gentle manner to all?" "Necessarily," said Glaucon. "But when, I suppose, he has come to terms with some of his exiled enemies, and has got others destroyed and is no longer disturbed by them, in the first place he is always stirring up some war so that the people may be in need of a leader." " That is likely." " And also that being impoverished by war-taxes they may have to devote themselves to their daily business and be less likely to plot against him ? " " Obviously." " And if, I presume, he suspects that there are free spirits who will not suffer his domination, his further object is to find pretexts for destroying them by exposing them to the enemy ? From all these motives a tyrant is compelled to be always provoking wars ? " " Yes, he is compelled to do so." " And by such conduct will he not the more readily incur the hostility of the citizens ? " " Of course." " And is it not likely that some of those who helped to establish and now share in his power, voicing their disapproval of the course of events, will speak out frankly to him and to one another—such of them as happen to be the bravest ? " " Yes, it is likely." " Then the tyrant must do away with all such if he is to maintain his rule, until he has left no one of any worth, friend or foe." "Obviously." "He must look sharp to see, then, who is brave, who is great-souled, who is wise, who is rich ; and such is his good fortune that, whether he wishes it or not, he must be their enemy and plot against them all until he purge the city." "A fine purgation," he said. "Yes," said I, "just the opposite of that which physicians practise on our bodies, for while they remove the worst and leave the best, he does the reverse." "Yes, for apparently he must," he said, "if he is to keep his power."[1]

This passage has certainly not staled with the lapse of time. It even gives the modern reader a certain thrill in re-reading it to come upon the precise word " purge " ($\kappa\alpha\theta\alpha\rho\mu\acute{o}s$) employed by twentieth-century dictators for the process by which they rid themselves of their more dangerous opponents.

The final stage is that the people will discover too late the kind of monster it has been fostering in its bosom, too late since by that time he will have taken away their arms and concentrated all power in his own hands.

It seems to me that these passages are quite as well worth reviving in these times as Plato's warnings against democracy. It may be added that Plato has no patience with the literary admirers of tyranny. He would banish the tragic poets who speak of tyranny as god-like. After all, he was an Athenian, and was it not an Athenian who said that the Greek words for freedom (*eleutheria isagoria, isonomia*) were beautiful words having the sound of music ?

---

[1] *Republic*, VIII, 567, trans. Professor Shorey, Loeb Classical Library.

CHAPTER X

THE LATER PLATO

I

TO follow Plato's thought to its conclusion we must glance briefly at two other dialogues which come after the *Republic*, the *Politicus* and the *Laws*. The *Republic* holds its place in his mind as the ideal best, but he finds it necessary to contemplate a certain dilution of its counsels of perfection to fit actual human conditions.

In his classification of States in the ninth book of the *Republic* he had said that he counted as one the monarchical and the aristocratic types of Government, but his preference then seemed to be for the aristocratic over the monarchical. The philosopher-kings or guardians of the *Republic* were to be not single but plural and all of them seemed to have equal responsibility. In the *Politicus*, the next of his political dialogues, he definitely makes his choice for one monarch. Why, indeed, should there be more than one if this one is a philosopher, the spectator of all time and all existence, the embodiment of perfect wisdom who "always knows what ought to be done." There follows an even bolder thought, but again perfectly logical—why should this all-wise and absolutely disinterested and unselfish being be hampered by what is called law? *Regis voluntis suprema lex* must be the right formula for such a being. Law is within him and he must have perfect freedom to dispense it as he chooses. "What is ordinarily called law is an impediment to knowledge, and knowledge is true sovereign." The monarch being endowed with all necessary knowledge must be not a constitutional sovereign owing allegiance to law, but the actual head of the State wielding all executive power and doing what in virtue of his supreme knowledge he deems right.

But Plato is aware, as he develops this theme, that he is moving farther and farther from reality. He has painted not a man but a god, all-knowing and absolutely disinterested, whose reign would certainly dispense with mortal-made law, which is an institution arising out of human fallibility. Unfortunately—or fortunately—there is no earthly monarch who possesses this knowledge or can be trusted with this absolute power. We are thus at length back in the region of the possible and practicable—the region in which compromises must be accepted, and the ideal suffers some eclipse because of the hardness of the human heart. In this region law must be permitted as a lesser evil than oligarchy, democracy, or tyranny unchecked by law. By the standard now adopted democracy, though far below the ideal monarchy or aristocracy, is regarded as superior to oligarchy and far preferable to tyranny, which, as the corruption of the monarchical best, is always in the deepest depths in Plato's classifications.

His major premiss is still that the rulers are, like the philosophers of the *Republic*, men of all-embracing knowledge and complete disinterestedness, who will abide by laws of their own making. But by this time he seems to have abandoned his reliance on suasion and education and to be willing to give them *carte blanche* to govern either by free-will or by compulsion so long as they govern according to knowledge. Yet he is equally clear that the worst results are reached when law is flouted by rulers who are unscientific and governed by self-interest. It has been suggested on the strength of certain passages which countenance the use of force by scientific rulers that he would have approved the ruthless sacrifice of life by modern dictators in their effort to make their will prevail. Nothing is less probable, but it is true that a subtle change is now going forward whereby the poet and philosopher dealing in parables and symbols and ministering to the spirit gives place to the less amiable but much more familiar figure of the doctrinaire seeking to enforce his specifics on a reluctant people.

2

The *Laws*, which is Plato's last word on the art of government, is supposed to reflect his disillusion after the failure of his visit to Sicily and his attempt to persuade the tyrant Dionysius to apply the principles of the *Republic* to the government of Syracuse. The story is embroidered with many details culled from the Platonic Epistles whose authenticity is still a subject of lively dispute among scholars. That Plato went to Sicily, that he was deeply disappointed with the results of his efforts, and that he returned with a lively sense of the need of training young men in the true philosophic foundations of political action and so was led to the establishment of his famous Academy is not in doubt. But none of this has any serious bearing upon his political thought. To the end the *Republic* remains in his mind as the " best thing " and the schemes proposed in the *Politicus* and the *Laws* as the " second best." The difference between the two is that he realizes that the best is unattainable in any likely circumstances and now devotes himself to making the best of the second-best. Like Burke, he considers it a great part of wisdom to discover how much of an evil it is necessary to tolerate. Nothing is revoked, but a new start is made on the ground of practical politics.

The special interest of the *Laws*, on which he is supposed to have been still at work when he died in 347 B.C., is that it poses the central problem of government in the terms in which it would still be stated after the lapse of more than 2000 years. If tyranny is an abomination and an all-wise monarchy is impossible, what remains but a " mixed polity " in which monarchy and democracy, authority and liberty are somehow reconciled ? The mixture must be not of the bad but of the good sides of both ; it must seek peace, not the kind of peace in which one party has destroyed the other, but the peace of harmony in which both are reconciled under one leader.[1] Plato speaks of " a moderate form of government under elected magistrates " as being vastly superior to " complete liberty unfettered by any authority," and in the sixth book of the *Laws* he is seen conscientiously striving to keep the balance even between the different principles. Communism and the community of wives and children now disappear from the picture, whether for the rulers or for ordinary citizens. Instead there are laws to prevent accumulations of property in a few hands and to secure its even distribution. There is to be free trade with other States, but it is to be conducted by aliens, for Plato is of opinion that the practice of commerce is beneath the dignity of a

---

[1] See on this subject, Ernest Barker, *Political Thought of Plato and Aristotle*, p. 187.

full Greek citizen. In regard to institutions there is to be what we should call a constituent Assembly to start the State and select the necessary officials. A Council of 360 is to be elected in four groups from different propertied classes, and the army is to be entirely self-governing. " All who belong to the military forces shall vote for the commanders, all who carry shields for the taxiarchs ; all the cavalry shall elect for themselves phylarchs ; the commanders shall appoint for themselves captains of skirmishers, archers, or any other branch of the service." [1] The modern advocates of soldiers' and sailors' councils could scarcely desire more.

In other respects it has been much debated whether Plato's solution in the *Laws* is oligarchic or democratic, but this is mainly a matter of words. A council numbering 360 in a State of the size [2] he was contemplating could scarcely be regarded as an oligarchy, even though elected on a property qualification. We are here at the beginning of what moderns call representative institutions. Instead of the pure democracy of Athens in which every citizen is a member of the Assembly and has an equal voice in it, we now have a council of limited numbers, elected by different classes of property-owners. But with this qualification the new State is all-powerful. Its law covers the whole of life, moral, religious, and material ; its Government can follow every individual into every nook and cranny of what we now call his private life. It is, in fact, what moderns call totalitarian. It is true that Plato still prefers that law shall be enforced not by punishment and the secular arm, but by education and the appeal of mind to mind, but he provides an apparatus of compulsion which raises a strong presumption that the State of the *Laws* would degenerate into the same kind of tyranny as the modern totalitarian State.

3

Still more so when we consider the enormous importance which Plato attaches to an education which shall take children of tender

---

[1] *Laws*, VI, 756.
[2] Apparently the number of enfranchised citizens was to be less than 6000.

years and, through music and gymnastic, mould them to the form desired by the State. They are to be so brought up as to assimilate their surroundings and to accept without question what their elders declare to be good and right. The original idea of the use of music in education is carried to its extremest length in the second book of the *Laws* where " choristry " and singing are all but identified with education. The law-giver is told that he " can, if he tries, persuade the souls of the young of anything, so that the only question he has to consider in his inventing is what would do most good to the State if it were believed." He must " devise all possible means to ensure that the whole of the community constantly, so long as they live, use exactly the same language, so far as is possible, about these matters in their songs, their tales, and their discourses." Choirs of boys, young men, and older men must " enchant the souls of children, while still young and tender, by rehearsing all the noble things which we have already recounted or shall recount hereafter," and all else that their elders may decide to be good and right.[1] The passage might almost be taken from a manual of propaganda prepared in Moscow, Berlin, or Rome in the twentieth century.

One reads on with a growing distaste. Plato is so obsessed with the idea that his law-givers will be infallible guides to what is good and right that he does not consider what would be the effect on the young if the myths and songs which they invented fell short of his ideal. In the light of modern experience I find it difficult to read the famous passages on education in the *Laws* or even in the *Republic* without feeling that the bloom has gone from them. They lend themselves all too easily to what in effect is an outrage on youth. The idea of catching the child in infancy and fixing certain ideas indelibly on the plastic surface of its mind, before it is of an age to think or choose for itself, has been a germinating seed of mischief in the subsequent years. The breathless pursuit of youth by religious and political sects, the enormous sums of money spent on it, the strife that it has provoked, the fanaticism that it creates when it succeeds, and the violent reactions to which it leads when it fails—all this is a heavy contra-account to an originally benevolent idea.

---

[1] *Laws*, II, 664.

In this philosophy youth only exists as plastic material in the hands of its seniors ; it has no rights of its own, least of all the right to question and inquire. The constitution propounded in the *Laws* is a tyranny of age over youth. There are age qualifications for all its principal offices; the "Nocturnal Council," which is the final guardian of the constitution, consists of old men ; the "Dionysiac chorus," which is in charge of the arts, is a body of seniors. To these is committed the maintenance of the *status quo* ; for all the remaining citizens the main requisite is a self-controlled and law-abiding disposition, governed by reverence (αἰδώς) and moderation (μετριότης), which yields unquestioning obedience to those in authority and which has been so imposed on children from their tenderest years as to be second nature when they grow up. In this way and this way only, Plato seems to say, can his Commonwealth be kept in equilibrium and prevented from declining.

4

In the end what chiefly strikes a modern on reading or re-reading Plato is that he seems always to have in his thoughts the decline and fall of States—their corruption from the good to the bad side of their constitutions—never their progress from the bad to the better, from the primitive to the civilized. His Nocturnal Council in the *Laws* is permitted to send missions to inquire of the practice of other States and to incorporate into their own constitution what they think to be good, but their object is rather to take warning and to prevent decay of a *status quo* which (*ex hypothesi*) is the best attainable in the imperfect human conditions. The society which Plato has in mind is a perfect but static unity, rendered such by the co-operation of all its citizens ; but needing to be carefully guarded from the danger of its balance being disturbed from within or without. The idea of its being an organism in the sense that it is capable of growth—capable of what a modern philosopher calls creative evolution—is no part of his thought.

Nor has he any conception of the ideas which moderns group together as toleration, freedom of opinion, and liberty of conscience. The measures against impiety in the tenth book of the *Laws* read like a perfect model for the Holy Inquisition.

If anyone commits impiety either by word or deed, he that meets with him shall defend the law by informing the magistrates, and the first magistrates who hear of it shall bring the man up before the court appointed to decide such cases, and if any magistrate on hearing of the matter fail to do this, he himself shall be liable to a charge of impiety at the hands of him who wishes to punish him on behalf of the laws.

A distinction is made between the atheist who is a just man and a hater of evil, and the atheist who is an evil liver ; yet both must be punished, and of the two the good atheist is the more dangerous, since he is more likely to convert other people. The impiety which results from ignorance but is not of evil disposition is to be treated by a special kind of incarceration for five years during which the offenders are to be visited only by the elders (members of the Nocturnal Council), who " will minister to their souls' salvation by admonition." If when the period of their incarceration is over, any of them seems to be reformed, " he shall dwell with those who are reformed, but if in reality he is not reformed and if he be convicted again on a like charge he shall be punished with death." The whole atmosphere of this and similar passages is ecclesiastical, even, we might say, mediæval. The book has been well quarried to provide justification for persecutors and heresy-hunters.

Yet, in spite of everything, Plato again and again repeats that true morality is the voluntary acceptance of the good by the rightly educated man. He makes Clinias, the Cretan spokesman in the *Laws* quote with approval the " common saying that good Athenians are always superlatively good," for " they alone are good not by outward compulsion but by inner disposition." How, then, it may be asked, does he justify the formidable apparatus for outward compulsion which he proposes in his latest constitution ? Conceivably he might answer that this is a " second-best " constitution, requiring a coercion of sinful mortals which would be unnecessary in the heavenly model, but his theory that right conduct depends on right knowledge leads logically to the conclusion that the man who is ignorant, whether from wilfulness or blindness, must be eliminated from a virtuous State if his ignorance proves invincible.

Thus at every turn we are driven back on the presupposition that there is a body of doctrine in the possession of one man or a group of men which the true believer will recognize and joyfully accept, and which unbelievers must be compelled to accept, if only to prevent them leading others astray. For the citizens of the heavenly city with the eyes of their souls turned to the light this may be a blessed revelation ; in the hands of fallible mortals ruling over their fellow-men it easily becomes an instrument of persecution and tyranny. It is impossible for a modern to read the *Laws* without perceiving in the light of mediæval and modern instances the ultimately pernicious consequences of the theory that politics is an exact science of which the principles and methods have been discovered by certain favoured beings. If that assumption is granted, all encroachments on their sphere and especially those which seek justification in the name of democracy must be resisted as intrusions of the inexpert, and political heresy becomes as much sin and crime as religious was in the eyes of mediæval ecclesiastics.

5

These observations in no way detract from the greatness of Plato as a political thinker. To read him again is to be impressed with his astonishing genius, his capacity for abstract thinking, his wide-ranging human interests, his humour, his wit, his eloquence, the beauty of his literary style. If only in some of these respects his successors could have followed in his footsteps, what a place by now might not philosophy have filled in the daily life of ordinary people ! It is as easy for a modern reactionary, Fascist or Communist, to quote Plato as for the devil to quote scripture, indeed, in some respects easier, for the dramatic form in which he writes often leaves it uncertain whether he is speaking for himself or putting some paradox which helps to develop his theme into the mouth of one of his characters. But to treat him literally as a guide to practical politics is to mistake our real debt to him. That debt—and it is immense—lies mainly in the fact that he took a great mass of unsorted material touching the govern-ment of mankind and from it extricated and stated explicitly the chief problems which have faced the world from his time till now. What is the true relation of rulers and ruled ? Can the exercise of authority by the former be reconciled with the enjoyment of liberty by the latter ? Are right and wrong, justice and injustice the same for the

of a genius and poet for that of a professor, lecturer, and tutor.[1] There are passages in which we can almost hear him rapping out his firstlies, secondlies, and thirdlies, and making the necessary pauses while his pupils take notes. Yet if we can get over a certain distaste for his pedagogic manner and a certain disappointment at the numerous lacunæ and seeming inconsequences in his political writings, as they have reached us, it is precisely these matter-of-fact qualities which help us forward in the history of political thought.

Aristotle opened his school at Athens in 335 B.C., about twelve years after Plato's death, and his principal works are supposed to have been written in the next ten years. He is in agreement with Plato in regarding ethics and politics as one study, in assigning moral and spiritual significance to the association of men in the State, in believing that the happy life, which is the life of virtue, is the end which God and nature have ordained both for the individual and the State—the end to which the whole creation moves. Where he parts company with Plato is in denying the virtue of an ideal which, as Plato admits, may not be realizable on earth. In Aristotle's view, as propounded in the *Politics*, political theorizing is only useful in so far as it keeps within the limits of the possible here and now. He analyses existing States and constitutions according as they conform to or depart from certain types, which in the end are fined down to democracy and oligarchy, but always keeps an eye on their practical results. Both the dominant types are departures from his ideal (which seems to be monarchy in the hands of an all-wise, perfectly disinterested, but non-existent monarch), but he thinks that in a combination of the two we may discover something which approximates to it as nearly as is possible in the conditions of mundane, practical politics.

Plato himself, as we have seen, had made a similar descent from the ideal to the actual in his later books, the *Politicus* and the *Laws*, where also an elaborate discussion may be found of the " second best " institutions possible in the actual world ; and if we are concerned to support him against his pupil, we may easily discover that he had anticipated a considerable number of Aristotle's criticisms. As

---

[1] This does not apply to the *Ethics,* which, especially in the later books, contains passages of almost apostolic fervour.

between the two philosophers it is sufficient to bear in mind that Aristotle is very often bringing to bear on Plato's philosophic parable standards fetched from the everyday life which Plato himself had, for his special purpose, deliberately discarded. The two men are in this respect moving on different planes, Plato (in the *Republic*) covering the whole field of religion and philosophy, Aristotle (in the *Politics*) concentrating on practical affairs.

2

It is with Aristotle the practical politician that this chapter is concerned. I will therefore leave aside his discussion of the origins of the State and his classifications and analyses of the existing governments of Greece, in order to concentrate on his sketch of the ideal State in Books VII and VIII of the *Politics*,[1] which may be presumed to contain his ideas of what ought to be within the limits of the possible. At the outset we find him, even more than Plato, shutting himself within the limits of the Greek city-state. Good law, by which he means a good constitution, is difficult if not impossible, he thinks, in an over-populous State. Who is to be the leader of any great multitude or its public crier if he has not the voice of a Stentor? The number of citizens is to be the largest possible in order to ensure independence of life, but not so large that it cannot be comprehended in a single view.

Of what human material should such a State be composed? It must have husbandmen who supply food, artisans, an army, a propertied class, a priesthood, and judges of questions of justice and policy. In an undiluted democracy all citizens are considered qualified to perform all these functions, but this is not to be desired. No fully enfranchised citizen should lead a mechanical and commercial life, for such a life is ignoble and opposed to virtue. Functions must be distributed according to age, experience and capacity. But certain practical considerations need to be borne in mind. Thus the classes which have arms in their hands have also in their hands the continuance or the dissolution of the constitution. Therefore both the

---

[1] The editions vary in the order in which they place the books. In some the books here numbered VII and VIII are placed as IV and V.

military and the deliberative or judicial functions should be assigned to the same persons, but not at the same time. The younger should serve in the army, the elder perform judicial and deliberative duties, and the old take up the priestly duties, the serving of the altars, the religious festivals, consulting the oracles, etc. It is as though in the modern world a man began his career as a subaltern in the Guards ; then at the age of thirty or thereabouts went into Parliament or became a civil servant or a judge, and finally about the age of sixty wound up his career by becoming a bishop or a dean or being appointed to a cure of souls in town or country.

Since the citizens who perform these functions are not to engage in mechanical or commercial activities, they must have enough property to enable them to live the life of leisure, which is the condition of good public work. Accordingly, the land is to be divided into two parts, public and private, the public for the worship of the gods, the private for the support of the free citizens who are to have two plots each. All this land is to be cultivated by slaves, or, if not slaves, by men of slavish disposition—a necessary precaution " if they are to be useful in labour and in no danger of rising against their masters." A certain affluence is the condition of good citizenship in a State which makes happiness its object, for " while no doubt the virtuous man will make a moral use of poverty, disease, and all other chances of life, still it is not in these, but in their opposites, that true happiness resides."

Common meals, for which special buildings should be provided, are desirable for the different classes of citizens, and, if the necessity of subscribing to them excludes the poor, that makes a desirable property qualification which the landowning citizen is able to meet. But care must be taken lest there should be a large class of subject citizens excluded from power, since they would have on their side all the unenfranchised inhabitants ready for revolt, and it is impossible that members of the governing class should be so numerous as to be stronger than the other two together. In the way suggested we shall obtain the desired mixed " polity " or constitutional government which is a fusion of democracy and oligarchy, the power being neither in the hands of the rich, as in oligarchy, nor in those of the poor, as in democracy, but in those of a body of free citizens enjoying some property and sufficient leisure. One condition, however, is all-important. This is that there should be a body of law the observance of which should be binding on the governing class. This in the end is the test of a true " polity " or, as moderns would say, of constitutional government, and it is to be found neither in a democracy, which overrides law or makes law as it chooses, nor in an oligarchy, which governs without law.

3

Virtue, in Aristotle's thought, is always a mean between two extremes, and his virtuous State finds salvation in the rule of moderately endowed men in accordance with law. He even says that the criterion of a good fusion or good mean between democracy and oligarchy " is the possibility of calling the same polity a democracy and an oligarchy, for it is evident that the cause of his uncertainty in language is the success of the fusion. It is, in fact, a general characteristic of the mean that the two extremes are discernible in it." [1] His final conclusion is that the best constitution is that which rests mainly on the middle-class of citizens. " For they do not, like paupers, lust after the goods of others, nor do others lust after theirs, as paupers after the property of the rich." Accordingly, it is an immense blessing to a State that the active citizens should possess an intermediate and sufficient amount of property ; for where there is a class of extremely wealthy people on the one hand and a class of absolute paupers on the other, the result is either democracy or an untempered oligarchy, and from either of these in their extreme form tyranny may result. A strong middle-class is the best guarantee against tyranny, but this class must see to it that the poor are not too poor, for if they fail in that their own position becomes insecure.

Should this model State have a foreign policy, and, if so, what sort of policy should it be ? Aristotle is astonishingly vehement in denouncing an aggressive or imperialist policy. He rebukes a contemporary writer for eulogizing the Spartan legislators, who " disciplined the citizens to endurance in order that they might enjoy external dominion." Such a principle, he says, is full of mischief,

---

[1] *Politics*, VI, 9.

since it would justify any citizen who had the power in endeavouring to make himself a tyrant :

No principle therefore and no law of this nature is either statesmanlike or profitable, nor is it true ; the same ideals are the best both for individuals and for communities, and the lawgiver should endeavour to implant them in the souls of mankind. The proper object of practising military training is not in order that men may enslave those who do not deserve slavery, but in order that first they may themselves avoid becoming enslaved to others ; then so that they may seek suzerainty for the benefit of the subject people, but not for the sake of world-wide despotism ; and thirdly to hold despotic power over those who deserve to be slaves. Experience supports the testimony of theory, that it is the duty of the lawgiver rather to study how he may frame his legislation both with regard to warfare and in other departments for the object of leisure and peace. Most military States remain safe while at war, but perish when they have won their empire ; in peace-time they lose their keen temper, like iron. The lawgiver is to blame, because he did not educate them to be able to employ leisure.[1]

The last sentence in this passage brings us to one of the central thoughts of the *Politics*—the necessity of leisure in the well-ordered State and the right use of it. " War," he says, " has its end in peace and business its end in leisure." The right conduct of business and the noble employment of leisure are both requisite. Leisure and virtue are closely allied : " A high degree of justice and temperance is necessary to persons who are reputed to be most prosperous and who enjoy all the goods for which men are accounted happy—to those, if such there be who dwell, as poets say, in the islands of the blessed ; for they above all will need culture, temperance, and justice, and in proportion as their life is one of leisure amidst a rich abundance of such goods. . . . It is our duty to cultivate the virtue which has its sphere in leisure and to do so for its own sake."

4

How shall the State be provided with citizens of the desired type ? Care and thought are needed from the moment of procreation on-wards. Men should marry about the age of thirty-seven, and women about the age of eighteen ; they will thus come at the same time to

---

[1] *Politics*, VII, 13 ; trans. H. Backham, Loeb Classical Library.

the period of life when they cease to beget children. Since the population must not exceed a certain number, a limit is to be set to the number of children born. How this is to be achieved is a question on which Aristotle, like Plato, is somewhat vague. There is to be a law against rearing cripples ; but for the rest he prefers abortion to the exposing of children born. In order to maintain the necessary physical standard, a man is not to be a parent after the age of fifty-four or fifty-five ; and children should have a diet containing plenty of milk, be inured to cold at an early age, and be allowed to stretch and scream as nature prompts them. Special precautions should be taken against their associating more than necessary with slaves ; there must be no talking about foul things in their presence and they must not be taken to satirical plays or comedies or be brought into contact with objects or pictures from which they might derive a taint of ungentlemanliness.

Aristotle is painfully impressed by the confusion of opinion about the subjects and methods of education. " Nobody knows whether the young should be trained in such studies as are merely useful as a means of livelihood or in such as tend to the promotion of virtue." But since he has laid down that mechanical and mercenary occupations " deprive the intellect of all leisure or dignity," studies which lead up to these must not be pursued with " excessive assiduity or endeavour after perfect mastery." Within these limits or if undertaken for one's own sake or the sake of one's friends or the attainment of virtue, they need not be deemed illiberal, but otherwise, and they may easily bear " a menial or slavish aspect." In these studies the object is everything. They must be pursued for their own sake and not for livelihood or profit.

The right manner of employing leisure thus becomes the main object of education for the free citizen. Reading and writing are necessary and the art of design has uses both as a means of forming judgments on works of art and so saving the citizens from being cheated in the purchase and sale of household goods, and even more because it renders them scientific observers of physical beauty. But music is the main factor in education for the employment of leisure, music as a modern understands the word, and not in the extended sense, to cover literature and poetry, in which Plato uses it.

always easy to draw the line between the two things, but he is unsparing in his condemnation of usury—the employment of money to make or breed money—as a wholly unnatural use of wealth.

It was this part of his doctrine in combination with his support of property and the family which brought Aristotle most into favour with the mediæval world, lay and ecclesiastical. In its confusion between money and wealth and its failure to recognize the essential part played by trade in the life of the State this special kind of conservatism may seem the most impracticable of all to the modern reader, but it fits in with his whole idea of the nature of citizenship. His free citizen was to be a man of culture and leisure, assured a comfortable existence by his possession of a certain limited quantity of land cultivated by slave-labour, but he was to be shut off from mere money-making and the vulgar occupations associated with it, among which usury was deemed to be the most debasing. No doctrine could have suited better the mediæval feudal aristocracy, which, ignoring the limit which Aristotle placed on the possession of land, found high sanction in the rest of his doctrine for the contempt of commerce and the commercial classes which helped them to claim and keep their privileged position. The sharp line drawn by Plato and Aristotle, in common with most Greek thinkers, between the gentleman on one side and the trader and mechanic on the other, and their insistence that the gentleman could not cross this line without losing virtue, has a large responsibility for the class distinctions of the modern world.

6

In keeping with the whole order of his ideas is Aristotle's doctrine of " distributive justice." He conceives the State as distributing functions and rewards to citizens who have claims on it in proportion to their contributions to it. But what standard shall it adopt in measuring these contributions ? A democracy will say freedom of birth, which would require it in justice to distribute its good things in exactly equal shares to all its citizens. An oligarchy will say wealth, which would require it to favour its citizens in proportion to their possessions, which are apparently assumed to be their contribution to the State. But the State which regards the promotion of virtue as its object will discard both these standards and seek to distribute its rewards and offices to those who will best help to pursue this object, that is to say, it will give most power to the most virtuous citizens. This will be the right kind of distributive justice, though it may result in a superficial inequality. It would be a positive injustice to the fit to give the offices that are due to them to the unfit.

At the same time Aristotle's idea of fitness or capacity is less specialized than ours. The good citizens must have " moral wisdom," military prowess, and a certain amount of property, as well as efficiency in a particular direction. But an important qualification is added. It would not be just to confine offices to the fit and few and leave the many out in the cold. For the many collectively make an important contribution to the State which deserves a proportionate return. Moreover, they have a capacity, for which scope ought to be given, in judging and deliberating, in electing the magistrates and examining their records and auditing their accounts. The best results may be expected when the many and the few are associated in these functions. Aristotle concedes, as Plato does not, that there are occasions when demos displays the kind of good sense in which experts are apt to fail. On these occasions *secura judicat urbs*. In any case, it would be dangerous to exclude the many, for they might cause serious trouble if they joined up with other dissatisfied elements or with slaves. The sense that the great beast is dangerous and needs to be appeased is never absent from Aristotle's thought. " More must be the number of those who wish a State to continue than of those who do not," but this wish to continue will only be assured if it is recognized that the majority have claims which ought to be respected and a certain political capacity which is of value to the State. Distributive justice will ensure this.

We have here the germs of what in modern language would be called a Liberal constitution, but the picture is unfinished and many points are left in doubt. In spite of his repeated insistence on the sovereignty of law—law being conceived as " reason unaffected by desire "—he leaves us in doubt about both the sources of law and the nature of the law-making authority which he has in view for his State. He considers that changes in law are to be avoided, if possible, and for that reason places the guardianship of law—upon which constitutionalism depends—in the hands of aged men, who are supposed to speak with the voice of experience detached from party-passion. But the idea of a legislative body exercising a law-making or law-reforming function is alien to Greek thought and practice and has no explicit place in Aristotle's scheme. In Athens, which he has most in view, the popular assembly shared in the proceedings preliminary to legislation, but not in legislation itself. It considered at a stated meeting each year whether the laws stood in need of revision, and if it so decided, any private citizen could give notice of amendments which were then tried by a court specially appointed *ad hoc*, and if approved by that court became law.[1] But a popular court appointed *ad hoc* could scarcely be regarded as a guarantee of law in the teeth of the popular assembly, and the result was, in fact, a popular sovereignty over law as over all else. The problem of guaranteeing law against popular assemblies and preventing the latter from overriding it by their decrees or arbitrary action is still very much in debate in the modern world, witness the struggle between President Roosevelt and the aged judges who are entrenched in the Supreme Court of the United States. Their antiquity, which was their main defect in the President's eyes, would have been their main qualification in Aristotle's State.

Aristotle is keenly alive to the evils and dangers of extreme poverty. While seeking to keep the property of the well-to-do within moderate limits, he would have a public fund for the purchasing of small farms or finding some sort of business for the very poor. He approves the life of the farmer, for the characteristic reason that he is generally too busy with his own affairs to want to take office or to interfere in politics.[2] The larger the non-political class who will be content to leave public affairs to the qualified few, the better in his view it will

---

[1] " The people has made itself sovereign in every respect, and determines every issue by its decrees or by courts in which it is itself supreme " : Ἀθηναίων πολιτεία XLI, 24-6, cited by Barker, *Political Thought of Plato and Aristotle*, p. 456.

[2] In criticizing Plato's idea of the community of wives and children Aristotle observes that " it would seem to be more serviceable for the farmer class than for the guardians, for there will be less friendship among them if their children and women are in common, and unfriendliness in the subject classes is a good thing with a view to their being submissive to authority and not making revolution." *Politics*, II, 1.

be for the State. To convert the idle and turbulent poor into industrious peasant-proprietors who will be all day at work in the fields is therefore extremely desirable. Throughout all this part of his argument we are conscious of a severely practical strain. He does not pity the outcasts or talk humanitarian language about them ; he wants to keep them quiet so that his virtuous citizens may conduct the affairs of the city in peace. He argues passionately for the necessity of slavery and its justification (outside the enslavement of Greeks) by the principle of rule and subjection which pervades all nature. A slave is an " animate instrument " and belongs wholly to his master in virtue of the latter's intrinsic moral superiority. The slave differs from his master in not possessing reason and from the lower animals in being able to understand it. Aristotle admits that there are exceptional cases which have somewhat confused the true doctrine ; but this doctrine is that, where the proper relation exists, slavery is beneficial both to the slave and to his owner. Since a slave is useful only in providing the necessaries of life, he need have no high degree of virtue, but only just so much as will prevent him failing in his duties from licentiousness or timidity.[1]

In the cool objectiveness of this argument we reach the limit of Greek thought. The thing that moderns speak of as " common humanity " does not exist for either Plato or Aristotle. Plato and (less certainly) Aristotle would seem to bar slavery for Greeks, but that men have rights in virtue of being men does not occur to either of them unless men are Greeks. And even among Greeks both have in view a favoured class possessing culture and virtue which entitle them to the service of others, who are excluded from equality with the favoured few precisely because they render these services and by so doing partake of the nature of slaves. The germ of the thought that moral worth might be exhibited in all material conditions and even perhaps shine the brighter in adverse conditions was presently to appear in the Stoic philosophy and later to blossom into one of the great central doctrines of Christianity, but it makes almost no appearance in Plato and Aristotle.[2] To them leisure, culture, and a certain degree

---

[1] *Politics,* I, 5.

[2] See *supra,* p. 100, for Aristotle's observation that a virtuous man will make the best of adversity.

of wealth were necessary conditions of a free and virtuous life, and though this life might only be led by a minority, it was part of the nature of things that these necessaries should be provided for this minority by lower orders of slavish men pursuing menial or banausic occupations.

CHAPTER XII

ARISTOTLE ON REVOLUTION

I

BOOK V[1] of the *Politics*, which deals with revolutions and their causes, is a bed of thorns for the impatient reader. It abounds in digressions and parentheses ; it gives full rein to the writer's passion for dividing and subdividing ; it illustrates by examples which have only an antiquarian interest for the modern reader. Yet if we persevere in spite of these discouragements we shall find in it some of Aristotle's most characteristic thoughts.

With a very little ingenuity it might be divided into two parts with separate objects in view. One would be a practical manual of behaviour for oligarchs, democrats, aristocrats, monarchs, and even tyrants, showing each according to his own suppositions and standards how to keep himself in power when he has gained power. The other would be a treatise on the philosophic basis of good government, a knowledge of which is necessary to the steady pursuit of the good life under any system. Part one we might suppose to be written by a man of the world who takes a cool view of what is expedient or necessary for those in authority, and who views the scene with an objectivity which might be called cynical and even Machiavellian. Part two, on the other hand, would be the work of a thinker who stands above the battle and admonishes all the parties to it about the principles of just government.

Let me cull a few maxims and warnings from the supposed Part I. Oligarchs (assumed to be men of property who have obtained control of government) are warned that they need to have a majority of

---

[1] Placed by some editors as Book VII and Book VIII.

people " (οὐκ ἀδικήσω τὸν δῆμον) ; and if the democrat wishes to endure, he too must do justice not only to the multitude, but to all classes. Whatever it is, a constitution must be rooted and grounded in the heart and will of the people ; if this fails, no mechanical rules will save it in the long run. There must be an established or pre-established harmony between a people and its constitution. For this reason a " system of education suited to the constitution is the greatest of all preservatives." For a people educated under such a system " to live in conformity with the constitution ought not to be considered slavery, but safety."[1] Aristotle to the end holds to his view that his mixed constitution, the judicious blend of democracy and oligarchy, is likeliest to commend itself to a rightly educated people, but harmony of people and constitution by means of such an education is the greatest preservative.

Here, in the end, he joins hands with Plato in a doctrine which is invoked equally by Liberal reformers who hold that a good education is the foundation of good citizenship and by dictators who see in it a potent and indispensable instrument for fashioning the young to the pattern of their institutions. " This," said Burke, " is the true touchstone of all theories which regard man and the affairs of men ; does it not suit his nature in general ?—does it suit his nature as modified by his habits ? " " On the contrary," say the Dictators, " the nature of men can and ought to be modified to suit our theories. Just as the churches have required religious education to suit their doctrine, so we require political education to suit ours." If we may judge by results Plato and Aristotle did not at all exaggerate what may be achieved by this instrument in shaping the human material, provided it is taken young enough and submitted year by year to a systematic discipline of thought and mind from which all conflicting ideas are excluded.

It is in the end what Pascal calls the *plis de la pensée*—the fold of the thought, the things that it takes for granted—which makes it so difficult to draw parallels between Greek and modern thinking. In many ways the Greek mind seems more enlightened than the modern, yet it

---

[1] Οὐ γάρ δεῖ οἴεσθαι δουλείαν εἶναι τὸ ζῆν πρὸς τὴν πολιτείαν ἄλλα σωτηρίαν.

accepts without question a view of life which shuts the immense majority of human kind out of the supposedly civilized world and makes distinctions between those whom it admits which, though justified on high philosophic grounds, seem to a modern pure snobbery. Whether he is talking of democracy or oligarchy, the people whom Aristotle has in mind are a privileged caste whose wants are supplied either by slaves or by inferior persons engaged in occupations which the superior regard as beneath them. I have listened to a lecture on the *Politics* in which a skilful comparison was drawn between Aristotle's ideal polity with its middle-class exercising the chief power and constitutional government as practised in mid-Victorian England. It could be made plausible so long as the term " middle-class " was made to embrace in the same category Aristotle's men of leisure and virtue and the great industrial magnates, merchants, and traders who had risen to power by their success in commercial pursuits in mid-Victorian England. But in fact nearly the whole of these would have been excluded by Aristotle's definitions from the privileged ranks of free and virtuous citizens, and relegated to an inferior position outside the franchise.

As with Plato, so with Aristotle, the value of what he has to tell us lies less in his analysis of institutions than in his shrewd and penetrating observations upon the behaviour of men in their efforts to govern their fellow-men, and the peculiar temptations and pitfalls which attend these efforts. Institutions change, but political human nature remains astonishingly the same. We may read Plato and Aristotle and in this respect find modern instances on almost every page. This, we say to ourselves, is what must happen if the democratic man pushes his doctrine to excess or the oligarchical man rides roughshod over his fellow-beings or the rich fail to satisfy the just claims of the poor. Here is the perfect picture of the tyrannical man and the necessity which he is under of purging his opponents and rivals ; or here, again, the warning of what happens when government breaks down and chaos follows. In all these respects we seem to be reading the books of the prophets revealing problems which during the next two thousand years and more were to face mankind in its endless quest of the kind of government which shall give it peace and justice.

CHAPTER XIII

CICERO

I

WHILE the philosophers were still arguing about the Greek city-state and seeking perfection in miniature for its self-sufficing institutions, forces were at work which were to destroy all the suppositions of their theory. The rise of Philip of Macedon required a vital decision from the Athenians. Should they make terms with him and empower him to lead the combined Greek world against the barbarian, or should they themselves rally the Greek world and lead it against Philip ? Either decision required a break with the theory of the self-sufficing city-state and a revival of Pan-Hellenism, as in the old days of the Persian war, whether under the leadership of Athens, if another Pericles could be found, or under that of the new genius who was rising up on the unlikely soil of Macedonia.

Athens wavered. Philip of Macedon was from her point of view only half a Greek, and to make terms with him seemed a humiliation. Demosthenes thundered against the very idea ; Isocrates, knowing his countrymen and their mood under the cautious leadership of the able administrator Eubulus, who then controlled their fortunes, was for appealing to Philip, who greatly admired Athens and would have made things easy for her if she had let him. Between the two she hesitated, and having blundered into war with Philip suffered the disaster of Chæronea, which rung the death-knell of the independent Greek city-state. The philosophers had had their say and the men of action were now on the scene. Greece became a dependency of Macedonia, and Alexander, the pupil of Aristotle, destroyed Persia and marched as far as India, founding many new Greek cities as he went. On his death his empire broke up, and after two centuries of confused struggle the rising power of Rome carried all before it. Having destroyed the Macedonian kingdom and wiped out Carthage, Rome became master of the whole Mediterranean basin. The Greeks had had some flickers of liberty and had sought safety now with one side and now with another in the long struggle, but their incurable inability to hold together was still their undoing, and in the end nothing remained for them but, in the words of Polybius, to obey the words of Rome.

The period is full of interest for the historian of war and conquest, and it may even be said to have scattered Greek culture and Greek civilization over a far wider area than would have been possible if the Greek cities had succeeded in maintaining their self-contained life and their aloof attitude to the outside world. But it has little or nothing to tell us of the development of political institutions. Conquering armies and governments improvised methods of administering the territories they annexed, employing severity or lenience as suited their purpose, which was to guard their new frontiers and prevent the conquered enemy from rebelling. The technique of conquest through the planting of new cities and the conversion of conquered territory into provinces with more or less of self-government, as the conquering Power proved unequal to the task of governing them from the centre, is the chief theme of history during this period. Success was to fall to the Power which was least wedded to any preconceived theory and best able to adapt itself to the rapidly changing circumstances.

2

This period, nevertheless, was to test one of the principal questions raised by Aristotle : Can a democracy govern an empire ? Can it acquire an empire and remain a democracy ? The history of Rome during these years might almost be written in the form of an answer to these questions. At the beginning of the period of conquest (roughly from 270 B.C. to 150 B.C.) the constitution of Rome was a near approach to Aristotle's idea of a moderate democracy. The Consuls, representing the monarchical element, were elected and held office only for a year. The patriciate had ceased to exist as a privileged class ; the Senate and the great offices were open to all citizens ; the will of the people in assembly was in theory and still to a large extent in fact supreme in the election of magistrates and the passing of laws, but the system was so checked and balanced as to prevent the multitude from obtaining supreme power. In the years that follow we see power passing gradually out of the hands of the assembly into that of the Senate, and the Senate itself falling under the control of a small class which more and more arrogates to itself an exclusive authority in defiance of law and constitution. The Assembly still in theory decides the question of peace and war, but almost invariably it acts on the prompting of the Senate, which keeps in its hands the appointment of generals, the conduct of war, the making of peace, the conclusion of alliances, and all that in modern times is called foreign policy. As the old nobility fades out of the picture a new class of " plebeian nobles," which has won its position by wealth and efficiency, appears on the scene, and stands together against all comers. This class was even more hostile to democracy than the old aristocracy. They had, says Livy, " begun to despise the people from the moment that they had ceased to be despised by the patricians." [1]

In the circumstances of these years this was the inevitable course of events. Only the Senate had the power of prompt and decisive action which the period of war and conquest required, and it had justified itself by the tenacity and courage with which it carried through the Punic wars. But the Senate itself broke down under the strain of the new problems which crowded on one another during this period. The enormous influx of wealth following on the conquests changed the whole structure of Roman society. Much of it had flowed into the pockets of private individuals, successful soldiers who had been permitted to despoil the conquered, traders and speculators who had followed in their wake, bankers and financiers who had thriven on both. But enough came into the coffers of the State to enable it to dispense with the orderly taxation of its subjects, while it bribed the town proletariat with bread and games and flooded the country with free corn produced by slave labour, to the ruin of Italian farmers. To grow rich quickly was now the object of the ruling class, and cor-

---

[1] " Plebeios nobiles contemnere plebem, ex quo contemni a patribus desierint, coepisse " : Livy, XXII, 34.

rupt governors let loose upon provinces reduced flourishing cities to ruin and bankruptcy within a comparatively short time.

Moralists inveighed against the decay of the old Roman tradition and the dissolute excesses of the new order. They were too late. The Republic by this time had become an oligarchy of wealth which by its misrule was rapidly goading the poorer citizens into rebellion. This was the opportunity of ambitious soldiers, who played off people against nobles and presented themselves as saviours of society. By the beginning of the first century B.C. the scene was laid for the struggles between rival soldiers, Marius and Sulla, Pompey and Cæsar, Octavius and Antony, and for the triumvirates and dictatorships which were to end the Republic and inaugurate the Empire.

Beware of the conqueror, said Aristotle, for he will not be content with lording it over subject races ; he will want also to lord it over his own people ; beware of letting the wealthy grow out of proportion to the poor, for they will produce rebellion and out of rebellion will come tyranny. Beware of aspiring to military success, for the States that do, although they are saved in time of war, generally collapse as soon as they have obtained imperial power. They "lose their temper like steel in time of peace. For this, however, the legislator is to blame, in that he did not educate them in the capacity for enjoying leisure." Capacity for enjoying leisure was certainly not included in the gifts with which the Romans had been endowed by nature. Nothing could have been in more striking contrast with the quiet life of the virtuous citizen in the self-contained and self-sufficient city-state of the Aristotelian model than the restless ambition and boundless activity of the makers of imperial Rome.

3

Aristotle had failed to perceive that the principle of rule and subjection which he found in all nature and used to glorify slavery had a far wider application than the particular case to which he limited it. If it was, as he said, " equally inevitable and beneficient " that the master, in virtue of his supposed superiority, should own and dominate the slave, why should not the Roman, equally conscious of his superiority, conquer and dominate his inferiors, especially when most of these were barbarians who would have destroyed him if he had not succeeded in destroying them ? What could he do, when conspiring circumstances even more than deliberate policy had committed him to this enterprise, how keep what he had got except by extending his boundaries to absorb those who threatened him ? Pride and misgiving mingle in the literature of these years, pride in the immense empire which is said to be discharging a predestined civilizing mission for the whole world, misgiving about the effects on national character and morals of the new wealth and the new apparatus of luxury imported by the returning conquerors. In Cicero and Livy we may discern something which in modern language may be termed a " recall to religion," an appeal to the old standards of honesty in government, the simpler life of Republican times.

At this point Greek thought came in some degree to its own again. But it is Greek thought with a remarkable change, effected in the main by the Stoics and especially Panætius, who had cut it off from its dependence on the now obsolete Greek city-state and made it a doctrine for the whole world. It was a doctrine which in its exaltation of civic duty was specially acceptable to thoughtful and cultivated Romans who were seeking some moral anchorage in the confused and hungry world of Roman conquest. Of the writings of Panætius we know little more than has come down to us in the moral and philosophical works of Cicero, but to judge from their influence it is scarcely an exaggeration to say that he did for Greek philosophy what St. Paul did afterwards for Christianity, i.e. gave it meaning and value for a far wider circle than the race from which it originally issued.

Cicero is the mouthpiece of this transformed Greek doctrine, and I take him, therefore, as the next great writer who contributed to thought on the art of government. He is so frank in his acknowledgment of his debt to the Greeks that it has become the fashion to dismiss him as a mere imitator and plagiarist. This, I believe, is to do him a serious injustice. What he gives us is—to use a modern term— a restatement of Greek doctrine with its Stoic enlargement, but adapted to the new conditions of the Roman world, an amalgam which, whatever its component parts, is in effect novel and original. If we judge by results, he was for centuries to come the most influential of Roman writers. The young Octavian, afterwards the Emperor Augustus, was a warm admirer of his political treatises and is supposed to have been greatly influenced by them in his policy of moderation and his respect for political forms when he became all-powerful. Quotations in St. Augustine and other Christian writers help to restore what is missing in his words. Next to Aristotle there is no ancient writer whom they more respect.

The first of his two political treatises, the *De Republica*, has come down to us in a greatly mutilated form. Much of it is missing, and many passages have to be reconstructed from subsequent quotations. Yet even thus imperfect, it contains eloquent and powerful passages which deserve their place in the great literature of the religious and moral foundations. The exordium contains a famous remonstrance with the too fastidious men of culture and learning who shirked their public duties and were tempted in evil times to wrap their cloaks around them, like Plato's philosophers, and take shelter under a wall until the storm was past. It is true, he says, that the public life may be dangerous ; it is true that States have been grossly ungrateful to those who served them best, witness a long line of martyrs at the hands of their countrymen in both Athens and Rome. But to retreat for fear of this fate is ignominious :

For, in truth, our country has not given us birth and education without expecting to receive some sustenance, as it were, from us in return ; nor has it been merely to serve our convenience that she has granted to our leisure a safe refuge and for our moments of repose a calm retreat ; on the contrary she has given us these advantages so that she may appropriate to her own use the greater and more important part of our courage, our talents, and our wisdom, leaving to us for our own private uses only so much as may be left after her needs have been satisfied.

Moreover, we ought certainly not to listen to the other excuses to which these men resort, that they may be more free to enjoy the quiet life. They say, for example, that it is mostly worthless men who take part in politics, men with whom it is degrading to be compared, while to have conflict with them, especially when the mob is aroused, is a wretched and dangerous task. Therefore, they maintain, a wise man should not attempt to take the reins, as he cannot restrain the insane and untamed fury of the common herd ; nor is it proper for a freeman, by contending with vile and wicked opponents, to submit to the scourgings of abuse or expose himself to wrongs which are intolerable to the wise—as if, in the view of good, brave, and high-minded men, there could be any nobler motive for entering public life than the resolution not to be ruled by wicked men and not to allow the republic to be destroyed by them, seeing that the philosophers themselves, even if they should desire to help, would be impotent.[1]

The dialogue which follows is modelled closely on the opening scenes of Plato's *Republic*, and Scipio, who is obviously speaking for Cicero, plays the part of Socrates. The opening is a discussion on the value of the study of astronomy, both as a means of allaying superstitious fears caused by eclipses and other natural happenings and as inducing humility :

How can any man regard anything in human affairs either as exalted, if he has examined into yonder realms of the gods ; or as of long duration, if he has realized the meaning of eternity ; or as glorious, if he has perceived how small is the earth—not only the earth as a whole, but especially that part of it which is inhabited by man—and has noticed how we Romans, though confined to a scanty portion of it and entirely unknown to many races of men, hope nevertheless that our name will be borne abroad on wings and will spread to the ends of the earth ? But as far as our lands, houses, herds, and immense stores of silver and gold are concerned, the man who never thinks of these things or speaks of them as " goods " because he sees that the enjoyment of them is slight, and has noticed that the vilest of men often possess them in unmeasured abundance—how fortunate is he to be esteemed ! For only such a man can really claim all things as his own, by virtue of the decision, not of the Roman people, but of the wise, not by any obligation of the civil law, but by the common law of nature, which forbids that anything shall belong to any man save to him that knows how to employ and to use it.[2]

Scipio then, at the request of his friends, takes up the question of the best form of government, and gives his vote for the Aristotelian mixed constitution as most likely to avoid the licence of the " untamed crowd " and the degradation of monarchy into tyranny. He condenses into a sentence the Platonic cycle of corruption :

The ruling power of the State, like a ball, is snatched from kings by tyrants, from tyrants by aristocrats or the people, and from them again by an oligarchical faction or a tyrant, so that no single form of government ever maintains itself very long.

---

[1] *De Republica*, I, pp. 4 and 5 ; trans. W. C. Walker Keyes, Loeb Classical Library.
[2] *Ibid.*, I, p. 17.

Scipio plunges into history and seeks to prove that the Roman people came nearest the ideal of Aristotle in the great days of their Republic. They " grew great not by chance, but by good counsel and discipline, though to be sure fortune has favoured them also." But " unless there is in the State an even balance of rights, duties, and functions, so that the magistrates have enough power, the counsels of the eminent citizens enough influence, and the people enough liberty, this kind of government cannot be safe from revolution." In the actual history of States one or other of these elements is always encroaching upon the others and by upsetting the balance exposing the State to revolution.

4

But the necessary concord, says Scipio, can never be brought about without the aid of justice, whereas it is the common opinion that the government of a State cannot be carried on without injustice. For the sake of argument, one of the company, Philus, consents to play the part of Thrasymachus in the *Republic* of Plato, and to defend injustice against Scipio who, like Socrates, is the advocate of justice. A large part of this argument is missing, but it can be pieced together sufficiently from what remains and from quotations of subsequent writers. Scipio bases himself on the definition of the State. *Res publica*, commonwealth, is the property of all its people. If it is the property of one man, a tyrant, it ceases to be a commonwealth. In proportion as it deprives any of its citizens of their just rights it falls below a commonwealth.

But this does not carry us far, and Philus, who sustains his part with great energy and skill, has questions to ask which Scipio seems to evade rather than answer. Who are these philosophers who prate to us about justice and statecraft ? Where would Rome have been if she had followed their advice—remained within her walls, abjured all wars except for self-defence, behaved " justly " to the neighbouring cities ? There is no such thing as natural justice or law. Utility is the measure both of law and policy. Rulers everywhere rule for their own advantage, not in the interests of the governed. Rome has won her empire by injustice both to gods and men ; had she pursued justice, she would have remained only the poverty-stricken village that she was at the beginning.

The same is true both of individuals and of States. Philus gives a Ciceronian version of the argument of Glaucon [1] in the second book of Plato's *Republic* :

> Suppose there are two men, one a pattern of virtue, fairness, justice and honour, and the other an example of extreme wickedness and audacity ; and suppose a nation is so mistaken as to believe the good man a wicked, treacherous criminal, and the wicked man on the other hand a model of probity and honour. Then let us imagine that, in accordance with this opinion held by all his fellow-citizens, the good man is harassed, attacked, and arrested ; blinded, sentenced, bound, branded, banished, and reduced to beggary ; and finally is also most justly deemed by all men to be most miserable. Then let the wicked man, on the contrary, be praised, courted, and universally loved ; let him receive all sorts of public offices, military commands, wealth and riches from every source ; and finally let him have the universal reputation of being the best man in the world and most worthy of all the favours of fortune. Now I ask you, who could be so insane as to doubt which of the two he would prefer to be ?
>
> The same thing is true of States as of persons ; no people would be so foolish as not to prefer to be unjust masters rather than just slaves. [2]

After some wavering over the supposed law of nature which makes it "just" that the better should rule the worse, as the master rules the slave, the defenders of justice fall back on the plea that it is its own reward.

> "What riches, what power, what kingdoms can you offer such a man (the man who is both wise and just) ? For he thinks these things are human, but deems his own possessions divine. . . . If universal ingratitude, or the envy of many, or the hostility of the powerful, deprive virtue of its proper rewards, yet it is soothed by many consolations and firmly upheld by its own excellence."

In the end Cicero, like Plato, finds himself driven step by step beyond time and space in his search for the ultimate sanctions. In Scipio's dream, the epilogue to his *Republic*, which is obviously on the model of but by no means a slavish copy of Plato's Vision of Er, Cicero returns again to the theme with which he opened his dialogue—the littleness of man and his earthly doings against the immensities and

---

[1] Plato, *Republic*, II, 361-2.
[2] Cicero, *Republic*, III, 17 ; Loeb Classical Library.

eternities of the universe. Scipio being out of the body on some Lord's Day looks down upon the human scene from a peak in space. He meets his father, who tells him that the life of justice is the road to the skies, to that gathering of those who have completed their earthly lives and been relieved of the body. From this height his father rebukes him for so often turning his eyes back to earth.

Keep your gaze fixed upon these heavenly things and scorn the earthly. For what fame can you gain from the speech of men or what glory that is worth the seeking ? Earth is one of the meanest of the planets and inhabited only in a few patches separated by vast deserts. See how small your Empire is in spite of its proud name. . . . Look on high, contemplate this eternal home and resting place and you will no longer attend to the gossip of the vulgar herd or put your trust in human rewards. Virtue herself, by her own charms, should lead you on to true glory. . . . No man's reputation will endure very long, for what men say dies with them and will be blotted out in the oblivion of posterity.

Cicero appears to have felt that in thus transferring the goal to another world he might be encouraging just that abdication from earthly duties against which he had protested in his opening passage. Scipio therefore is made to say " if, indeed, a path to heaven is opened to those who have served their country well, I will strive more than ever," to which his father replies :

Strive on, indeed, and be sure that it is not you that is mortal, but only your body. For that man whom your outward form reveals is not yourself ; the spirit is the true self, not that physical figure which can be pointed out by the finger. Know, then, that you are a god, if a god is that which lives, feels, remembers, and foresees, and which rules, governs, and moves the body over which it is set, just as the supreme God above us rules this universe. And just as the eternal God moves the universe, which is partly mortal, so an immortal spirit moves the frail body.[1]

Such is Cicero's reconciliation of idealism and practical politics. By this time Stoicism, Epicureanism, and the religion of the Mysteries have all mingled with Plato and Aristotle in the thought of a cultured Roman of the first century B.C. Something of each of them enters into the Ciceronian doctrine.

---

[1] Cicero, *Republic*, VI, 24 ; Loeb Classical Library.

5

The idea of a mystical union between God and man is taken up in the *Laws* and made the foundation of Cicero's theory of law. Reason is that which men have in common with God ; right reason is law which men have in common with God. As the argument proceeds, nature and God become interchangeable terms. The most valuable of the teachings of philosophy is that " we are born for justice, and that right is based not upon men's opinion but upon nature." " Those creatures," therefore, " who have received the gift of reason from nature have also received right reason and therefore they have also received the gift of Law, which is right reason applied to command and prohibition." The virtues originate in " a natural inclination to love our fellow-men," [1] and this is the foundation of justice which must be sought and cultivated for her own sake. " The very height of injustice is to seek pay for justice." There follows the " praise of wisdom " which enables us to know ourselves :

He who knows himself will realize, in the first place, that he has a divine element within him, and will think of his own inner nature as a kind of con-secrated image of God ; and so he will always act and think in a way worthy of so great a gift of the gods, and, when he has examined and thoroughly tested himself, he will understand how nobly equipped by Nature he has entered life, and what manifold means he possesses for the attainment and acquisition of wisdom. For from the very first he began to form in his mind and spirit shadowy concepts, as it were, of all sorts, and when these have been illuminated under the guidance of wisdom, he perceives that he will be a good man, and, for that very reason, happy.[2]

It may be objected that by identifying God with nature and affirming both to be the sources of virtue and justice Cicero assumes what he sets out to prove. But this does not diminish the glow and splendour of the rhetoric—almost Pauline in its fervour—with which he expounds the great commonplaces of religion and morals. The high respect in which he was held by St. Augustine and early Christian writers is its own witness to his influence, not only in his own time but for many centuries later.

---

[1] Haec nascuntur ex eo, quia natura propensi sumus, ad diligendos homines, quod fundamentum juris est.

[2] Cicero, *Laws*, I, 22 ; Loeb Classical Library.

Yet, once more, as we read on into the *Laws*, it presents us with the paradox so often found in ancient writers. Is it possible, we ask, that the man who has expounded these lofty views with inspired eloquence can seriously believe in divination and auspices, can deliberately propose to place great decisions of state and even of peace and war at the mercy of augurs consulting the stars or examining the entrails of birds?

The highest and most important authority in the State is that of the augurs, to whom is accorded great influence. But it is not because I myself am an augur that I have this opinion, but because the facts compel us to think so. For if we consider their legal rights, what power is greater than that of adjourning assemblies and meetings convened by the highest officials, with or without *imperium*, or that of declaring null and void the acts of assemblies presided over by such officials? What is of graver import than the abandonment of any business already begun, if a single augur says " On another day "? What power is more impressive than that of forcing the consuls to resign their offices? What right is more sacred than that of giving or refusing permission to hold an assembly of the people or of the plebeians, or that of abrogating laws illegally passed? Thus the Titian Law was annulled by a decree of the college of augurs, and the Livian Laws by the wise direction of Philippus, a consul and augur. Indeed, no act of any magistrate at home or in the field can have any validity for any person without their authority.[1]

It is the method of the witch-doctor in an African tribe[2], and all the stranger because introduced suddenly at the close of an eloquent plea

---

[1] Cicero, *Laws*, II, 12 ; Loeb Classical Library. See also Book III, 12 : " The right of taking the auspices (granted to magistrates) is intended to bring about the adjournment of many unprofitable meetings of the assembly through plausible excuses for delay ; for the immortal gods have often suppressed unjust aggressions of the people by means of the auspices." Plutarch says that Aemilius Paulus on being made augur " so carefully studied the ancient customs of his country and so thoroughly understood the religion of his ancestors that this office, which was before only esteemed a title of honour and merely upon that account sought after, by this means rose to the rank of one of the highest of the arts, and gave a confirmation of the correctness of the definition, which some philosophers have given of religion, that it is the science of worshipping the gods."

[2] It is difficult to believe that Cicero, himself an augur, is not winking in some of these passages. A few years ago I happened to be camping in the territory of an African tribe which entrusted the appointment of its headmen and

for the ordering of the State on principles of reason, justice, and knowledge. We ask, as we read these passages, is the elaborate organization of primitive rites and ceremonies proposed in them part of the useful myth which Plato countenanced for State purposes, or does it express genuine belief and piety? The answer probably lies somewhere between these two extremes. Conservative Romans took a sincere pride in the rites and ceremonies which they believed to be uniquely Roman and a legacy from the greatest time, and were alarmed at the possible consequences upon the popular mind of the scepticism started by the New Academy which was bringing them into question. "Let us," says Cicero, "implore the Academy— the new one, formed by Arcesilaus and Carneades—to be silent, since it contributes nothing but confusion to all these problems, for if it should attack what seems to us to have been formed and arranged with knowledge, it would play too great havoc." The pragmatic value of religion as an instrument of State policy seems in this and several other passages to be an implied part of Cicero's thought, but with it is mingled reverence for the ancient rites as part of the patriotic heritage of a Roman citizen. The immense lost work of Varro— the forty-one volumes on the *Antiquities Divine and Human*—and the vogue it had at this time and for centuries later attests the strength of this sentiment and the hold it had even on educated Romans. In Virgil too we note the importance attached to the careful performance of the prescribed rites at all critical moments in the *Æneid*.

6

Cicero himself wavers, if we may judge from his other philosophical works. In the *De Divinatione* he is sceptical about the practices which he accepts as beyond question in the *Laws*. In the *De Natura Deorum* he had developed even more mystically the theme of the union between the human and divine spirit, which reappears in the *Laws*

---

the decision of its more important matters to witch-doctors, who manifested the will of the tribal spirit by foaming at the mouth. I asked the British Administrator how this system worked. He said it worked very well, since the witch-doctors were generally sensible men who were acquainted with the means of producing the necessary manifestation, and used them, on the whole, judiciously.

and in that setting seems to be in sharp contrast with the proposed apparatus of religion. It is as though the same writer had been the author of the Book of Leviticus and the books of the prophet Isaiah. There is evidently a conflict between the philosopher seeking truth and the conservative politician impressed with the importance of the orthodox religion as a buttress of the State. A reconciliation was possible on what to-day are called modernist principles. All these rites and ceremonies, it might have been said, were symbols of an underlying reality. Just as in the Greek State the oracle and the lot reserved a place for God in human affairs, so in the Roman was this place provided by the pontiff and the augur.

Lucretius, meanwhile, had laid the axe at the root of the tree in the great poem which Cicero had read (and admired) when he wrote the *Laws*. Is it fanciful to see a certain defiance of that thundering manifesto against superstition in his adhesion to the old rites and ceremonies ? Cicero greatly disliked Epicurus, whose speculative theories Lucretius adopted, but he could have had little quarrel with the Stoical conclusions which the poet drew from his theory of the universe :

> Apparet divum numen sedesque quietæ
> Quas neque concutiunt venti nec nubila nimbis
> Aspergunt neque nix acri concreta pruina
> Cana cadens violat semperque innubilis æther
> Integit, et large diffuso lumine rident.
> Omnia suppeditat porro natura neque ulla
> Res animi pacem delibat tempore in ullo.

It is not the life of pleasure—eat, drink, and be merry—which this austere sceptic enjoins, but the life of the soul set free to pursue virtue and reason in the presence of the *divum numen* and the calm of beauty which it sheds around. Cicero's higher flights are often in the mood of Lucretius, and mingling with his ritual rules are sudden outbursts of high doctrine which for thousands of years to come were in advance of religious practice. "Donis impii ne placare audeant deos. Platonem audiant qui vetat dubitare qua sit mente futurus deus, cum vir nemo bonus ab improbo se donari velit " : " Let not the wicked dare to think of appeasing the gods with gifts. Let them hear Plato, who will not let us doubt what the mind of God would be about such an approach to Him, for no good man would wish to receive gifts from the wicked." Had the mediæval Church lived up to this maxim, Erasmus and Luther would have been deprived of a large part of their case and many of the struggles between the secular and ecclesiastical powers have been avoided.

In reading Cicero we become aware, as in scarcely any other Latin author of the great contribution which the Roman Republic had made to the art of the government. It had gone far to reconcile liberty with authority—liberty the "inalienable possession" of the individual, guaranteed by law and custom, with the paramount claims of the State—and kept the quarrels of its political factions within bounds laid down by something recognised as the public interest. Compared with the firm and solid building by which the Roman expanded his city into a nation, and his nation into an Empire the Greek achievement seems brief and transitory. Roman law was to pass through as many vicissitudes as the Roman State and finally to lay a stress on authority which favoured despotism. But the sense of order, continuity, permanence from which it sprang persisted through all its phases and provided the foundation for the coherent legal systems varying with local conditions on which modern civilisation is built.

The maxims expounded in Cicero's *Laws* are not what we should call law, but counsels of political commonsense—to be moderate in word and deed, to eschew violence, to preserve the balance of the constitution, and therefore to beware of enroachments by the plebs on the Senate and Consulship, or attempts to oppress the plebs by the wealthy and privileged. But with all his practicality Cicero remains to the end a mystic, and in that also represents a side of the Roman outlook on life which was to pass through centuries of change and struggle into the modern world. In his writings the identification of religion and politics is still complete. For him it is not a question of the relation of Church and State : the two are one, there is no boundary between their functions ; religion is part of the machinery of the State, pontiffs and augurs are State officials with high political as well as religious functions ; magistrates are invested with the rights of augurs in order to give them authority in their secular duties. To disentangle the secular from the religious, to assign separate functions to Church and State was to be the unfinished work of centuries—a work attended by incessant conflicts, and liable even in modern times to revive in unexpected forms. We shall understand it best if we think of it as starting from an almost complete identity of religion and politics. The Roman pontiff, when he had become Pope, had a long historical tradition behind him in resisting the process which finally stripped him of his political functions.

CHAPTER XIV

THE ROMAN EMPIRE IN ACTION

I

IN one of his writings Cicero tells the story of a certain Lucius Gellius, a good-natured and practical man of affairs, who going to Athens as proconsul was moved to wonder and pity at the large number of philosophers he found there, and the vexation of spirit and waste of time that they inflicted on one another by their interminable arguments. He therefore called them together and urgently advised them to come at length to some settlement of their controversies, and in case they should need outside assistance good-naturedly offered his own services. It was as though Lord Kitchener had offered to arbitrate between Hegelians and Utilitarians. Rome in the first century B.C. was thronged, we may even say infested, with philosophers of all the schools—Peripatetic, Stoic, Epicurean, Old Academy, and New Academy.[1] A select company of highbrows seems to have been enormously interested in their disputations and to have patronised their voluminous and unreadable writings.[2] But the Roman man of action regarded them much as Lucius Gellius did the philosophers of Athens, if indeed he troubled at all about their doings. Now and for many generations to come the Roman contribution was in the field of action and experience.

In approving Aristotle's "mixed constitution" Cicero had passed lightly over Aristotle's warning against imperialism. Rome was to

---

[1] Varro, according to St. Augustine, said there were 288 sects of philosophers in Rome.

[2] When the Villa of the Faun was excavated at Herculaneum, its library, to the great disappointment of the excavators, was found to contain nothing but worthless and voluminous works of unknown Epicurean writers.

verify this warning, but in the beginning it was less the ambition of conquering generals than the compelling force of circumstances which made havoc of her constitution. Recent historians seem to be agreed that Augustus had greatness thrust upon him. They believe that when his power had been firmly established by the Battle of Actium, he showed a genuine desire to return to the constitutional form of government. To the end of his days he declined all titles which might appear to reflect on the legal sovereignty of senate and people and observed all forms which kept the theory of that sovereignty in being. If he permitted himself to be called *princeps* and continued to hold the position of *imperator*—the name which in the subsequent centuries became the symbol of imperial rule—it was precisely because these titles did not conflict, in theory or appearance, with the legal rights of senate and people. After the campaign in which he followed up the victory of Actium and obtained the submission of the Eastern provinces, he ostentatiously closed the Temple of Janus and formally laid down all other extraordinary powers which he had held in the previous years. In his own words he " handed over the republic to the control of the Senate and people of Rome."

But the temple of Janus did not long remain closed ; and it soon became clear that one and the same man could not be master of the legions, with the sole responsibility of guarding and extending the great circle of imperial frontiers, and remain a Republican official among Republican officials in Rome itself. Senate and people were quite unequal to the task of governing the Empire and were well aware of their incapacity and of the chaos that would follow if the princeps were really to abdicate. It was they who piled on him the honours and dignities which he seemed reluctant to take, who decreed that he should be called Augustus, connived at his exercising in the city the rights which belonged to him in the provinces, and transferred to him the *tribunicia potestas* which gave him the power of legislating under Republican forms. The process came to its climax in the worship of " Rome and Augustus," first instituted in Asia Minor within two years of the battle of Actium and gradually diffused through the provinces as a symbol of imperial unity. This, too, though probably intended at the beginning as an Oriental flourish to impress Orientals, gradually percolated into Italy, and though officially unauthorized was practised in Italian towns even in the lifetime of Augustus and became in subsequent years one of the official tests of loyalty to the Empire.

Augustus, in fact, had no choice between actually abdicating, as more than once he seemed sincerely anxious to do, and going the whole length to complete personal rule. Having started on this road, he followed it to the end with extraordinary skill and craft, if also with sincere patriotism. But the end was fated from the beginning, and it was, as Aristotle said, that the man who exercised the power of external dominion would also—indeed must—make himself the ruler of his own State. Aristotle's other prophecy, that States " generally collapse, as soon as they have obtained imperial power, for they lose their temper in time of peace," may have seemed far from fulfilment in these years. But the seeds of that also had been sown. The ancient Rome, proud of its institutions, determined to govern itself and to guard its independence against all who would encroach on it from within or without, had already passed away. The new Rome, gorged with the plunder of conquered provinces, was only too willing to hand over its affairs to an able man who would save it both from civil war and external enemies, and leave it to pursue its life of money-getting, luxury, sport, and vice without being troubled with public affairs.

So with the accession of Augustus doubts and self-searchings die down, and poets and prose-writers vie with one another in hymning the glories of the Empire and its supreme good fortune in finding a God-sent ruler. Augustus was a man of extraordinary ability. In his grasp of the whole, his eye for detail, his choice of the moments when to strike and when to spare, he seemed almost infallible in his best years. His organization of Asia Minor, of the Parthian Empire, and of Gaul was masterly ; the stubborn Germans alone resisted the Romanization effected elsewhere with a comparatively small force. But the success of Augustus lay largely in his capacity for enlisting able men and giving them discretion to use their judgment in circumstances which were necessarily beyond his control. Rome in these days presents us with the paradox of increasing corruption at the centre and remarkable vigour, ability, and dutifulness in the provinces. As we look over the Roman world, we may wonder at the almost unending supply of able soldier-administrators which continued through centuries which are commonly supposed to be the period of its decline and fall. Gibbon says of the immediate successors of Augustus that nothing saved them from oblivion but " their unparalled vices and the splendid theatre in which they acted." He has no mercy on the " dark, unrelenting Tiberius, the furious Caligula, the feeble Claudius, the profligate and cruel Nero, the beastly Vitellius, the timid Claudius, and inhuman Domitian." These monsters, nevertheless, had the good fortune to be served in the provinces by men of the highest ability, who helped to create for Rome that tremendous prestige which survived the most crushing disasters and was carried far down into the Middle Ages. It is possible that this transfusion of her blood over so wide an area was an actual cause of the brain-exhaustion and decadence which afflicted her centre. But as time went on, her history more and more illustrated Aristotle's maxim that conquering generals are a danger to the State. Every Emperor had to beware of successful commanders in control of armies and dreaming that the purple was within their grasp. In seventy years there were twenty-three Emperors, more than half of whom perished by violence.

2

The story of our own country, now, thanks to the labour of archæologists, being more and more revealed, may be taken as an example of Roman activities in these years. We have Cæsar's account of the fierce people with their painted bodies, long moustaches, and streaming hair, their formidable chariots and amazing skill with horses, who awaited him when he landed on the Kentish coast in 55 B.C. They were by no means savages, but their towns were of the neolithic type, and some of them practised a community of wives, living in groups of ten or twelve, especially brothers with brothers and fathers with sons. They were extremely pugnacious, and though they healed their feuds to combine against the Romans, those north of the Thames were often at war with those to the south. Within a few generations the Romans had created on this unpromising soil an almost perfect model in miniature of their own civilization ; and in this effort they seem to have enlisted the good will and co-operation of the British themselves.

The labours of the late Professor Haverfield and subsequent researches which are described by Professor R. G. Collingwood in a recently published book,[1] reveal Roman Britain as an elaborately planned State within its limits. The greater part of it was divided into self-governing cantons in which the old tribal capital or a newly built town became the seat of Government. There were about a dozen of such capitals and about fifty smaller towns, varying from busy industrial centres to mere stations, and all were joined up with paved roads. The capitals themselves were small according to our standards ; except London, none of them seems to have had more than 2,000 inhabitants. But nearly all were perfect models of Roman urban culture, serving as examples of what life was in Imperial Rome and what it might become if the less civilized British followed her example.

Evidently the walled town served as a centre of business, education, and amusement for the surrounding country, for its lay-out was altogether out of proportion to the population within its walls. Near the centre of each town was a forum, a market square surrounded on three sides by shops and flanked on the fourth by a basilica, an aisled and colonnaded hall such as very few towns possess in the twentieth century. In the little tribal capital of Silchester the basilica measured 240 ft. by nearly 60 ft., and it is supposed to have been 60 ft. high. Seated in the modern fashion it would have held 4,000 people.

In nearly all were public baths, in which hundreds could bathe at once. At Wroxeter there were hot and cold rooms, each measuring 80 ft. by 35 ft. Outside all the chief towns were amphitheatres with banks of earth carrying wooden seats capable of holding some thousands of spectators. Just as Emperors provided amusements for the population of Rome, so, according to their scale, did each local government of the provincial districts try to make its own city a miniature Rome, and to provide the same gifts for the people within its boundaries. The best houses in the towns were large, roomy, richly decorated with tesselated pavements and frescoed walls, and had spacious gardens behind them. In some there were buildings which have been identified as hotels. There were numerous temples

---

[1] *Roman Britain and the English Settlements,* by Professor R. G. Collingwood and Mr. N. L. Myres (Oxford, Clarendon Press).

in which hospitality was offered with Roman tolerance to all the cults, and at the end of the period Christian churches began to appear. Outside the towns were the great villas, centrally heated, sumptuously decorated, served by large numbers of slaves, working the adjacent properties. Scattered about were the villages, where the non-Romanized British lived in beehive huts with thatched roofs and generally on a lower level of culture. No doubt they benefited somewhat from the urban and villa civilization, but it is suspected that they were overtaxed for the benefit of the towns, and that their resistance, or their inability to give the towns the necessary support was one of the reasons for the decay of the towns which can be traced before the departure of the Romans.

Roman Britain had a chequered and at times a rather exciting history of its own. In the first and early second century A.D. the Roman occupation was rough and ready, and most of the buildings erected by the conquerors were still of wood. Sporadic disturbances on the part of the British had to be kept under, and at least once at the cost of heavy casualties.[1] It was not until Hadrian visited Britain (A.D. 123) and started the building of the Great Wall that the Romans introduced their practice of building in stone, and built up the town and eventually the villa civilization of which the archæologists are now presenting so clear a picture. In later years the appearances suggest a decay in the urban civilization, while the villa civilization persisted, but there were considerable periods when the two existed side by side.

Not infrequently Roman Britain was caught up into the troubled politics of Imperial Rome and the struggles of rival Emperors. Septimius Severus died at York after a costly and only temporarily successful expedition into Caledonia, but Britain seems to have been unaffected by the savage struggle which followed between his sons in Rome. For about ten years at the end of the third century Britain set herself up as an independent Empire under Carausius, and if he or any successor could have kept the command of the sea, it might have retained this position. But Carausius was murdered by his finance minister, Allectus, who, being a fraudulent financier and not a naval strategist,

---

[1] For the unexplained disappearance of the Ninth Legion and other evidences of rebellion against Roman rule see Collingwood and Myers, *op. cit.*, pp. 128-9.

looked on while Constantius prepared the fleet which enabled him to land a disciplined army which easily routed the motley barbarian force that Allectus had got together to oppose him. Britain was now again drawn into the Roman system, and by a reform of civil and military administration rendered safe, at least for the time being, from invaders by land or sea. But her fortunes were now indissolubly linked with those of Rome, and when the legions were withdrawn at the beginning of the fifth century, she was left with her back to the wall to carry on a losing fight against raiders and rebels. Even then there was no sudden collapse, but a gradual decline redeemed by many moments of heroic resistance. Not till the sixth century did the darkness of barbarism finally descend on the country.[1]

In spite of these vicissitudes there seem to have been two and a half centuries—as long as from the end of the seventeenth century to the present day—for the greater part of which Britain was the centre of a highly finished civilization which, being exempt from the inroads of barbarians that were plaguing Europe, offered a more secure and more settled existence than almost any other part of the Roman Empire. Before the end of the period the older Roman villas would have had the same stately antiquity as a Jacobean country house in our own time.

The remains point to the conclusion that much of this period was a time of culture, comfort, and even luxury, in which the British population participated with no sense of being a conquered or servile people. The form of government appears to have been very much the same in Britain as in Gaul, the towns having their municipal senates and officials bearing the Roman titles quæstor, ædile, duumvir, and quattuovir ; and in Britain, as in Gaul, the well-to-do British families appear to have learnt Latin, adopted Latin nan.es and customs, and played a large part in the local government. The system of roads, the imposing remains of the Roman cities of London, York, Chester, and Colchester, and of the great bathing establishment of Bath, much of it lying beneath the Abbey and still uncovered, bear their own witness to the kind of life lived by the well-to-do. It is probable that not only the Roman-British, but many other rich people from Gaul and even from Italy came to the healing springs of Bath in

---

[1] Gibbon, I, Chap. XIII. Collingwood and Myres, *op. cit.,* Chap. XVII.

the great days of the occupation. For general comfort and official organization nothing like it was to be seen again in the island till near the end of the eighteenth century. Even now the great population of the twentieth century lacks some of the amenities provided for the small population in Roman times.

Suppose the Legions had not gone back—suppose they had decided to remain and make Britain an oasis of Roman culture safe from Goth and Visigoth and in later days from Saxon and Dane ! This surely deserves a modest place among the might-have-beens of history.

3

I have digressed from the main theme, but it is important to bear in mind the contrast between the power and prestige of Rome as seen ˙n the provinces in these centuries and the corruption which even in the early days was at work in the capital.

In Rome Emperors and plutocrats between them exhibited both the vices that Plato and Aristotle had ascribed to tyranny and the waste and profligacy which they had associated with an oligarchy of wealth. All the excesses and corruptions of all the possible systems seemed to be working together in the capital from the accession of Tiberius to the death of Domitian ; yet during a large part of this period the great provinces were never more flourishing or better governed. In North Africa, in Syria, in Asia Minor the remains of beautiful Roman towns built by the legions tell their own tale. There followed the great renascence of the Antonine period of which Gibbon has said in a famous sentence that " if a man was called upon to fix a period in the history of the world during which the condition of the human race was most happy and prosperous, he would, without hesitation, name that which elapsed from the death of Domitian to the accession of Commodus (A.D. 90–180). The vast extent of the Roman Empire was governed by absolute power under the guidance of virtue and wisdom." Yet, if we look outside Rome itself a large part of the Empire shows the same appearance of prosperity and good government under the bad Emperors as under the good. After the annihilation of the legions of Varus in the Teutoburg there was no serious military disaster ; the seas which Augustus had cleared of pirates remained open to an ever-growing commerce ; the riches of the

East poured into the West, manufactures multiplied especially in Gaul ; the fury and folly of the bad Emperors seems to have spent itself in Rome and the adjacent parts of Italy.

In these years philosophy turned inwards. Despotic rulers do not encourage free thought about political institution. Those who ventured on that ground had to walk warily ; the reputation of being engaged in a conspiracy against the Emperor was too easily acquired and too many were in waiting to pass it on. Under the bad Emperors, not what the State should do or what was wrong with its institutions, but how an individual might live tolerably and be at peace with himself was the main subject of inquiry by the philosophic sects, whether Stoic or Epicurean, Sceptic or Eclectic. The differences between these schools were less important than their general agreement that salvation was only to be found in the life of the spirit. The idea of a kingdom not of this world—not " dear city of Cecrops but dear city of God "—grows vivid precisely as the worldly kingdom seems cruel and wicked. More and more the philosopher comes to fill the place of the spiritual director or confessor of later time. He is attached as court chaplain to the Emperor, as domestic chaplain to great generals and nobles. In his brilliant study of this period which should be familar to all students, Dr. Samuel Dill[1] has an illuminating passage on this subject :

Seneca, the tutor and minister of Nero, is the greatest of these spiritual directors, and undoubtedly he deserves credit for the Quinquennium Neronis, the good five years with which the reign was inaugurated. His success in keeping his balance and saving his enormous wealth during the subsequent orgies of his imperial pupil, and his cringing attitude to Claudius, have somewhat tarnished the lustre of his ethical writings in the eyes of posterity ; but a terrible and difficult part fell to him in very evil times, and he acquitted himself creditably in the end. In Seneca's philosophical works the God of the Stoics came so near the God of the Christians that an ingenious ecclesiastic of later days forged a supposed correspondence between him and St. Paul to account for the affinity. But the millionaire Stoic who kept in with Nero and

---

[1] Dill, *Roman Society from Nero to Marcus Aurelius* (Macmillan & Co.), pp. 293–4.

flattered Claudius could scarcely be surprised if some of his contemporaries discovered a gap between his creed and his life.

Religious ferment was unceasing in these years. Immense numbers were attracted by the mystery religions—the cults of Isis and Serapis, of the Magna Mater, of Mithra with its horrid taurobolium, or purification through the blood of bulls. Piety was often a cover for lubricity, and the most exalted sentiments attended some of the foulest practices. Among the more intelligent philosophy gained by the contrast between its simpler and purer doctrine and the extravagance and orientalism of these cults. Stoics pointed to the inner witness, Cynics claimed to be ambassadors of God and enjoined an ascetism akin to that of Christian monks ; revivalists like Apollonius of Tyana preached to immense audiences from temple steps and rebuked their sins ; Plutarch lectured on morals, formulating a new theology of Paganism in which dæmonology played a central part. Through it all the Emperors, following the example of Augustus, laboured to preserve and even amplify the old Roman religion. The sacred college of which, as Pontifex Maximus, the Emperor was head, exercised supreme control over the whole field of religion. To restore temples, to revive ancient rites, to be profuse in expenditure on festivals and ceremonies, were the aims of all the Princes, with the possible exception of Nero, who was more concerned about his own houses and palaces than about the temples of the gods. Marcus Aurelius performed all the sacred offices as Pontifex Maximus, reciting from memory every word of the ancient liturgy, which by this time had become almost incomprehensible to the vulgar.[1]

Such in general was the part played by philosophy, religion and superstition in Rome at the end of the first and begining of the second century A.D.

---

[1] *Dill*, p. 535.

CHAPTER XV

THE COMING OF CHRISTIANITY

I

INTO the *colluvies* of religions and superstitions described in the last chapter Christianity was now working its way. So decisive a factor as it proved itself to be in the evolution of government from the fourth century down to our own time needs as much attention from the students of politics as of theology.

It might be supposed that the Christian doctrine had everything to commend it to intelligent people of pious disposition. It offered certainties about God and the nature of things in place of the speculations of philosophers ; it practised a pure and simple mysticism in contrast with the extravagances and barbarities of the other mystery religions ; its adherents lived blameless lives, at all events in the early days. Why, then, in these early days was it excluded from the genial tolerance which Rome extended to so many strange cults and even to the Jews, of whom originally Christians were supposed to be a sect ? There is no easy answer to this question. Harnack has made a collection of the denunciations and opprobrious epithets showered upon Christians by writers of the highest repute, Tacitus, Suetonius, Pliny,[1] and they strike us not merely by their violence but by their grotesque inappropriateness to the followers of Jesus Christ. These men and women whose gospel was love and who overflowed with charity to all mankind, who walked humbly and modestly, were charged

---

[1] *Mission and Expansion of Christianity*, Engl. trans. by Dr. James Moffat (London, Williams and Norgate), I, p. 267. " Superstitio nova et malefica " ; " superstitio prava immodica " ; " exitiabilis superstitio " are expressions used respectively by Suetonius, Pliny, and Tacitus.

with hatred of the human race and said to be guilty of abominable crimes.

There is a note of fear in these denunciations. Early in the day the Christians gained the reputation of being politically dangerous as no other religious sect. They held together ; they increased in a mysterious way. They were a people, cried the pagan Cæcillius, who loved darkness and shunned the light, who were silent in public and whispered in corners, who recognized one another by secret signs and tokens, and fell in love almost before they were acquainted. Why had they no altars, no temples, no recognized images, like other religions, unless the object of their worship deserved punishment or was something to be ashamed of ? Who was this unique, solitary, forlorn god whom no free people, no realm, and no Roman cult or superstition had ever known ? The lonely and wretched race of the Jews worshipped one god by themselves, but they did it openly, with temples, altars, victims, and ceremonies, and their god had so little strength and power that he and all his nation were in bondage to the deities of Rome ! But the Christians ! What monstrosities, what portents were they pretending to have discovered ?

The comparison with the Jews furnishes one of the principal clues. The Jews might be disliked, but they were supposed to be harmless fanatics whose operations were above-board. The Christians were underground workers who needed constant watching lest they should be dangerous to the State. For this reason the Jews seem never to have been submitted to the test of Emperor-worship, but the Christians very soon were. Were they loyal to the Empire or were they not ? If they were, they could not possibly object to offering incense and wine to the image of the Cæsar—a thing to which no sensible Roman, however religious he might be and whatever gods he might worship, took exception. It was like standing when the national anthem was sung or saluting the flag of the regiment. If the Christian did object, it was proof positive that he was really engaged in the treasonable conspiracy which his furtive ways and whispering in corners suggested. Enough did object to increase suspicion ; the tests grew harder, the suspect was ordered to say explicitly whether he was or was not a Christian, to deny his Master on pain of instant execution.

2

Readers of Gibbon's famous chapters have the material for forming their judgment about the magnitude of the persecutions and the motives of the persecuting Emperors, who included the good Emperors as well as the bad, Trajan, Diocletian, and Marcus Aurelius, as well as Nero, Caligula, and Domitian. If we follow Gibbon's figures, which seem to be generally accepted by theological writers, the total number of Christians who were put to death during the ten years of the Diocletian persecution was not more than 2000, and on the same scale the total number of all the martyrs in the various persecutions would scarcely be more than three times that number. Gibbon concludes his chapter (XVI) with reflections on the " melancholy truth " that Christians " in the course of their intestine dissensions have inflicted far greater severities on each other than they had experienced from the zeal of infidels." A modern might add that the new pagans of these latter days have slaughtered bishops and priests on an even greater scale and with a more indiscriminate ferocity than their predecessors in Roman times.

Intervals of tolerance were followed by renewal of persecutions, and often when we should least expect it. The good Emperors acted with obvious reluctance. Pliny, in seeking the advice of Trajan, puts the best case he can for the Christians and says that he only acted when he had no doubt that " obstinacy and invincible contumacy deserved punishment." He gives a touching account, evidently intended to soften the Emperor's heart, of their demeanour on trial :

They maintain that their guilt or folly had amounted only to this : That on a fixed day they had been wont to meet before sunrise—to repeat in alternate verses a form of words in honour of Christ, as of a God—and to bind themselves by a solemn vow not to do any wickedness, but against stealing, against brigandage, against adultery, against breaches of faith, against repudiations of truth ; that after these rites it had been their custom to separate, and then to meet again for the pupose of taking food, ordinary and innocent food, but that they had ceased even to do this after the edict in which, obeying your instructions, I had forbid political societies. I thought it all the more necessary to examine two maid-servants, who were styled deaconesses, with the further aid of torture, but I discovered nothing except perverse and extravagant superstition. I therefore adjourned the inquiry and had instant recourse to your counsel.[1]

The Emperor replied that though when they are reported and convicted they must be punished, they must not be sought out, and in no case must anonymous accusations be used against any of them. Even when convicted they should be pardoned and their past record wiped out, if they will show their repentance by worshipping " our gods."

It will be observed that the edict under which Pliny is acting is one " forbidding political societies." To be a Christian was undoubtedly, as the officials of the Empire saw it, to be a member of a political society, and one particularly difficult to deal with. Christians were not only in Rome, where they could be watched ; they were all over the Empire and might easily act as " cells," in the modern phrase, to promote sedition in outlying regions. As time went on they were credibly reported to have penetrated the households of nobles and officials and to have large followings among women and slaves. The different centres corresponded with one another, using symbols and unintelligible expressions which might well arouse suspicion when their letters fell into the hands of the police, and transmitted considerable sums of money from one " cell " to another. All such proceedings are hateful to despotism, and in the atmosphere of alarm in which most of the Emperors lived it needed very little to interpret them as evidence of a dangerous secret conspiracy. The innocent but—for its purpose—extremely efficient organization of the churches easily lent itself to that interpretation. Their pagan fellow-citizens dubbed the Christians a " third race " standing apart from the rest of the community and its civic obligations ; and officials of the Empire judged them to be an alien and indigestible element, much as the modern German judges the Jews. The pagan crowds shouted " Usque quo genus tertium ? " " How long are we to endure the third race ? "[2]

It added to their offence that they continued to grow in numbers whether the official policy was one of repression or tolerance. Repression kindled a passion for martyrdom—in the official mind one of the

---

[1] Pliny, *Epistles*, X, 77 ; trans. R. C. Jebb.
[2] Harnack, *op. cit.*, I, p. 273.

most inexplicable and exasperating characteristics of the sect—and never went far enough to destroy them. Tolerance drew them out of their shelter and gave them the opportunity of spreading their doctrines openly and defiantly. In the third century, though still a relatively small minority compared with the whole number of citizens, they were by far the largest of the religious or philosophical sects. The catacombs in Rome, which served as their burial grounds, were already of enormous extent and bear their own witness to the magnitude of their numbers in the city itself. Excavations on the scale of these catacombs could only have been executed by a large and active community with the knowledge of the authorities. In normal times Christians carried on their funeral rites and performed their memorial services without any concealment, but the winding underground passages with secret ways in and ways out offered them hiding-places and means of escape which were a serious complication for the police when they were officially banned.

3

In refusing to accept the test of Emperor-worship the Christians had, unknown to themselves, opened a controversy which to this day remains the central issue between religion and State. Harnack goes to the root of the matter :

From the practical point of view, what was of still greater moment than the campaign against the world and worship of the gods was the campaign against *the apotheosis of men*. This struggle which reached its height in the uncompromising rejection of the imperial cultus, marked at the same time the resolute protest of Christianity against *the blending of religion and patriotism*, and consequently against that cultus of the State in which the State (personified in the Emperor) itself formed the object of the cultus. One of the cardinal aims and issues of the Christian religion was to draw a sharp line between the worship of God and the honour due to the State and to its leaders. Christianity tore up political religion by the roots.[1]

With the alteration of a very few words this passage (published in 1908) would apply almost exactly to the struggle between the German Confessional churches and the German totalitarian State,

---

[1] Harnack, *op. cit.*, I, p. 295.

which, personified in the "leader," claims the submission of its Christian subjects, as did the Roman State personified in the Emperor.

But then, as later, the question arose, could the Christians live up to their own high doctrine? The pagan observed all through the third century that while they rejected the apotheosis of the Emperor, they apparently had no objection to the deification of their own apostles, patriarchs, martyrs, and archangels. Theoretically the line between the worship of God and the cult of saints, intercessors, and deliverers might be clear to the Christians, but it was very far from clear to the pagan. "If," asked the pagan Porphyry, "you declare that beside God there are angels who are not subject to suffering and death and are incorruptible in nature—*just the beings we call gods*, inasmuch as they stand near the god-head—then what is all the dispute about? Are we to consider it merely a difference of terminology?"[1] For all its monotheism, Christianity at the close of the third century abounded in objects of devotion and adoration, and on this ground it was the equal of any other cult.

Christianity, in fact, was in active, though possibly unconscious, competition with paganism during the last half of the third century. It was in this period chiefly that Christians multiplied. Harnack estimates their number in Rome at or about 250 A.D. at 30,000, and thinks it probable that it had "doubled, perhaps quadrupled" by the beginning of the fourth century.[2] The Decian and Diocletian persecutions appear to have done nothing but increase their numbers. The less heroic withdrew while the persecution lasted, but reappeared and were reinforced by large numbers of new converts as soon as it was over. By the beginning of the fourth century, practically the whole of Asia Minor was Christianized, and in Antioch, Egypt, Africa, and southern Gaul Christians were both numerous and powerful. Constantine's Edict of Milan in 313, granting tolerance to all religions, and his practical adoption of Christianity as the official religion ten years later, when his victory over Licinius had given him sole domination over the Roman world, were believed in ancient times to have been sudden and miraculous events. But in the position which Christianity had won a Constantine was bound to come. An official religion was

[1] Harnack, *op. cit.*, I, pp. 299–300. [2] *Ibid.*, II, p. 459.

throughout the history of both Republic and Empire. In an age of universal superstition it was impossible that the State should let pass out of its hands into the hands of an independent caste of bishops and priests the exercise of the tremendous power, which, according to Christian belief, was vested in the Church. That might too easily be used to the discomfiture of the secular authorities.

There was yet another difficulty which the Emperor had not foreseen. In pagan times the test of orthodoxy was the simple one of Emperor-worship. Those who conformed in this one respect were free to believe what they chose. They might worship at the old shrines, follow the cult of Mithra, profess the Christian faith or one of the agnostic philosophies. All the faiths were tolerant of one another and it was no concern of the State to decide which of them possessed the truth. With the adoption of Christianity all this was changed. The Church claimed to be the sole depository of something conceived as absolute truth, and the State in adopting the Church found itself committed to the guardianship of this truth. It was an unpleasant surprise to Constantine, who seems to have contemplated tolerance of the old beliefs as part at all events of the initial stage and who imagined that in the Edict of Milan he had conferred on all citizens of the Roman world the privilege of choosing and professing their own religion. He now found himself under strong pressure to make large concessions to Christians at the expense of pagans, and even to aid and abet them in what was to all intents and purposes a persecution of pagans. Tolerance of infidels regarded as enemies of Christ and the truth was no part of Christian charity in those days.

More embarrassing still, the Emperor next discovered that, though claiming to be in possession of absolute truth, the Christians were rent with conflicts about the definition of this truth. Gibbon drily observes that " a Roman general, whose religion might still be a subject of doubt and whose mind had not been enlightened either by study or by inspiration, was indifferently qualified to discuss, in the Greek language, a metaphysical question or an article of faith." But Constantine had to face the fact that the controversy about the nature of the Trinity threatened violence and disorder in large parts of the Empire, and that some settlement of it was a State necessity. He approached this part of his task in the spirit of the Roman proconsul

Lucius Gellius, mentioned in a previous chapter, who, as Cicero tells us, was moved to wonder and pity at the large number of philosophers he found in Athens and the vexation of spirit and waste of time they inflicted on one another by their interminable arguments. He therefore, as Cicero goes on to say, called them together and urgently advised them to come at length to some settlement of their controversies, and in case they should need outside assistance, good-naturedly offered his own services. Just so did Constantine summon the bishops to conferences at Rome, Arles, at Nice, at Rimini, to settle the doctrine of the Trinity, and came himself to listen to their disputes, sitting humbly on a stool before the assembled bishops. But the Councils failed to restore peace, for though they might declare their authority to be supreme, there always remained a minority who considered it a matter of conscience to refuse submission and did not scruple to have recourse to violence in support of their views. Constantine began by counselling moderation and attributing the trouble to a trifling and subtle question concerning an incomprehensible point of law. But as the controversy developed the parties compelled him to take sides, and being thoroughly confused about the differences between orthodoxy and Arianism, " homoousion " and " homoiousion," and the other numerous fine points made by the different sects, he found himself protecting the heretical Arians, persecuting the orthodox Athanasians, upholding the council of Nice as the bulwark of the Christian faith ; and in the end receiving baptism at the hands of an Arian bishop.

5

The same facts make amazingly different impressions on different minds. Events which move Gibbon to his sardonic comments on ecclesiastical human nature appeal to John Henry Newman as conclusive proof of divine guidance leading the Church to infallible truth :

" It is the vast Catholic body itself, and it only," says Newman,[1] " which affords an arena for both combatants in the awful, never-ending duel (between Authority and Private Judgment). It is necessary for the very life of religion, viewed in its large operations and its history, that the warfare should be inces-

---

[1] *Apologia*, original edition, p. 391.

the comprehensive hospitality which admitted "barbarians" to Roman citizenship and enlisted them in the imperial service throughout the Provinces had largely obliterated the line between Romans and the subject races. Intermarriage was common and by no means frowned upon. Several of the Emperors themselves were "barbarians." Trajan was a Spaniard; Septimius Severus an African, his son Caracalla and nephew Heliogabalus were barbarians in manners as well as in origin; Philip was another African; Maximin a Pannonian. In and after the reign of Theodosius German chiefs not only obtained great military commands, but were practically rulers of the Empire when the Emperors were weaklings. It would be possible without much straining of the facts to write the story of the decline and fall as an interminable civil war between the men who for the time being were in control in the capital and the powerful military chiefs who held the chief commands in the provinces. There were numerous "barbarians" in both camps, but most of them, so far from objecting to Roman rule, were ready to go all lengths to obtain the prizes that the Empire had to offer.

We have evidence of the extent to which Rome itself was being Germanized in the legislation of this period. Dr. Dill, who has made a careful study of the subject, quotes [1] three edicts of Honorius between 397 and 416 which forbid the wearing of trousers, long hair, and fur coats of the barbarian style within the precincts of the city. The tone of the law of 416 leaves no doubt that the rage for German fashions was widespread, and that the previous edicts had been disregarded. Argobastes, the Frank, a member of a German tribe, who had been appointed Master-General of Gaul, probably instigated the murder of Valentinian II, and according to Gibbon was determined " either to rule or to ruin " the Western Empire. Alaric the Visigoth was a Roman-trained soldier who had commanded the Gothic auxiliaries in Theodosius's last campaign, and it is surmised that he too had a quarrel with his Roman superiors. The preliminary phase to the first sack of Rome was a stubborn conflict between two " barbarians " Alaric the Visigoth and Stilicho the Vandal, who was to all intents and purposes Emperor of the West. If Honorius, the nominal

---

[1] *Roman Society in the Last Century of the Western Empire*, IV, Chaps. I and II

Emperor, had not been foolish enough to procure the assassination of Stilicho, it is improbable that Alaric would ever have entered Rome.

In the next forty years Attila and his Huns were thrown back at the battle of Chalons by Aetius—himself probably of "barbarian" origin—with a mixed force of Romans, Visigoths, Burgundians, and other "barbarian" *fœderati*. Then again history repeated itself. The Emperor (Valentinian III) procured the assassination of Aetius (whose friends avenged him by assassinating the Emperor), and in the turmoil which followed the Vandals sailed across from Carthage under Gaiseric and looted the city (455 A.D.).

2

For the next twenty years "barbarian" generals installed in Rome were masters of the Western Empire, and created and deposed Emperors at will. For the first sixteen years of this period the German Ricimer, of Suevic and Visigothic descent, having murdered Majorian, the last of the ruling Emperors, held the reins with a succession of puppet Emperors. After him came Odoacer, a Danubian of the tribe of Scyrri, leader of the "barbarians" from beyond the Danube, who now made up the greater part of the German army in Italy. Having a keener sense of reality than most of his predecessors, he deposed the last of the puppet Emperors, contemptuously called Romulus the little Augustus, and so made an end of the Western Empire. In theory the deposition of the western Emperor restored the unity of the Empire and made the Emperor in the East once more supreme over all. This was only a theory and, as it turned out in the end, a disastrous one, for the Eastern Emperor was unable to assert his authority and both injured himself and brought disaster on Rome in his endeavours to do so.

Odoacer was now master of Italy, though he considered it prudent to recognize the nominal authority of the Emperor in the East. But he too, after thirteen years, was threatened by other "barbarians," this time the Ostrogoths under their extremely capable leader Theodoric, who had spent much of his youth as a hostage in Constantinople and had there gained a thorough knowledge of Roman institutions which had inspired him with a great respect for the name and tradition of Rome, and at the same time shown him the weakness of the existing Empire.   Unfortunately for Odoacer, Zeno, the Emperor of the East, was not a puppet but a shrewd, capable, and jealous man, who saw the opportunity of smiting the Empire in the West and removing the Ostrogoths and their leader to a comfortable distance from Constantinople.   Zeno accordingly commissioned Theodoric to invade Italy and dispose of Odoacer—which he did by luring him, out of his impregnable stronghold at Ravenna and assassinating him (A.D. 493).   Despite this and one or two other blots on his record Theodoric proved the wisest and most capable ruler seen in the West since the age of the Antonines.   " His manner of ruling over his subjects," says Procopius, who, as the historian of the Eastern Empire may be taken as a disinterested witness, " was worthy of a great Emperor ;   for he maintained justice, made good laws, protected his country from invasion, and gave proof of extraordinary prudence and valour."   Under his rule Italy prospered, the ravages of the barbarians were repaired, and Rome was largely rebuilt.

In his *History of Europe*, Fisher raises the interesting question whether, but for the untimely action of Justinian in invading Italy (A.D. 553), the Ostrogoths might not have been established there and altered the whole course of history, both by saving the country from the horrors of the invasions by Franks, Alemans, and Lombards, which now awaited it, and by effecting an Italian unity which would have avoided the revival of the Empire in the West and the creation of the Papal State.   Theodoric, however, was a very exceptional kind of Ostrogoth, and the usual disruption appears to have set in soon after his death and to have made considerable progress before Belisarius and Narses appeared on the scene.

3

The lure of Rome, even when the seat of Government had been moved to Milan or Ravenna, Rome, the great name, surviving in memory and tradition all loss of actual power and dominion, was for centuries to come to exercise a fatal fascination upon the ambitious and to be the last infirmity of more than one noble mind.   Justinian had far better have devoted to the Eastern Empire the men and treasure which he wasted on a vain endeavour to make himself master of the old Roman Empire.   The realities of that had long passed away ;

the struggles were now only for names and shadows. Who in the sixth century could be certified as " Roman " and who branded as " barbarian " ?

The question now was whether any of the races either in Italy or the Provinces could form a nucleus round which the others could rally, or any ruler not merely establish himself against rivals and aggressors in his lifetime but create a dynasty which would secure continuous administration after his death.

The damage done to Rome and Italy by the barbarian invasions has probably been somewhat exaggerated. St. Augustine makes it part of his defence of Christianity that Alaric, being a Christian (albeit an Arian), did comparatively little damage. Rutilius, writing six years after Alaric's raid, paints a picture of the city in which the great palaces and temples are still standing, and this " fair queen of the world " is hailed in her splendour as the symbol of a world-wide and God-like sway. The barbarian raiders went almost as quickly as they came ; their armies were comparatively small, and though they ravaged the countryside they appear to have left many of the great villas untouched.

The worst havoc was wrought by Justinian's generals, Belisarius and Narses. The force they commanded was nominally Roman, but in reality, as Fisher says, " even more alien to the native population of Italy than the Gothic swordsmen who had been peaceably settled in the country for half a century." Its advance was attended by devastation and massacre on the largest scale. Fisher paints a gloomy picture of the plight of Rome when it had finished its work.

The teeming capital with its luxurious public baths, its system of food doles and popular amusements, had disappeared. In its place a few thousand impoverished beings, many of them clerics, lingered on among the monuments of ancient greatness, henceforth and for many centuries to come to be girdled by undrained and malarious wastes. No more was there a Roman Senate. The last circus had been held, the last triumph celebrated, the last consul elected. [1]

This, nevertheless, was the city the very sight of which, with its great churches and shrines, its tombs of the apostles and saints and other

---

[1] Fisher, *History of Europe*, p. 130.

noble buildings, was to throw Charlemagne into ecstasies 200 years later. Apparently in the intervening period the great change had been accomplished which converted it from the capital of the Pagan Empire into the centre of Catholic Christianity.

The resilience of Rome after its disasters is one of the miracles of history. Apollinaris Sidonius, the Gallo-Roman, who in one of his letters gives us an account of his visit to the city in the year 468, says not a word about its sack by the Vandals twelve years earlier. The city is en fête, for the marriage of Ricimer, the Visigoth and *de facto* ruler of the Empire, to Alypia the daughter of Anthemius, one of the puppet Emperors, and Sidonius sees " the wealth of two Empires blown to the winds in the process." High society is enjoying itself as carelessly and extravagantly under the rule of the Visigoth as in the great days. Markets and theatres are thronged, crowds of clients fill the halls of the Senatorial magnates. The only hint of trouble is that when Sidonius is appointed Prefect of the city he becomes anxious about the food-supplies, for which, as a set-off to this high distinction, he becomes responsible. " I rather fear," he says, " that there may be an uproar in the theatres if the supplies of grain run short, and that the hunger of all the Romans may be laid to my account." His fears were well justified, for Africa, the principal granary of the Empire was now in the hands of the Vandals, who certainly were not concerned to see that Rome was supplied. But in these days the great majority were totally ignorant of what was happening outside a very narrow circle, and seem to have lived care-free between one raid and the next. [1]

4

We may get some light on these centuries by considering our own experience as an Imperial Power. In India we have passed through

---

[1] Sidonias, *Epistles*, I-VII ; see also Dill, *op. cit.*, p. 260. Orosius, the Spanish priest and disciple of St. Augustine, speaks of the capture of Rome as a single act of brigandage in a world enjoying general tranquillity. The Goths, says Dill, " in their first onset might be fierce and rapacious, but they were after all fellow-Christians. Their chief had kept inviolate the Christian churches ; the soldiers in the midst of their pillage had formed a singular procession to escort the sacred vessels to the basilica of St. Peter, singing hymns as they went."

two stages, first in dealing with the people as we found them and next in dealing with the people as we made them. The first stage was comparatively simple. It was a question of conquest and submission. After that there might be a rebellion if unwittingly or otherwise we offended religious susceptibilities, and in that case the problem was again one of suppression and punishment requiring a certain amount of force. But with the one exception of the Mutiny the officials of the East India Company and their successors in the Indian Civil Service administered the country on a friendly footing with the Indian people for nearly a century. The next stage, when these people had learnt from their rulers Western traditions and ways of life was much more difficult. We had educated them and led them in this direction and they wished to know why they should not govern themselves as we did ourselves. We answered with concessions leading up to self-government within the framework of the British Empire, but there have been new and perplexing problems all the way, and it is impossible to say that we have reached anything like a final solution. The question for us is not merely whether a democracy can govern an Empire, but whether independent or semi-independent democracies can work in the same Empire.

In late Republican and early Empire times Rome produced a large number of highly capable soldier-administrators who had the faculty, as the British in like case, of getting on with the peoples they had conquered. But they too, like the British, passed by degrees into a second stage in which these people had become Romanized. Their solution, like ours, was a liberal one ; they sought to bring their new subjects into the circle of Roman citizenships and to give them local and municipal self-government, and to open all offices, even the highest, to men of capacity among them without compromising the theory that Rome was over all. But these subjects were not divided from them by any gulf of race and blood or even of religion, as the East is from the West. When Rome adopted Christianity, most of them became Christians of one sect or another ; intermarriage mixed all the races and as the years went on it became more and more difficult to distinguish between Roman and " barbarian." In some respects Roman Gaul, if we may judge from the descriptions of its beautiful cities, its great villas, and its social and cultural life given by writers like Apollinaris Sidonius more than held its own with Italy. Many of the wealthiest and most cultivated Romans seem actually to have preferred to live in Gaul.

This upset the balance of the Empire, but Rome by its immense prestige continued to cast its spell over all. To be consul or prefect, even to wear the purple, became the ambition of gifted and able provincials, whether they were Roman or barbarian in origin. What Tacitus called the *arcanum imperii*—that an Emperor could be made elsewhere than at Rome—became a fatal weakness in later years. The distracting ambitions, conspiracies, and intrigues which attended the pursuit of the great prize shattered the central organization and was fatal to the orderly administration of the provinces. It was as though an Indian Prince or the Prime Minister of a Dominion were to turn his back on his own country and arrive in London with a fleet or an army making a bid for the British crown or the position of Prime Minister. The later history of the Roman Empire is that of an incessant struggle for a prize which was being destroyed by those who were fighting for it.

5

The one thing which might have saved the Empire at the eleventh hour was undoubtedly, as Fisher has suggested, a working partnership between Roman and Visigoth. Neither could have endured alone, but the two together might have supplied one another's deficiencies. Often we seem to be on the edge of it. There are traces of a movement to establish an independent Gallo-Roman state under Visigoth leadership about the middle of the fifth century, and even Apollinaris Sidonius, one of the most loyal of Roman citizens, appears to have dallied with it. The letter in which he paints the character and describes the court of Theodoric II [1] at Arles about this time describes him as a benevolent and comparatively civilized monarch who made himself acceptable to the Gallo-Roman people. Seeing that he had left them in possession of their villas and a large part of their estates and permitted them to remain under their own form of administra-

---

[1] Not, of course, the great Theodoric, who ruled in Rome 493-526, but an earlier member of the same house. Sidonius, *Ep.*, I., 2.

tion, there was much to be said in these years from their point of view for letting well alone. Life certainly was easier for them than if they were exposed to the sudden and arbitrary exactions of the weak central government. If the Emperor Majorian had held his hand there need have been none of the fierce fightin, which fell so heavily on Lyons and the neighbourhood in the next few years. And if at this late date the Western Empire could have been kept together, it would have been by the Visigoths with Roman acquiescence or assistance. Theodoric the Great came as near performing that miracle as was possible at the end of the sixth and beginning of the seventh century, but the old Roman prejudice against the " barbarian "—now a perfectly meaningless word—reasserted itself on his death and fired Justinian with the disastrous ambition to reconquer Italy.

6

How much the old Roman stock needed replenishing is only too evident from the records of the fifth and sixth centuries. Some Western Emperors, like Valentinian III and Majorian, were well aware of the facts and seem to have faced them courageously. Their codes, which have come down to us, are a scathing indictment of the accumulating scandals which were now coming to their climax. In them we can read the story of the decadence of the Senatorial class—cut off equally from military service and commerce ; of the ruin of the middle-class and their martyrdom at the hands of rascally and rapacious officials ; of the degradation of the lower class in their abject dependence on public doles and amusements at the public cost. Valentinian and Majorian were unsparing in denunciation, but they had no power to effect reforms. It is a familiar story and we can trace it back to its beginnings in the abominable system of feeding the capital with the plunders of conquered nations and supplying a large part of its needs with slave labour. This was the ruin both of orderly finance and of industrial development on any logical and progressive lines, and it led inevitably to the corruption and confusion of the later years.

Yet to get to the source we must go behind these symptoms and ask how it was that the old Roman virtues of honesty and frugality decayed. They survived under Augustus and even Tiberius ; they had a renascence under the great Emperors ; they reappeared in a last flicker under Theodoric. Plato and Aristotle would probably have answered that the great size of the Empire made what they considered good government impossible. I think it may be said that the fund of ability necessary both to govern the provinces and to keep an orderly central administration in Rome ran short as the Empire expanded. To find capable and honest administrators in numbers sufficient to govern the provinces and man the central government became more and more difficult. The abler and more ambitious men sought careers in the provinces with the ultimate idea of winning the prizes of the capital, but they drained the capital of its brains and left it in a weakened condition to become the sport of their ambition. There were limits to Roman patriotism when it conflicted with ambition. From the days of Marius and Sulla, *stasis*, to use the appropriate Greek word, had been a perpetually recurring vice of the leading Romans, and rebellion against some of the monsters who wore the purple may have seemed a civic duty even to good men. But the incessant tumults in the city and the breach of continuity when Emperors were assassinated and rivals were fighting their way to the throne were fatal to good government. In these conflicts the spoils were to the victors, who rewarded themselves by plunder under various official disguises. The sacks of the city were as often as not scrambles for spoils by its own high officials and soldiers.

Yet while we pile up the indictment we can never forget the amazing services which the Roman Empire performed for the world. It had constructed great roads through pathless forests and swamps, built beautiful cities, provided water-supplies and sanitation on a scale scarcely equalled by modern engineering. It was presently to bequeath a system of law which was to prove the greatest and most durable of its gifts to the modern world. It had a grossly brutal side. Its sports included the human sacrifices of the arena ; it had no compunction about selling the conquered, including women and children, into slavery ; it had a contempt for the multitude whom it fed with bread and circuses. The speculative faculty seemed to be omitted from its nature. It contributed little to philosophy, and its art was imitative ; it loved the grandiose rather than the beautiful. It improvised as it went along, seldom pausing to think about itself or what lay ahead when the next corner was turned. In the pioneering days there was great virtue in the variety and flexibility of Roman method, but it lacked systematic organization, and the central control became spasmodic and irregular. Rome was, geographically speaking, an admirable centre for the original Empire, spreading south and east as well as north and west, but it was less well suited to the Western Empire after the separation from the East. A capital cut off from the greater part of the Empire by the great barrier of the Alps was in the least favourable position to control the centrifugal tendencies which were now setting in, and which in due time were to lead to the formation of nations as moderns understand that word. If Rome was to remain the capital of the Empire in the West, decentralization had become an urgent necessity after the schism with the East. The lesson leaps to the eyes of the modern who reads the story in the light of later experience, but the actual rulers were absorbed in the emergencies which crowded in upon them as conflict and chaos followed the breakdown of the administrative machine. After the age of the Antonines no statesman of the first rank appeared who was capable of seeing the problem steadily and seeing it whole. It is the failure of brains much more than of military power or any physical decadence in the population that appears to set a limit to the survival of Empires.

prosperity. Each accepted the existence of the other's deities, regarding them as beneficent or malevolent, angels or demons, according to their point of view. Judicious selections of the triumphs and disasters recorded in the long history of Republic and Empire could prove either case.

But the pagans had at least one point of substance which even now is far from settlement. Could a devout Christian be a good citizen of any earthly State? Would his conscience permit him to take up arms in defence of his country? St. Augustine argued that the Gospel was not opposed to war waged justly and mercifully, but he had against him a great company of monks and ascetics who had turned their backs upon the scene of warfare and shared the views which St. Paulinus had set out in his famous letter [1] to the soldier who had felt drawn to the higher Christian life. In that letter Christian obedience was boldly declared to be incompatible both with the duties of citizenship and the relations of family life. There was no possibility, said the saint, of serving both Christ and Cæsar. The soldier was a mere shedder of blood, doomed to eternal torment. The love of father or mother, wife or child, the desire for wealth or conquest were so many obstacles to the Christian life. In that faith thousands in the last years of the fourth century had followed St. Jerome to Bethlehem or fled to hermitages in the deserts of Syria and Egypt and monasteries on islands in the Tuscan sea. Upon all these the execrations of the mob and the contempt of the old pagan nobility were poured out in the fullest measure. It was these and the likes of them, said their assailants, who had corrupted the old Roman virtues and brought ruin on the State.

Rutilius Namatianus, one of this old nobility, who flung out of Rome in a rage at its Christian decadence and sought a pagan oasis in Gaul, has expressed what he and his friends thought of monks in a poem describing his voyage to his new home. He describes Caprasia as an " island filthy with men who shun the light, who call themselves by the Greek name of monk, because they wish to live alone with none to look on. They fear the rewards and dread the losses of

---

[1] St. Paulinus, Ep. XXV, quoted by Dill, *Roman Society in the Last Century of the Roman Empire*, p. 10.

fortune." [1] As he sails away Rutilius delivers himself of a high-flown panegyric of Rome and her Empire and her ancient gods, thereby drawing down on himself a sharp rebuke from Gibbon, who thinks the year 416 ill-chosen for such a theme.[2] Yet if not to despair of the Empire may be considered as meritorious as not to despair of the Republic, Rutilius holds a high place among the optimists of history. In any case, his poem is evidence of the hold which even then paganism had in both the aristocracy and the mob in Rome itself. When all allowance has been made for poetic licence, it is unlikely that even the most extravagant rhetorician could have written in just these terms in the year 416 A.D. if there had not been a certain swing back to the old religion after the great disaster. The rhetoric is impressive, even beautiful, and there is a real thrill in the passage in which the pagan writer imagines that he still hears the shouts rising up from the circus and the arena. This is one of the passages in classical literature which seem suddenly to bring the ancient world to life.[3]

2

While Rutilius was singing the praises of the old order, St. Augustine was writing his great work, the *De Civitate Dei*, and in passing from the one to the other we leap the gulf that divides pagan from Christian. The famous Bishop of Hippo had watched the sack of Rome from the relative security (till then) of his African diocese, and it filled him, as it did St. Jerome in his retreat at Bethlehem, with horror and dismay. But he quickly roused himself to champion the Christian cause, and his *City of God* is his reply to the pagan onslaught. As a counter-attack much of it is little above the level of the attack. It ransacks history for arguments good or bad, it moves in a world of demons and devils, angels and archangels ; it is at once romantic and mystical, superstitious and materialistic. But St. Augustine—and this is the

---

1 Rutilius, *De Reditu Suo*, ll. 439-43.
2 *Miscellaneous Works,* vol. 5, p. 435 (1814 edition).
3 Sæpius attonitæ resonant circensibus aures
   Nuntiat accensus plena theatra favor.
   Pulsato notæ redduntur ab æthere voces
   Vel quia perveniunt, vel quia fingit amor.—*Rutilius,* 201-4.

of outworn superstitions, careless of Plato's rule that nothing should be imputed to God which would be discreditable if attributed to man. In all these respects he is the child of his time, with the peculiar sensitiveness of the man of genius to the mood which for the time being possesses him. In the writings of such a man it is easy by judicious selection to find support for almost any interpretation.

To me St. Augustine's general view of the relation of the city of God to the earthly State suggests an analogy with Plato's idea of the relation of his *Republic* to the practical constitution propounded in his *Laws*. The *Republic* is the pattern laid up in heaven, the first-best, of which the vision is never to be lost sight of; the *Laws* a second-best, to be tolerated in the actual condition of the world, but always to be brought into judgment by comparison with the first-best. So to St. Augustine the City of God is the ideal, whether in heaven or on earth, by which actual human institutions are to be measured and judged. Both have their virtues and values, but the values of the City of God are absolute and those of the earthly city only relative. Order there must be and justice in the latter—for take away justice and what are the kingdoms of the earth but great bands of robbers?—but the earthly virtues and values are tainted with the alloys of sin and selfishness, whereas in the heavenly city there is only one object of love, and that is the universal good. In the earthly city order must be kept, property must be allowed, if only to keep greed within bounds; slavery must be permitted and human institutions fitted to the hardness of human hearts, but all these things are decreed by God as remedies for sin, and it is only in the heavenly city that absolute righteousness can be realized. The heavenly city can co-operate with the earthly and the citizens of the one may be citizens of the other, but the earthly virtues temperance, prudence, justice, fortitude, praised by the pagans, are only mortal virtues; there can be no lasting element of felicity in them, such as faith in God and the hope of eternal life provide in the heavenly city.

Thus conceived, neither the earthly city nor the heavenly corresponds to anything material and tangible. The former is not the Roman Empire, the latter is not the existing Church. But even though the writer might not have intended it, it was inevitable that his readers should apply it to existing institutions, to the Empire and to the Church. St. Augustine himself, it must be said, frequently lends himself to this construction. He speaks of a " house which is being built to the Lord in every land, that is the city of God which is the Holy Church," and in presenting this as the alternative to the pagan State, he would naturally be taken to mean that he thought of the actual and visible Church as successor to the Roman Empire. To the Christian readers who had learnt to think of " the Holy Church " as the ecclesiastical organization of bishops and priests and who may even have seen St. Augustine himself administering justice in his African diocese, this would have been a natural and highly acceptable interpretation. St. Augustine, says Harnack, " roused the conviction that the empirical Catholic Church *sans phrase* was the kingdom of God, and the independent State that of the devil." [1]

4

There is, in any case, no doubt that subsequent generations did so interpret his book, and in that, as we shall see hereafter, lies its importance in the history of Church and Empire. It fixed Catholic Christian orthodoxy in the form in which it was to be generally accepted, taking up into it the doctrine of original sin and redemption through grace and the sacrament of baptism. To this doctrine it attached a system of pains and penalties threatening the non-elect, the unbeliever, and the backslider with eternal torture from which escape is only to be found in the Church or through the Church and the acceptance of its discipline. The chapters in the *De Civitate* condemning the wicked to an eternity of pain, the long and ingenious argument to prove it to be an acceptable belief that the fleshly body may by a special providence be submitted for ever to the pains of burning without being consumed, and other passages in which the saint dwells in careful detail on the terrors awaiting the sinful and unfaithful, are sometimes dismissed as expressing ideas which were generally shared in the fifth century and have no bearing on the main argument of the book. In this way we may get eventually a truer as well as a more humane version of the Christian faith, but there is no shirking the fact that the doctrine of eternal punishment from

---

[1] *History of Dogma*, V, p. 151 ; English translation.

which the Church alone offered the means of escape became under St. Augustine's influence an integral part of Christian theology, and that it had enormous importance in subsequent history. It was this eventually which gave the Church its power over both the individual and the State.

The pagan State had been tolerant of all beliefs ; it had never presumed to say that departure from an official belief or offences against morality would be attended by pains and penalties in the after-world. The Church not only said this, but claimed to be in a position to send into outer darkness those whom it judged to be sinners and heretics. In the pagan world individuals might feel the sense of sin and seek in the mystery religions the means of appeasing the powers of light and darkness, but this was entirely at their own discretion ; the only heresy known to the State and punishable by it was the disloyalty to itself, which might be inferred from refusal to burn incense at the shrine of the Emperors. Sin it knew only as offences against the law, for which penalties were prescribed here and now. The whole idea of punishment in another world to which it might doom or from which it might release the offender was remote from its thoughts. Thus when the Church had once obtained the acceptance of its claim that it held the keys of heaven and hell—that it had the power of loosing and binding—it was bound to become a serious rival to secular rulers, who could only kill the body. In this respect the State had prepared its own undoing, for it had not merely adopted Christianity as the official religion ; it had placed the civil power behind the Church for the punishment of heretics and at the same time made it a powerful secular organization by giving it the right to acquire property, which very soon came to it in abundance from the faithful, who were persuaded that in this way they could obtain absolution and release from suffering in the after-world. The doctrine of purgatory came in gradually to mitigate the crude alternatives of eternal bliss or eternal damnation, but in either case the dispensing power supposed to be exercised by the Church and the tremendous results which followed even in this world from its sentence of excommunication were to be the chief sources of its temporal and material power and its frequent collisions with the State.

For this reason it is impossible to discard the doctrine of eternal punishment in the after life as something temporary and local belonging to a primitive state of thought and imagination. As expounded by St. Augustine and his contemporaries it was one of the foundation doctrines of the faith, derived in strict and literal logic from words attributed to Christ ; and an immense structure, some of which survives to this day, has been raised upon it. In the form which it took it may even be said to be original to Christianity as interpreted at this time. The Jews thought of Sheol as a place of dim dreariness and Homer makes the shade of Achilles tell Ulysses that he would " rather live upon the soil as the hireling of another, even with a landless man who had no great livelihood, than bear sway among all the dead who are no more." [1] Virgil in his sixth *Æneid* paints lurid pictures of tortures devised for mythical beings who had offended the gods. The Eleusinian mysteries promised happiness hereafter to those who had been initiated and left those who had not to " fade away utterly in the dark gloom." [2] There were also impostors both in Athens and Rome who went from house to house selling charms to rich people to save them from the pain awaiting the unitiated in Hades.[3] But there is little or no analogy between these ideas of happiness to be gained by the magic of initiation and the Christian doctrine of the pains of hell as penalties for sin. Superficially the two ideas might seem to meet in the performance of some rite or ceremony said to be the way of salvation, but the idea of a world steeped in sin and doomed to eternal suffering except through the means of grace provided for the faithful by the Church was original to Augustinian Christianity, and had developments and consequences undreamt of by pagans.

For it not merely made the Church immensely powerful as an organized institution ; it introduced into the Western world a conception of human life which had hitherto been confined to the East, and even in the East mainly to India. To immense numbers the life of this world now appeared of vastly less importance than the eternal life in the world to come. Human beings were on pilgrimage to eternity, and what they suffered here and what they vainly imagined they were doing in their quest of wealth or power or fame counted

---

[1] *Odyssey*, XI, pp. 499 *et seq.*

[2] Fragment of Sophocles quoted by F. Legge in *Forerunners and Rivals in Christianity*, I, p. 59.

[3] *Ibid.*, p. 140.

for nothing in comparison with the happiness or damnation that awaited them hereafter. Morally there were great advantages in a doctrine which made all men equal before the Lord, and all, whether bond or free, Roman or barbarian, the subjects of His wrath and, if they were Christians, of His love and mercy. For the first time it introduced the idea of humanity as one, and of a great society of the faithful transcending the bounds of any earthly State. But since the sojourn of this society on earth was only a fleeting moment in its eternal existence, the same doctrine reduced to relative unimportance what could be done for it or to it by earthly sovereigns and rulers. Its sufferings might even be regarded as a necessary and predestined probation for the glory which awaited it hereafter.

The whole tendency of this line of thought was adverse to what moderns call progress. Both the practical Roman spirit for building, improving, and developing and the scientific Greek spirit for inquiring and discovering were sharply checked, and for centuries intellectual and scientific development was to pass over to Arabs and non-Christians, while the Christian world devoted an immense part of its energy and wealth to the building of churches and cathedrals, the founding and endowing of monasteries, and the support of priests, one of whose chief functions was the saying of masses for the souls of the departed. The dead and the other world now exercised the same sort of sway over the peoples of Europe as in the Egypt of the Pyramids.

5

We have seen in a previous chapter how the necessity of keeping order in doctrinal tumults brought the State to the support of the Church. Ecclesiastics, however, were not content that it should be merely, so to speak, at call for these emergencies. They wished it definitely brought into the scheme whereby, in their belief, the world was or ought to be governed. This is the critical fact for the student of political institutions. We now enter upon the enormous complication of politics and religion which is the chief part of the history of government in the next thousand years. From this time forward the marriage of State and religion was indissoluble, but it was not an identity of the civil and religious powers or the subordination of the religious to the civil, as in pagan times ; it was the union of two

partners, Church and State, of which the Church tended to become
the predominant partner in virtue of its supernatural powers.   In the
previous centuries the State had used the pagan religion as part of the
official apparatus of government, a part as completely within its
control as any branch of secular administration.   The same officials
discharged both civil and spiritual functions ; the Emperor could be
quite sure that his writ would run in both spheres, if it ran in either.
With the adoption of Christianity, all this was changed.   There was
now an order of bishops and priests claiming supremacy in the
spiritual sphere in virtue of miraculous powers ensured by the Apostolic succession to them and to them alone, powers which inevitably,
like that of excommunication, encroached on the civil sphere and
required its acquiescence and support.

The bishop was, in Gibbon's words, " the perpetual censor of the
morals of his people.   The discipline of penance was digested into a
system of canonical jurisprudence, which accurately defined the duty
of private or public confession, the rules of evidence, the degrees of
guilt, and the measure of punishment.   It was impossible to execute
this spiritual censure if the Christian pontiff who punished the obscure
sins of the multitude respected the conspicuous vices and destructive
crimes of the magistrate ; but it was impossible to arraign the conduct
of the magistrate without controlling the administration of civil
government.   In the early days some consideration of loyalty or fear
protected the sacred persons of the Emperors from the zeal or resent-
ment of the bishops ; but they boldly censured and excommunicated
the subordinate tyrants who were not invested with the majesty of the
purple.   St. Athanasius excommunicated one of the ministers of
Egypt ; and the interdict which he pronounced of fire and water was
solemnly transmitted to the Churches of Cappadocia."   Gibbon
quotes other instances such as that of Synesius, Bishop of Ptolemais,
and the venal and rascally Andronicus whom he doomed to the abhor-
rence of earth and heaven. But side by side with this heroic testifying for
right and justice there were other cases which proved that bishops could,
no more than other men, be trusted to exercise arbitrary power at their
own discretion. Within a very few years of the adoption of Christianity
it was clear that a powerful State was growing up within the State and
threatening a dangerous duality in civil and criminal jurisdiction.

without compromising their political independence. For opposite reasons the Popes desired the material support of the Franks, but were extremely jealous about their spiritual ascendency.

The final breach in the continuity of the Roman Empire in the West was the work of the Lombards, an East German nation which swept down upon Italy in the middle of the sixth century and, unlike previous invaders, made no pretence of respect for the Roman Empire. When they had done their work they had conquered all Italy with the exception of the country round Ravenna, Rome, Naples, and the extreme southern end of the Peninsula. The representative of the great Roman Empire was now only the Exarch of Ravenna, and he was reduced to the position of a local chieftain. The Papacy alone retained any semblance of the ancient authority, and to a certain extent had gained by the Lombard conquests, which had released it from its dependence on the Emperors. Gregory the Great, who became Pope in 590, seized the opportunity to rebuild its authority both spiritual and temporal by his administrative ability and reforming zeal, and in the next two centuries it made a bold bid to be the supreme power in the civilized world.

But to maintain this position, and especially after its excommunication of the Iconoclasts and consequent complete breach with the Emperor in the East (731), the support either of the Lombards, who were now firmly established in Italy and also professed the orthodox faith, or of the Franks became an absolute necessity to the Papacy. Pope Gregory III very shrewdly decided that if the Lombards became masters of Italy he would become their vassal, whereas the remoter Franks would be well occupied at a convenient distance from Rome. Thus in 739 he sent the keys of the tomb of St. Peter to Charles Martel and invited him to replace the Emperor in the East as the legal suzerain in Rome, *i.e.* practically declare himself Emperor in the West. This was too great a leap for Charles, who though virtually ruler of the Franks, was still legally only mayor of the Palace, exercising his power through the puppet sovereign who was the lawful heir of Clovis. But his son Pepin saw his way to a series of profitable transactions with the Papacy. He had earned much merit by his real or supposed piety, and his support of the Englishman, Boniface, who was carrying the gospel into Germany. He wished to make an end of the nominal sovereignty of the puppet kings and to make himself *de jure* as well as *de facto* ruler of France. But what power was there which could legitimize a monarch and give him sanctity in the eyes of his subjects?

Only one, Pepin decided, and that was the Pope of Rome, the head of the Orthodox Christian Church. To Pope Zacchary, therefore, he had recourse, putting a discreet question, such as a Greek might have addressed to the Delphic oracle. Was it not right that the real ruler should also be the acknowledged ruler? Zacchary replied that assuredly it was right. It seemed an innocent question and received a man-of-the-world answer. But the answer was momentous, and on the strength of it Pepin deposed the legitimate Merovingian and got himself anointed king by his friend, Boniface, in the cathedral at Soisson. Thus, *coram populo*, Pepin acknowledged the power of the Pope to make and unmake secular rulers and the Papacy established a precedent which was to be one of its chief weapons for the next thousand years.

By this stroke the Pope had exalted his own position and done Pepin the considerable service of legitimizing his position as a monarch. But his dependence on the Lombards left him in a precarious position, and he now looked to Pepin to release him from this bondage. Pepin responded by undertaking two expeditions against the Lombards, and forced them not only to secure the Pope in the Duchy of Rome but also to give up to him all the territory of the late Exarchate stretching from Rome to Ravenna. Thus by the " donation of Pepin," which the Pope complacently accepted as his due under that monstrous forgery the supposed " Donation of Constantine " (giving all Italy to the Pope), the Papal States, or " States of the Church," were set up as an independent Italian principality, to the fatal prejudice for the next 1100 years of Italian unity.

2

Before the end of the eighth century the Popes were again in difficulty both from their own rebellious subjects and from the Lombards. Pepin's greater son, Charles the Great, now came to the rescue, and in 773 on the call of Pope Hadrian he marched into Italy, defeated and deposed the Lombard king, declared himself King of Lombardy, and marched in triumph to Rome, where he renewed the " donation of Pepin." During the next twenty years the power of Charles was immensely increased by his numerous campaigns against Saracens and Avars, Saxons, Danes, and Slavs, and before the century ended he was master of all Catholic Christendom except the British Isles. But now once more a Pope, Leo III, was in difficulties. Accusing him of cruelty and oppression, his subjects had risen against him (798) as he was going in solemn procession through the streets of Rome and wounded him and left him for dead. He escaped, however, and made his way to the Frankish King, who sent him back to Rome under escort, promising to follow himself a little later.

He did follow, and on Christmas Day 800 there was enacted in the old church of St. Peter the extraordinary scene of his coronation. It was not a coronation as that rite is commonly supposed to be. The Pope had got himself acquitted or whitewashed ; his innocence, already vindicated by a miracle, had been pronounced in full synod by Charles acting as " patrician," and Charles having done this business, had waited to spend Christmas in Rome. He attended high mass on Christmas Day in the garb and place of the " patrician " and nothing more had been expected by the clergy and laity in attendance than the pomp and ceremony usual on such an occasion. But suddenly after the reading of the gospel, the Pope came off his throne and placed on Charles's brow, as he knelt before the high altar, the diadem of the Cæsars and knelt in obeisance before him. Immediately there rose a great shout from the multitude assembled in the church : " Karolo Augusto a Deo coronato magno et pacifico imperatori vita et victoria."

" In that shout," says Bryce, " echoed by the Franks without, was pronounced the Union, so long in preparation, so mighty in its consequences, of the Roman and the Teuton, of the memories and the civilization of the south with the fresh energy of the north, and from that moment modern history begins."[1]

In that shout, we may add, the uneasy marriage of Church and State, with its inextricable tangle of the secular and the spiritual, was imposed for another 700 years on both the parties to it.

Readers of Bryce's study of this event are familiar with the historical problem and the subtle arguments to which it gave rise. It was certainly a well-prepared scene, so far as the Pope was concerned, but

---

[1] *Holy Roman Empire,* sixth *ed.. p.* 49.

was Charles taken by surprise, as his biographer Eginhard seems to suggest, and, if so, was it a pleasant or an unpleasant surprise? We can only say that Charles had some strong motives for making it appear a surprise. He was engaged at the moment in a tortuous negotiation with the Eastern Empire, and was even supposed to have toyed with the idea of marrying the abominable Empress Irene (who had deposed and blinded her son) as the easiest way of reuniting East and West and getting himself acknowledged undisputed Emperor of the whole original Empire. The coronation flung defiance at the East, which had never abandoned its claim to be master and overlord in West as well as East. In the circumstances it may have suited Charles to let it appear that his hand had been forced by the Pope. Still more it may have suited him not to have acknowledged, by suing for it, the ight which the Pope had tacitly asserted of making an Emperor by the act of coronation. His father, Pepin, had gone as far in that direction as was convenient for a Frankish monarch, when he had persuaded the Pope to give an opinion about his relation to the puppet kings. This was helpful as the advice of the greatest moral force of the age, but it was very far from a claim on the Pope's part to have the power of creating an Emperor or the acknowledgment of such a claim by his nominee. Yet both the claim and its acknowledgment were implicit in the act of coronation, and it was the universal opinion of the ecclesiastical world that since Charles had accepted the crown at the hands of Leo III, he had assented to the doctrine that no Emperor could be made without the fiat of the Pope. The importance of this doctrine at a time when there was no secular law of succession to any throne need not be emphasized. For those monarchs who were fortunate enough to found a dynasty with hereditary rights of succession, as the French finally did, it was of little consequence what the Pope thought or did, but for Emperors who depended on election or held a precarious position in dependence on nobles and ecclesiastics, his support might be a matter of life and death.

3

If the coronation was inconvenient to Charles, in that it ended his dream of fusion with the East, it was of the highest importance to him in all else. By his immense success as a conqueror and administrator

Charles had seemed to be the man of destiny, the man designated by God and history to revive the glories of the Roman Empire. That Empire was still (in the West at all events) one and indivisible in the minds of all who engaged in affairs at this time, and he who presided over it needed to have a spiritual as well as a secular title, a title which could only be conferred by the Pope, who alone represented the continuous Christian tradition untainted by schism or heresy. Charles was a sincerely pious man and he was zealous in carrying on the work of his grandfather and father, who had warmly supported the saintly Boniface in converting Saxons, Frisians, Thuringians, and Hessians to the orthodox Christian faith and had lent the support of their armies when the converts proved reluctant. To have the support of the Church greatly enhanced his position in his own eyes and in those of his Catholic subjects. He was now not merely the conquering monarch of the Frankish people but Emperor *jure divino*. The unity of his Empire depended largely on the religious bond. Every Christian—Frank, Gaul, German, or Italian—owed loyalty to the Pope as head of his religion, and if to the Pope, then to the Emperor whom the Pope had crowned as the secular agent of his spiritual rule.

The doctrine had its severely practical as well as its spiritual aspect. The bishops were more and more encroaching on the secular sphere. They had great estates ; they claimed the right to govern them in their own way and to administer their own kind of justice ; even to raise forces for their own defence. Many were rich and worldly and ranked with dukes and counts, even in some cases being themselves dukes and counts, who were beginning to create the new thing called the feudal system. With the Pope on his side, the Emperor could work his will on them ; with the Pope against him, they were potential centres of rebellion ready to stab him in the back whenever he was in difficulites if he did not do their will. The dominating personality of Charles kept the Church in a subordinate place during the fourteen years that remained to him. There was only one will and that was his. He brought it to bear with excellent results upon the much overdue task of educating the bishops and priests, being aided thereto by his favourite instructor, the English Alcuin. But when Charles departed, the inherent difficulties of the Pope-Emperor combination began to appear.

CHAPTER XIX

THE PORTRAIT OF CHARLEMAGNE

I

LET me pause here to dwell for a moment on the one perfect portrait of a great ruler by a contemporary which has come down to us from this time. I mean Eginhard's *Life of Charlemagne*. It may be compared with the portrait of the Visigoth Theodoric II, a much inferior, but still interesting figure, by Sidonius Apollinaris glanced at in a previous chapter. Both show us the intimate life and routine of courts which by the old Roman standards would have been counted " barbarian," but which are a characteristic blend of the old tradition and the nascent new order.

Eginhard starts with a lively sketch of the plight to which the Merovingian Kings had been reduced by the mayors of the palace. Childeric, the last of them, had beyond his title nothing but the satisfaction of sitting on his throne with long hair and hanging beard, trying to look like a sovereign, giving audience to ambassadors and charging them to deliver in his name replies which had been dictated to him. The mayor allowed him only one small property and the minimum of servants to attend to his wants. When he went out, it was in an oxen wagon driven by a herdsman in the rustic manner, and in this vehicle he had to present himself to the annual assembly of his people. This farce had been prolonged to the point of scandal when, about the year 750, the " Franks " (as the Royal annals say) or, more probably, the ruling mayor of the palace, Pepin, consulted the Pope, who (as recorded in the previous chapter) said very sensibly that the man who had the kingly power had better be king, and suggested that Childeric should have his hair cut and be sent to a monastery and Pepin be crowned king.

Pepin reigned for eighteen years and died in Paris in 768, leaving two sons, Charles and Carloman, between whom, according to the dangerous custom of the Franks, Pepin's kingdom had to be divided. Fortunately for the unity of the Frankish kingdom, Carloman, the second son, died after two years, and Charles became sole king. The narrative now becomes a catalogue of incessant wars against Lombards, Saxons, Bavarians, Slavs, Huns, the Normans called " Danes," Spaniards, and Bretons, brought invariably, according to the biographer, to triumphant conclusions. The Saxons are presented as obstinately resisting the efforts of the great king to tame them and Christianize them. They are said, " like nearly all the nations of Germany," to have been " of a ferocious nature, practising the cult of demons, enemies of our religion who saw nothing dishonourable in violating and transgressing laws human and divine." They were finally compelled to abandon the cult of demons and other tribal ceremonies, to adopt the faith and sacraments of the Christian religion, and to become one people with the Franks.

2

The King is represented as a man of unceasing activity, who " surpassed in wisdom and greatness of soul all the sovereigns of his time." He shrank from no labour or danger ; he knew how to combat adversity ; and when fortune smiled on him, never yielded to her seductions. He was wise enough to cultivate the friendship of the Powers which it was not convenient to challenge. He concluded treaties with the Constantinople Emperors and was at much pains to disarm their suspicion that he meant to challenge their prerogatives in being crowned Emperor in Rome. He received embassies from Haroun Al Raschid, the King of Persia, who (according to Eginhard) gave him the keys of the Holy Sepulchre and the only elephant he had then in his possession.

He made himself the guardian of the seas, built a fleet to fight the Norman (or Nordic) pirates, placing guard-posts at the mouths of the rivers to prevent them escaping after their up-river excursions, doing this equally for the northern and southern seas, saving Italy from the Moors as well as France and Germany from the Saxons and Danes. For nearly forty years this indefatigable man was prancing about

Europe, making for himself a resounding name, reviving the glories of ancient Rome, reinforcing the temporal power with the spiritual through his skilful manipulation and timely patronage of the Papacy.

He married a Lombard princess, divorced her at the end of a year ; then took to wife a Swabian, Hildegarde ; and after her Frastrada, a German lady of the Eastern Franks ; and after her again the Alamann, Liutgarde. The last two bore him three sons and six daughters. When all four of his wives had died, he took four concubines, who between them gave him four more children. He was most careful about the education of these children, all being instructed in the liberal arts, and the sons being taught to ride, hunt, and handle arms, and the daughters to spin and embroider. He was fortunate in that only three of his children died—two sons and a daughter—but he wept copiously at their death, and wept again as at the loss of a son or brother on hearing of the death of Pope Hadrian. His daughters were so beautiful that he refused to let them marry, but kept them living in a house near his till the time of his death. His biographer hints darkly at certain catastrophes having followed this method of dealing with beautiful young women, but he adds that the father never showed the slightest sign of having heard anything to his or their dishonour. When the son of one of his concubines (Pepin the Hump-backed) was caught in a conspiracy while he was away on one of his campaigns, he permitted him to retire to a monastery and there dedicate himself to the religious life. As a rule he was merciful to his enemies and to conspirators, but there were exceptional occasions when he yielded to an unjust violence, on the prompting—says Eginhard—of Queen Frastrada. His liking for strangers and foreigners was so great that the hospitality lavished on them was a serious burden not only on the palace but on the realm.

His figure was ample and robust, and it was agreed that his height was seven times the length of his feet. He had a round head, great vivid eyes, a longish nose, beautiful white hair ; whether standing or sitting he gave the impression of dignity and authority ; his limbs were so well proportioned that you did not notice that his neck was fat and short and his stomach a little projecting. Until the last years of his life he had excellent health. He built his palace at Aix because he loved bathing in the warm water, and was an excellent swimmer.

When he bathed a large company, consisting of his children, friends, nobles, members of his bodyguard—often as many as a hundred—were in the water with him and joined in the frolics.

He wore the national dress of the Franks, a linen shirt and drawers and over them breeches and a tunic with silk border, his feet and legs in putties. In winter a waistcoat of otter or rat-skin over his shoulders and chest. He carried a sword with gold or silver hilt, which on festive occasions or when he was receiving ambassadors was studded with precious stones. He disliked the costumes of other countries, and, except that he humoured Pope Hadrian by dressing in the Roman style when in Rome, he declined to put them on in any circumstances. On fête days he wore cloth of gold, a gold crown encrusted with jewels, and jewelled shoes, but on all other days his dress differed little from that of the common people.

He was extremely sober and forbade drunkenness, either in his own house or among his friends, but he had a big appetite and often complained of being hungry. During meals he listened to music and reading. He liked history and stories of ancient times, but above all the works of St. Augustine, especially the *De Civitate Dei*.

He undressed and slept for two hours during the day, but woke three or four times in the night. While he was dressing he not only received his friends but even heard the parties to a suit and delivered judgment. He was a good and clear speaker, with a facility which bordered on prolixity. He took lessons from Alcuin, the Briton, the most learned man of his time, and tried hard to learn to write, keeping tablets and sheets of parchment under his pillow so as to practise his hand in forming letters at any spare moment he might have. But he had little success in this, having started too late.

3

He was extremely devout ; he built the beautiful Basilica of Aix, with its massive bronze balustrades and doors, and lavished gold and silver on its adornment. Being unable to obtain the necessary marbles on the spot, he brought them from Rome and Ravenna. He attended the offices morning and evening as well as the daily mass, and provided the church so abundantly with vestments that not even the door-keepers were compelled to do their service in their ordinary clothes. He gave himself much trouble in correcting the styles of reading and chanting, for he was an expert in this matter, though he did not read in public and only joined in with the rest of the congregation in the singing. More than all other holy and venerable places the Church of the Blessed Apostle Peter at Rome was the object of his devotion. He devoted to its endowment a great quantity of gold, silver, and precious stones ; he sent the Popes innumerable rich presents and at no moment of his reign had anything more at heart than to work with all his means and resources to re-establish the ancient glory of Rome and by his generosity to assure the Church of St. Peter not only security and protection but a position above all other churches in the world. Yet in spite of this expenditure he only succeeded in visiting it four times in the course of his reign of forty-seven years.

His last journey was to rescue Pope Leo from the violence of the Roman mob. Having done this business and re-established the Church, which had been greatly compromised by this incident, he remained all the winter in Rome. It was then that he received the titles of " Emperor " and " Augustus." He was at first so annoyed that he said that he would never have entered the church, even on the high festival of Christmas, if he had known what the Pope intended to do. But he bore with great patience the anger of the Roman Emperors (in Constantinople) at his assumption of this title and bore down their opposition (*contumaciam*) by the magnanimity in which he greatly surpassed them, sending them frequent embassies and calling them " brothers " in his letters.

Having taken the title of Emperor he proceeded to fill up the gaps which he observed in the laws of his own people—for the Franks had a double system of law which differed greatly in different places—and these he unified and corrected where the text was corrupt (*prava*) or erroneously transcribed. But in substance he added nothing except a small number of additional articles. He ordered, however, all the nations under his rule whose laws were not written to reduce them to writing.[1]

Similarly he had " barbarous " and ancient songs celebrating the deeds and wars of the ancient kings written down and learnt by heart.

---

[1] For the Frankish and other barbarian codes, see Gibbon, ch. XXXVIII.

He also started a grammar of the national language and provided names of the months for the people in their own tongue.

Seeing his end approaching, he sent for his son Louis, King of Aquitania, and having solemnly assembled the nobles (*primores*) from the entire Frankish kingdom, associated him in the government of the whole kingdom, named him heir of the Imperial title, and decreed that he should henceforth be called Emperor and Augustus. This decision was received with high favour by all present, for it seemed to be inspired by God for the good of the realm. This greatly increased his prestige and struck terror into foreign nations. He then sent his son back to Aquitania and spent the autumn as usual hunting in the country round his palace at Aix. In November he returned to Aix and, his fever increasing and being complicated by the pain in the side which the Greeks called pleurisy, he took to his bed, and seven days later, after receiving Holy Communion, died, in the seventy-second year of his life and the forty-seventh of his reign.

4

Readers who remember Gibbon's comment on the moral and other characteristics of this great man may add some qualifications to the eulogy of his faithful biographer and son-in-law.[1] We may ascribe to the manners of his time the fact that this pious sovereign had nine wives and concubines, to say nothing of the more transient amours, the fruits of which are traced in the multitude of bastards whom he bestowed on the Church. But historical charity is strained beyond its limit if we try to condone the beheading on the same day of the sons of his brother, Carloman, the Merovingian princes of Aquitania, and 4,500 Saxons, whose murder was an abuse of the laws of conquest as acknowledged even in these primitive times. Eginhard ascribes these occasional acts of inhumanity to the prompting of his wife Frastrada, but he seems to be sole authority for this suggestion and Charlemagne was not the kind of man who was likely to be persuaded by his wife to anything that he was at all reluctant to do. Contemporary opinion appears to have judged that all things were lawful to an Emperor. Not only was the title " great " permanently attached to his name, but

---

[1] Eginhard married Imma, one of the daughters of Charlemagne.

when he died it was inserted in the Roman calendar with the addition " Saint," and it is actually a fact that churches were dedicated to him.

The interest of Eginhard's *Life*, however, is not its judgment on Charlemagne's character, but the light which it throws on the manners and methods of government at this time. The differences between the classical and the barbarous, the Roman and the Frank, are subtly conveyed to us in Eginhard's little book. His French editor, M. Holphen, points out that it follows closely Suetonius's *Life of Augustus*, with the obvious intention of drawing a parallel between the two Emperors. But in substance anything less like the dignity and culture of the Roman than the feverish and unceasing activity of the Frank could scarcely be imagined. In his anxiety to prove him equal to everything, Eginhard gives the impression that Charlemagne was incurably restless and scatter-brained. Napoleon said that force organized nothing, and within a century of Charlemagne's death practically nothing remained of most of his far-flung expeditions.

In two places we get the shadow of something which may be called constitutional. We are told that the puppet king was driven in an ox-wagon to " present himself to the annual assembly of the people." We are told that when Charlemagne himself nominated Louis as his successor he " solemnly assembled the nobles from the entire Frankish people." Constitutionalism in the Greek sense was dead, but new methods of checking the absolute rule of individuals were to grow out of the tribal assemblies and gatherings of chiefs customary with the Frankish and German tribes. Already the " counts," so lavishly created by the later Roman Emperors, threatened to encroach on the power of the monarch. Charles kept them in check by his system of *missi dominici*, his own emissaries, consisting generally of a count and a bishop, who visited all the counts, reported on their administration, and insisted on their carrying out the instructions of the monarch. This served well enough during his lifetime, but it had no lasting results after his departure. Some of the " Capitularies," or decrees embodying these instructions have survived, and they have been held to justify his title as " the greatest legislator of the Middle Ages." They were not, however, legislation at all in the strict sense of the word. They were extensions of the personal power of the ruler and depended entirely on his ability to enforce them.

CHAPTER XX

THE HOLY ROMAN EMPIRE

I

CHARLEMAGNE, we are asked to believe—and the claim was generally conceded in the Middle Ages—was a deeply religious man, and his favourite reading was the *De Civitate Dei* of St. Augustine. That great book seems to have lain dormant for several centuries, but it was now coming to life again, and by degrees we see it inspiring the idea of government which was to find explicit expression in the Holy Roman Empire as established by Otto the Great in 961. Had the Frankish Empire endured and Charlemagne established a dynasty, we should probably have dated that event from his coronation in 800. He as much as any of the German Emperors had based his rule on a Pope-Emperor partnership, and he was much more skilful than many of his German successors in turning it to his own advantage.

To apply these crudely mundane terms to St. Augustine's vision of the City of God may seem harsh to a devout reader. Yet they do convey the substantial truth about the use or abuse of this ideal as recorded in history. St. Augustine, to repeat what was said in a previous chapter, was a poet and mystic, and he left a large penumbra of doubt about the interpretation of his meaning. But what he evidently had in mind was a unity in which the earthly and the heavenly should be in such complete harmony that there would be no need to draw boundaries between them. In the few sentences in which he has summed it up, Bryce has probably come as near as is possible to the original Augustinian idea.

" It is," he says, " under the emblem of soul and body that the relation of the Papal and Imperial power is presented to us through the Middle Ages.

The Pope, as God's Vicar in matters spiritual, is to lead men to eternal life ; the Emperor, as vicar in matters temporal, must so control them in their dealings with one another that they may be able to pursue undisturbed the spiritual life, and thereby attain the same supreme and common end of ever-lasting happiness. Thus the Holy Roman Church and the Holy Roman Empire are one and the same thing seen from different sides ; and Catholicism, the principle of the universal Christian society, is also Romanism ; that is, rests upon Rome as the origin and type of its universalism ; manifesting itself in a mystic dualism which corresponds to the two natures of its Founder. As divine and eternal its head is the Pope, to whom souls have been entrusted ; as human and temporal, the Emperor, commissioned to rule men's bodies and acts." [1]

The dualism, as Bryce says, was to be a " mystical " one, and I think it is fair to apply that word to St. Augustine's intentions. But the Middle Ages were quite incapable of seeing anything so practical as government in mystical terms. To them the dualism was actual and concrete. There was the Government of the Emperor, supreme in secular affairs, and the Government of the Pope, supreme in spiritual affairs. St. Augustine had always in mind a higher unity harmonizing both and resolving their contradictions and clashes, but in actual fact the spiritual was perpetually colliding with the secular, and the secular with the spiritual, and there was no superior authority which both acknowledged. The Pope, moreover, was not merely a spiritual ruler ; he also had his temporal power, about which he became more and more jealous and acquisitive. Further, with his tremendous spiritual weapons he could always make temporal trouble for the secular powers, whose subjects might be torn between the damnation which he threatened and the penalties to which they were exposed at the hands of their civil rulers.

It is fair to say that through it all the Church created and kept alive in men's minds the sense of a human unity transcending physical or political boundaries. Nor should we forget the service that it rendered in breaking ground among the pagan tribes and in keeping alive scholarship and culture—even the simple arts of reading and writing—in centuries in which they were threatened with extinction. There were periods in which there was something like a recall to religion under the influence of reforming Popes, and still more of the great

---

[1] Bryce, *The Holy Roman Empire*, 1904 edition, pp. 103–5.

orders, Benedictine and Franciscan, with their passive—and some-times active—rebuke to the corruptions of the ruling ecclesiastics. The debit and credit account is no simple one, if we are thinking only of the contributions to civilization made respectively by Church and State in these centuries. But if we are thinking of the political conse-quences, it must, I think, be said that the Augustinian theory as embodied in the Holy Roman Empire proved in practice to be a disastrous dualism which prevented the Emperor from concentrating on his proper task of administering and developing the countries of which he had an effective control, and the Pope from his duty of promoting the spiritual welfare of his scattered flock. Each needed the other ; neither, according to the theory, could do his perfect work without the other. It sounded well, but the need was also to ambitious men the opportunity of intriguing, hindering, frustrating, the source of endless conflicts in which each of the two Powers sought to assert itself at the expense of the other, and the spiritual objects, if any, which lay behind their contentions became totally submerged in the predatory passions of sinful men. Never was the lamp held higher than in the heory of the Holy Roman Empire ; seldom did practice descend to lower depths, whether in politics or morals.

2

To rewrite the history of this or any period is far from the object of this book, but a few illustrations may help to elucidate its political aspects.

It was an acknowledged part of the theory of the Holy Roman Empire that in order to validate his position, the Emperor needed coronation by the Pope. But as soon as the Emperor was crowned, the same theory, or at least the Emperor's version of it, made him master of the Pope, who was now only the first of his subjects. Otto the Great having been crowned by John XII almost immediately asserted his authority by deposing the Pope. His sons bettered his example. Otto III, " the wonder of the world," purified the Papacy and appointed three Popes before his death ; Henry III found three rival bishops at Rome, deposed them all and appointed a German bishop, Leo IX, who proved to be a good man and a reforming Pope. On the other hand, a strong Pope might take his revenge by excom-municating or threatening to excommunicate an Emperor, and when both were strong, terrible struggles followed. The classical example is the grim duel between Henry IV and the famous Hildebrand, Pope Gregory VII (1077 A.D.) On Henry's side everything depended on whether he could rely on his princes and dukes and the wealthy and powerful and extremely combatant bishops and archbishops on whose support since the days of Charlemagne imperial power had been built up, or whether they would be overawed by the fulminations of the Pope. Henry had to go to Canossa and stand barefoot in the snow suing for admission and absolution lest his rebellious subjects should overthrow him at the call of the Pope. But this was only the beginning. Gregory too overreached himself and was driven from his throne and died in exile at Salerno eight years later, handing on the vendetta to his successor, who raised up a rebellious son to depose Henry, who also died in exile.

Gregory claimed to have loved justice and hated iniquity, and in so far as he waged war against simony and corruption and denounced the licentiousness of the clergy, his claim was good. But by prescribing celibacy for the clergy he had broken up the family life of the German clergy, with the unconcealed design of converting them into a body of militant priests wholly devoted to the service of the Church. And finally, by declaring it sinful for an ecclesiastic to receive his benefice from a layman, he aimed a deadly blow at all secular authority. Half of the land and wealth of Germany was in the hands of bishops and abbots, who, if Gregory had had his way, would have passed from the Emperor's control to that of the Pope. For centuries this " investiture " controversy, as it came to be called, was to trouble the peace of Europe. There was a plausible amount of right on the ecclesiastical side. It was said that the care of souls should be kept free from secular contamination, and therefore that it was imperative for the Church to guard its spiritual authority against all secular invasion. But the Church was an enormously powerful vested interest in which the spiritual and the secular were inextricably mixed. Success in asserting this claim would have brought civil government to a standstill.

3

The struggle between Empire and Papacy went on with varying fortunes all through the succeeding reigns. The necessity which he

was under or thought himself under to subdue the Papacy drew
Frederick Barbarossa to waste his power on fruitless expeditions into
Italy and involved his grandson, Frederic II, in a conflict with Popes
Gregory IX and Innocent IV which brought ruin on the Empire
(1250). Not the least of the weapons in the hands of the Popes in the
latter part of this period was that of stirring up the peoples to go on
crusade and discrediting their rulers if they were unable or refused to
go. Frederic II was excommunicated by Gregory IX for not going
to Palestine, excommunicated a second time for going without
waiting for the approval of the Pope, and a third time for returning
without Papal authority, after concluding what he thought to be an
advantageous peace. After Frederic's death the Papacy seemed to be
triumphant, but new forces were growing up, especially the increasing
power of England and France and the growth in numbers and importance of the independent city-states, which were to prove a formidable
check on the pretensions of both Emperors and Popes.

In the end it may be said that the combination of two Powers, one
claiming to rule the body and other the soul, was the least practicable
of all the possible forms of government. Still more the combination
of two sanctions, one in time exercised by the secular power and the
other in eternity exercised by the spiritual. Whatever it might be,
this could not be the solution of the eternal problem how to render
unto God the things that are God's and unto Cæsar the things that
are Cæsar's. In a superstitious age the sanctions in eternity might be
brought to bear with overpowering effect against those who disposed
only of the temporal sanctions. As between the civil authority,
which could only kill the body, and the spiritual which claimed the
power of inflicting eternal torment on the soul, the humblest might
take all risks to keep in with the spiritual powers.

The Popes, moreover, had one considerable advantage. They
provided for their continuity through election by the College of
Cardinals, which, even though at times it might be flouted and
challenged by the Emperors, provided in the end the standard of valid
succession and kept within the narrowest limits any internal trouble
there might be about it. The Empire, on the other hand, was perpetually in trouble about the succession of the Emperor. Just when a
powerful family, like the Hohenstaufens, seemed to have established

a dynasty in which the throne would pass from father to son, the German chieftains asserted their right to act as " electors " and proceeded generally on the principle that the supreme power should not be vested too long in the hands of one family. Unending feuds and intrigues followed from this cause and, long after the Empire had ceased to have any real existence as a world power, prevented it from settling down into a kingdom with a hereditary monarchy. The " electors " became rival powers to the Emperor and some of them, like the Hohenzollerns, the actual founders of the modern nations. Here, again, the Emperor was in a dilemma. His evident dependence on his local electors made nonsense of his claim to world-wide dominion, while the maintenance of that claim dissipated his energy and left him at the mercy of local factions.

The Golden Bull which Charles IV published at the Diet of 1356 has been described as the constitution of the Holy Roman Empire, but it was directed solely to the conditions in which the electors were to exercise their power, and, if it averted wars of succession, it did so at heavy cost to the unity of the Empire, and therefore to the prospect of any unified government of Europe. The seven electors [1] who alone in future were to have a voice in the choice of the Emperors were to be guaranteed full sovereign rights within their respective territories ; the secular electors were to inherit according to the rule of primogeniture, and their territories were on no account to be broken up. In such circumstances they more and more tended to be independent sovereigns overshadowing the Emperor and still further reducing his authority. The only possible move in a constitutional direction would have been the development of the Diet—an assemblage of the princes who were nominally vassals of the Emperor—into a Parliament to advise and check the Emperor. But then, as later, the Germans seemed incapable of combining for the kind of action the English call parliamentary, and in the fourteenth century the Diet was hopelessly discredited and quite powerless.

---

[1] They consisted of three ecclesiastical princes (the Archbishops of Maintz, Cologne, and Frier) and four secular princes (the Count Palatine of the Rhine, the Margrave of Brandenburg, the Duke of Saxony, and the King of Bohemia).

CHAPTER XXI

THE MIDDLE AGES AND DANTE

I

THE principal development in the methods of government during the Middle Ages was the revival of town life. This was the natural result of the increase of trade and commerce in the tenth, eleventh, and twelfth centuries and of the new intercourse with the East established through the Crusades in the subsequent years. The fairs which had served the purpose of bringing merchants and traders together in the early Middle Ages were unequal to this expanding trade. Merchants could not always be on the move; the skilled artisans class, now coming to the fore, required centres for mutual assistance and protection and for specializing in their chosen trades. All along the trade-routes, by the rivers, at sea-ports, at the crossroads, new walled towns sprang up, and many old Roman cities which had survived as centres of civil or episcopal administration gathered a new population of merchants and craftsmen about them.

By degrees these city-states produced a new type of men claiming and successfully asserting their right to be free. Many of them had escaped from the hereditary servitude of the feudal manor, and now shared the freedom which was the recognized right of all dwellers within the walls. Within the city were also the merchant and craft guilds, with their monopolies of particular trades and crafts and their complete control of the commercial and industrial side of its life. It was thus an independent, self-contained unit governed by its own burghers, who for all practical purposes went their own way. In theory they acknowledged the political authority of emperor, king, or prince and undertook to pay certain taxes to him or to their lord, but all their obligations and other conditions were definitely fixed and limited by charters for which substantial sums had often been paid to these potentates. One famous city, Venice, established itself as an independent republic and the centre of a trading empire ; others like the Hanseatic League of the North German towns, became powerful Federations standing together in mutual defence and the promotion of their common interests.

2

In describing these developments we are obliged to use terms—administration, law, justice, and so forth—which have fixed meanings in modern times, but they need many qualifications when applied to primitive or mediæval institutions. For long periods in the ninth century and later there was almost no government over a large part of Europe. Force, said Napoleon, organizes nothing, and this was specially true of the empire of Charlemagne. His conquests covered great spaces on the map, and while he lived his personal emissaries (*missi dominici*) maintained a minimum of law and order. But nothing was organized on a permanent basis. On his death both the central and the local administration fell rapidly into decay, and his feeble successors were unable to protect their poorer subjects from either the raids of the northmen or the violence of their own nobles. The latter literally took the law into their own hands, and usurped many of the functions of government. Being otherwise at the mercy of marauders, the poor submitted and got some security at the sacrifice of their freedom.

Hence the extension of the feudal system and the growth of the landed aristocracy, still further limiting the power of king and emperor. The association of military service with land-holding dated back from Roman times and in the long run proved ruinous to the peasants. Compelled to go campaigning without pay and at their own cost during the months when the land most needed their labour, they were soon sunk in debt from which they could only release themselves by selling their land to some noble or rich man. With the loss of their land they lost their status as freemen, and were now bound to a lord to whom they gave a large part of their labour or its produce. There were many grades and varieties of the system, which differed from country to country and even from village to village and manor to manor. At the top of the scale were the free tenants, a small class who did little more than pay rent to the landlord ; at the bottom the serfs, who were entirely without civil rights ; and between them the villeins, who had all the rights of freemen except that they could not leave the land without the lord's consent. Nearly all were compelled to work for the landlord on certain days and to pay him (generally in kind) for certain services that he provided, such as the use of his mill or of the great oven in which the bread was baked.

In this system we see the serf gradually coming to play the part of the slave in the Roman Empire. As the period of Roman conquest ended, the importation of slaves ceased, and of those who were in the country many became freedmen and the remainder acquired a scarcity value which ensured them a certain consideration. By the fourth century there was little distinction between them and the *coloni*, classes of persons who, though nominally free, were bound to the land and liable to be forcibly brought back if they attempted to move from it. In the end both slaves and *coloni* became merged in the serf class. It would, I suppose, be technically true to say that slavery as practised in the Roman Empire had ceased to exist from about the seventh century onwards, but an immense number were in a position which can only be described as unfree, chained to the soil, obliged to work without wages for a large part of their time, and living in conditions of the utmost squalor and poverty. Not merely the secular aristocracy but the monasteries and great ecclesiastical corporations were parties to this system, and the authority of the Church was constantly invoked to prove it to be ordained by God, who had assigned to each rank in the social order the station in life with which it was a religious duty to be content. The only legal escape from this system was by flight from the country to the town. It was a general rule that a man who had succeeded in maintaining himself for a year in a town without being detected could not be reclaimed by his lord. Since labour was in demand in the towns, large numbers no doubt escaped this way with the connivance of those who employed them.

3

For philosophic history or reflective writing on government or politics the Middle Ages are a desert. Its historians are largely bishops and priests, who are chiefly concerned with ecclesiastical events or who write in praise of some monarch or outstanding figure. There is no Thucydides, no Tacitus, no Livy, no onlooker who sees the drift of events and passes judgment. Boethius announced his " fixed intention, if the potent favour of the deity would so grant," to translate into Latin every work of Aristotle that came into his hand and to furnish it with a Latin commentary. He meant thus to present " whatever insight into natural truth may be gathered from Aristotle." A translation of the *Politics* with his commentary might have been a work of rare value, but unfortunately he fell into disgrace with Theodoric and was executed before he came to it.

The consideration of secular politics as an art or science with rules and principles of its own was altogether beyond the reach of the mediæval mind. The Scriptures as interpreted by the Church and the Fathers contained everything that was necessary for salvation in this world or the next. Wickedness in high places would be rebuked by holy Church ; oppression beyond a certain point would be followed by rebellion. Beyond this there was little to say. An immense number seemed to accept the depravity of Popes and princes as inevitable imperfections of a mundane order which was only an ante-chamber to the world beyond, the city of man soon to be superseded by the city of God.

The rediscovery of Aristotle and the intellectual awakening in the thirteenth century brought the theory of politics to life again and gave a new trend to the controversy between Popes and Emperors. St. Thomas Aquinas embraces government, as all other human activities, in the immense sweep of his *Summa Theologiae*. In his treatment it is no longer a question of striving and competing human beings in collision with one another ; all alike are subservient to the divine purpose whereby God rules the world, and through the co-operation of many callings ordains the good life for His creatures. If St. Thomas defends monarchy, he insists that the monarch shall regard himself as trustee for the whole community, leading the good life himself and seeking the welfare of all his subjects. He must act according to law described " as an ordinance of reason for the common good, made by him who has care of the community and promulgated it." Much of this is a transcript from Aristotle, who spoke of law as

" reason unaffected by desire." St. Thomas shares Aristotle's hatred of tyranny, and in his *de Regimine Principum*, while giving his preference to monarchy, he warns the monarch in truly Aristotelian style against making himself a tyrant.

We are back again in the region of the ideal, and St. Thomas, like Plato, might have said that his pattern was laid up in heaven. But he is not dogmatic about the nature of secular rule. There are many kinds of government and many kinds of law, and he does not presume to tell us which is best, for different kinds may be good for different countries and different conditions. He is strong on the subject of civil obedience to a good ruler, and he definitely says that the Christian subjects of a pagan prince are not justified in refusing him obedience. On the other hand, his horror of heresy is such that he holds the Church to be justified in absolving the subjects of an apostate or heretic ruler. There are many curious details in his writings which throw light on the mediæval mind and its ways of thinking, but the main point is that this greatest of Catholic doctrinal authorities definitely places government in the religious sphere, and requires the same standard of conduct in rulers as in other men who profess the Christian faith. This was to be of great importance at a later stage. A modern Pope has St. Thomas in mind when he challenges the doctrine of the Totalitarian States.

After a period of spasmodic activity in which it established itself in southern Italy and placed Charles Anjou on the throne of Naples, the Papacy fell back into its old confusion. For three years there were no Popes ; then followed a succession of evil Popes who brought the Church into deep discredit while loudly asserting their claims to supremacy over the Emperors. The Italian cities, meanwhile, were plunged into conflict according as they sided with Emperor or Pope, with the Ghibelline nobles, who maintained their allegiance to the Emperors, or with the Guelfs, who supported the Pope, or with the factious Blacks and Whites who came on the scene in Florence when the Ghibellines had been chased off it. The general judgment was that the state of things was intolerable. The Empire was more and more a shadow, but so long as it existed the religious kind of monarchy governing a limited sphere which Aquinas contemplated was impossible, and the Papacy, consumed with its mundane ambitions and corruptions, was merely one warring power among the many which were making havoc in Europe. By this time it was not even master in its own Catholic household, for the Gallican church had broken away and proclaimed its independence in matters of government and discipline. The English, too, were going their own way—the way which led them eventually to the conclusion that they would not be ruled by any foreigner and least of all by foreign ecclesiastics.

<h2 style="text-align:center">4</h2>

It was upon this scene that Dante Alighieri (1265-1321) made his first appearance as a writer. How, exactly, he had become involved in the tangled politics of Florence is somewhat in doubt. In his youth he served as a soldier in the war against the Aretines, and about the age of thirty he joined the popular party which had taken the power out of the hands of the Guelf nobles, and became one of the six Priors who were the supreme council of government. Though wholly Guelf in virtue of its adhesion to the Papal cause, the city was now sharply divided into Blacks and Whites, the latter being a constitutional party with what may be called a liberal policy, the former an aristocratic and reactionary group waiting its opportunity to seize power. This it succeeded in doing by a *coup d'état* in 1301, and Dante, being a White, was driven into life-long exile.

The picture of the poet eating his heart out in exile and wreaking an immortal vengeance upon the political opponents who sent him there has often been painted—and over-painted. It has even been suggested that his political treatise, the *De Monarchia*, which is the first reflective work on the meaning and purpose of human government since Augustine wrote his *City of God*, is a political pamphlet written to justify his appeal to a foreign potentate to depose his enemies in Florence. There is undoubtedly both in this work and in the *Divine Comedy* itself an element of bitterness which may be traced to this personal grievance, but the greatness of the theme and the passionate sincerity with which he approaches it forbid the thought that Dante was actuated chiefly or to any considerable extent by any petty motive.

Florence and its troubles (which in the *Inferno* he summarily attributed to " new people and wealth suddenly gained ") sink into insignificance as the theme is developed. This, in the *De Monarchia*, is in the direct descent from St. Augustine, even from Plato, and embraces the whole human race and its salvation here and hereafter in its sweep. Looking out on the vast confusion and turbulence of the times, Dante can only see one remedy—the establishment of unity under one Government. This is the divine order manifested in the heavens, which move under one impulse, the *primum mobile* which is God. Human beings, being the children of heaven, should conform to this pattern. He quotes Boethius :

> O felix hominum genus
> Si vestros animos amor,
> Quo coelum regitur, regat.

Love and law (as a principle of nature) were identical in the mediæval mind ; and humanity, therefore, should be governed by the love which is law.

St. Augustine had left in doubt how his ideal city should be achieved on the earthly plane. Not so Dante. A monarchy and a universal one was necessary to his idea. What else could it be than the Holy Roman Empire, not as it was, but restored to its ancient pre-eminence and reviving the glories of Rome at its greatest period. In a long argument Dante seeks to prove that the Providence of God was made manifest in Roman history. He is as fervent in maintaining that the Romans were God's chosen people as any Hebrew prophet in making that claim for the Jewish race. The world process had so far been one of conflict for the *imperium mundi*. Assyrians, Egyptians, Persians, Macedonians had each in turn striven for this prize, but Rome alone had achieved it. If her means had been war, that also was the way of Providence, which conferred a legal title on what was acquired by war. (*Quod per duellum adquiritur, de jure adquiritur.*) In view of the argument which was to follow, Dante is not quite easy about this reasoning, for he adds that war should only be resorted to in the last resort, and then only when the belligerents are inspired by a zeal for justice. There have been few belligerents who have not made a claim that they were so inspired, and Dante must have turned a blind eye to large spaces of Roman history if he seriously believed that these were the guiding principles of Roman conquerors. He was on safer ground when he said simply that the Roman people were ordained by nature for empire (*Romanus populus ad imperandum ordinatus fuit a natura*), and from this assertion inferred that the divine intelligence which decreed the end must have sanctioned the means.

A singular argument follows to prove that Christ's atonement for the sin of Adam would have been impossible unless the Judge who condemned Him had possessed jurisdiction over the whole human race. His Crucifixion would otherwise have been a local event with no universal significance. In willing to be born under Roman authority and to suffer under Pontius Pilate, Christ foresaw this necessary condition. Pilate was the agent of Tiberius, and Tiberius had jurisdiction over the whole human race, which he could not have had unless the Roman Empire was *de jure* (in the eyes of God). Christ, therefore (the argument seems to be), gave His sanction to the legality and rightfulness of the Roman Empire, for only so, as He knew, could His purpose in the atonement be accomplished. Dante himself is deeply impressed with this argument, for at the end of it he says almost defiantly, " Let those who think themselves sons of the Church cease to rail at the Roman Empire when they see it sponsored by Christ both at the beginning and at the end of His earthly career."

5

From these subtleties we pass to the practical conclusion. This is that the Empire receives its authority immediately from God, and not from the Church, which is not and cannot be the source of the Imperial power. To authorize or create Empire is contrary to the nature of the Church. If the " donation of Constantine "—the great mediæval forgery which was supposed to have given the Popes their title to secular power—was a fact, which Dante seems to doubt, Constantine had no right to rend the seamless garment of the Empire by giving it away to the Pope. The Church, moreover, being forbidden by Christ to possess gold and silver, could not have received the " donation " even if the Emperor had been entitled to give it. If the Pope claimed to have made Charlemagne Emperor by the act of crowning him, it was a *usurpatio juris* on his part which had no validity. If these instances are to be cited there are many others which would equally prove the right of the Emperor to appoint or depose Popes. Pope and Emperor each has his own sphere and each stands in a special relation to the human race. Both are subordinate to God, who is the supreme Unity, but that the Empire existed before the Papacy and independently of it is proved by the words of Christ Himself and of the Apostle who appealed unto Cæsar.

A certain duality is recognized as existing within this essential unity, for man has to keep his mind fixed on two kinds of blessedness, that of the earthly and that of the heavenly paradise. To the first he attains by the moral and intellectual virtues, to the second by the theological, faith, hope, and charity. It is for the temporal authority, *i.e.* the Emperor, to guide men to earthly happiness, but the spiritual authority is needed to bring them to their further goal of supernatural eternal happiness. Dante departs from mediæval ecclesiastical theory in never disparaging the value of the earthly paradise. It is part of the divine counsel (*dentro al consiglio divino*) that man should be happy in the earthly and hereafter in the heavenly paradise. But he seems often to be in trouble about keeping his balance as a faithful son of the Church who is true to her doctrine and yet desires her to be free from the alloy of temporal power and ambition. He cannot rule her out from the sphere of mortal happiness, for that is bound up with the prospect of immortal happiness. The two domains, therefore, are not separate but interpenetrant. The suggested solution is that the Supreme Pontiff should

bestow the light of grace on the temporal power, and that the Emperor in return should observe towards Peter the reverence which a first-born son ought to observe to his father, so that illumined with the light of the paternal grace he may the more effectively irradiate the world over which he is set to rule by Him who is the ruler of all things spiritual and temporal.

6

If we take it literally, we are obliged to say that never was a tract for the times less timely than Dante's *De Monarchia*. There could scarcely have been ideas more remote from practical politics than that the Popes of this period would accept the passive role assigned to them in this scheme,[1] or that the Emperors of this period—men like Albert

---

[1] In 1302 Boniface VIII had launched the Bull *Unam Sanctam*, claiming supremacy for the Church.

the Hapsburg or Henry of Luxembourg—could aspire to the desired universal monarchy. The universal Roman Empire was dead beyond resurrection, the Holy Roman Empire was scarcely the shadow of the great name and its pretensions excited open derision. To Italian patriots Dante summoning the German Emperor to play the role of Augustus may well have seemed no better than the Popes appealing to the French Kings.

Yet stripped of what is mediæval and scholastic and local and temporary, the central ideas of the *De Monarchia* have inexhaustible vitality. Dante sees the world in a chronic state of contention through its division into numerous States, each of which claims to be judge in its own cause :

Wherever contention may arise, there should also be the means of adjudicating it. Otherwise there would be imperfection, which is impossible, since God and nature are never lacking in things that are necessary. Between any two princes, of whom the one is not subject to the other, it is evident that there may be contentions either through their own fault or that of their subjects. Therefore there ought to be means of adjudicating between all such. And since the one, not being the superior or inferior of the other, cannot take cognizance of the other's affairs—for a peer has no rule over a peer—there ought to be a third of larger jurisdiction who by the scope of his authority is superior to both. This will either be a supreme monarch or not. If the former, the end is achieved (*habetur propositum*) ; if not, he will have another co-equal with himself, and once more another third party will be necessary. And so on to infinity, which is impossible.

A plurality of princes is an evil, except so far as it serves the purpose of local government ; for all other purposes there should be one prince or emperor.

This is the way and the only way of peace. Peace, universal peace, is necessary to the life of freedom, which is the greatest gift of God to man (*maximum donum humanæ naturæ a Deo collatum*). Through freedom we have our happiness here as men, through it our happiness elsewhere as gods (*De Mon.* I, 12). The monarch being alone completely disinterested will not pervert men to his own uses, as do tyrants, nobles, and democrats ; he will leave them free to pursue the good life of their own volition. Under the wrong constitution, as Aristotle says, a good man may be a bad citizen, but under the right constitution the good man is always the good citizen. "Right constitutions work for freedom in order that men may exist for their own sakes." Citizens are not made for the sake of consuls nor nations for the sake of kings, but on the contrary consuls for the sake of citizens, and the king for the sake of the nation. In respect of the road on which they are travelling, consuls and kings may be the masters of others, but in respect of the end to which they are moving, they are the servants of all. Most of all is the monarch to be regarded as the servant of all.

With a very little modernizing whole passages of the *De Monarchia* might be reconstructed as a plea for the League of Nations or some other authority standing above the national sovereignties, whose refusal to accept the arbitration of a third power is still the chief obstacle to world peace. Freedom, in Dante's view, "by which we have our happiness here as men and elsewhere as gods," is only to be realized in a world at peace ; peace can only be secure where justice reigns, and justice means in the end doing the will of God. It is one of the great themes of the *Divine Comedy*, emerging again and again from all that is mediæval and obscure or personal and prejudiced in that stupendous poem. *In la sua voluntade e nostra pace.*

Dante's treatise, it will be seen, is a highly idealized conception, far beyond anything that he, immersed in the squalid politics of his time, could have dreamt of as possible. Where in the welter of the thirteenth and fourteenth centuries was this transcedent being so universally acknowledged, so high above all other principalities and powers as not even to excite envy, so removed from the necessities of ordinary monarchs and princes as to be under no temptation to corrupt his subjects or to favour some at the expense of others ? It is possible, as some commentators have suggested, that the dream of a "second coming" and the reign of the Messiah on earth, which had come to life again in these centuries, was flitting through Dante's mind, but this supposition is by no means necessary. He was a poet and an allegorist and this ideal figure served him for a grand remonstrance against the corruptions of his time, the hopeless entanglement of the religious and the secular, the degradation of the Papacy to a political faction using its spiritual weapons to promote its temporal ambitions, the incurable schismatic and fissiparous tendencies which were taking the world farther and farther from the unity which was the professed purpose of the Holy Roman Empire, and is still the greatest of all the things necessary for the peace and happiness of mankind. The historian is obliged to say that the world had got far beyond the point at which it could be recalled either to the political unity of the original Roman Empire or to the mystical unity of the City of God and polity of men contemplated by St. Augustine. But the ideal is one which has not lost and cannot lose its virtue, and it thrills us to come upon this poignant expression of it in the mouth of the greatest of mediæval poets and thinkers.

CHAPTER XXII

THE END OF A DREAM

I

THE Papacy reached the climax of its pretensions at the end of the twelfth century. It now claimed to be supreme over all secular powers, whether emperors or kings, and to be empowered to order them to do its bidding. In 1195 Innocent III placed France under an interdict ; and in 1206 he pronounced the same sentence upon England, and ordered his vassal, Philip of France, to enforce it by invading the country. King John submitted, and for centuries to come England was in theory a fief of the Papal Empire and paid tribute to the Pope. The Papal claim, however, had one very considerable drawback. It became the object of kings and emperors to annex the authority which wielded these magical powers. If they dared not defy a Pope, they might capture him, bring him under their nfluence, use him for their own purposes. In 1309 the French did exactly this, and transferred the seat of the Papacy from Rome to Avignon, where it remained for the next seventy years and served for an instrument of French policy.

In 1399 Pope Gregory XI got back to Rome, but from this time onwards there were often two Popes and sometimes even three disputing with one another for the succession. The scandalous behaviour and incompetence of some of them kept the Roman people on the verge of rebellion ; they drove one Pope, Eugenius IV, into exile and rose in arms against his successor, Nicholas V. The "Restoration Popes" did not feel themselves precluded by sentiments of Christian piety from applying to these disorders the harshest treatment which the refined cruelty of their mercenary captains and executioners could invent. They slew, tortured, hanged their opponents.[1] In the meantime, by skilful intrigues with kings and emperors, who walked in fear of their influence with the superstitious masses, the Popes had defeated all the efforts of General Councils to bring them under control and compel them to set their own house in order.

Though the profligacy and criminality of the Popes and their entourage had become a byword in Europe, though priests and cardinals in the Holy City expressed a cynical disbelief in their own miraculous powers, the Church continued to assert its claims to supremacy over all secular authorities and to treat kings and emperors as vassals of its imaginary empire. The infamous Borgia Alexander VI insisted that in virtue of " the authority Almighty God granted unto us in St. Peter and by the office which we bear on the earth in the stead of Jesus Christ " it was for him and for him alone to apportion the territories discovered by Columbus and Vasco Da Gama, and the Kings of Spain and Portugal meekly admitted his pretensions. Previous Popes had accepted what was alleged to be the " donation of Constantine " or the " donation of Pepin." Alexander insisted that all the territories of secular sovereigns were the donation of the Papacy, " speaking by the authority of Almighty God."

So inordinate a pretension could not last. It rested purely on the belief that the Church had the power of salvation and that excommunication carried with it irreparable pains and penalties in another world. The modern spirit now dawning was less and less inclined to believe that Almighty God had authorized men of the type of the Borgias to administer these pains and penalties, even if He had provided them for His erring children. In the fifteenth and sixteenth centuries the Papal claim found itself in sharper and sharper conflict both with the independent nationalism which resented foreign intrusion and with the spirit of the Reformation which challenged the entire doctrine on which the power and wealth of the priesthood stood. The English were pioneers in both respects, in the movement of John Wycliffe and the Lollards, which blazed the trail for the Reformers of a later generation, and in the determination of their stubborn Tudor sovereigns, Henry VIII and Elizabeth, to be masters or mistresses in their own houses.

---

[1] Fisher, pp. 363-4.

Though the opponents of the Papal tyranny have won and deserve the applause of history, the breakdown at the hands of corrupt politicians and ecclesiastics of the great ideal which inspired St. Augustine and Dante and struggled vainly to find expression in the Holy Roman Empire must rank among the great calamities of history. With that perished for centuries the idea of a European unity rising above national sovereignties and gathering all into a bond of peace. The choicer spirits had risen to the point of dreaming this dream, but it was beyond the thought of either the ecclesiastical or secular politicians of these centuries. The Church, which in the dreamland of the saints would have been the instrument of a benevolent will to peace and the Christian life, strove for a secular supremacy in competition with the secular powers ; ambitious kings and princes sought to annex its supernatural powers and use them for their own advantage. Lacking the means of asserting its will over recalcitrant worldlings, the Kingdom not of this world challenged them on their own ground and descended to their level. The idea of a super-national unity was to be revived at the end of the Great War in the proposal of a League of Nations to abolish war and assert the supremacy of law over aggressors and transgressors. But this also was to prove premature. The secular Powers were no more able than the ecclesiastical to guard their ideal from the incursion of the mundane passions of envy, fear, jealousy, revenge.

CHAPTER XXIII

MACHIAVELLI

I

D ANTE'S *De Monarchia* is the last voice from the Middle Ages. The next political treatise, *The Prince* of Machiavelli, comes from an entirely different world. In the two hundred years which divide the two, the principal monarchies of modern Europe had emerged from the flux of mediæval feudalism and were attracting to their side the " new men," the men of commerce and industry, who looked to kings to defend them against the nobles. England and France after their exhausting Hundred Years' War had settled down into something like their final form ; the Turks had captured Constantinople and made an end of the Eastern Empire ; Columbus had discovered America ; Ferdinand and Isabella had extinguished the Moorish kingdom in Spain. Cities had multiplied and become large centres of a new kind of independent life and culture. The Holy Roman Empire was shortly to enter upon a new phase with the election of Charles V as Emperor, and to obtain an enormous accession to its nominal territories through a series of royal marriages. Printing had been invented, gunpowder was coming into use. The Papacy had suffered an irreparable loss of prestige through its submission to the French kings and its " Babylonian captivity " at Avignon (1309–1377). By the beginning of the sixteenth century the Popes had become little more than Italian princes, and some of them were the worst of their kind. They, nevertheless, continued to hurl their spiritual thunderbolts over all Europe, but with rapidly diminishing results.

The moral and intellectual upheaval was on the same scale. Italy had plunged into the neo-paganism of the Renaissance, as if to find a substitute in humanism for the religion it had discarded. Together

We are reminded that Machiavelli, as shown in his correspondence, was an amiable man and, according to his own lights, a public-spirited patriot. He desired to free Italy from foreign rule and to release its princes from their dependence on hired armies. On this and many other matters he gave them excellent advice. The men he admired, Alexander VI, Cæsar Borgia, Julius II, were, it is said, with all their vices, men of great ability and power—Cæsar especially, who, as Macaulay says,

found a powerful and durable excitement in the intense thirst of empire and revenge . . . who formed a gallant army out of the dregs of an unwarlike people, who, after acquiring sovereignty by destroying his enemies, acquired popularity by destroying his tools ; who had begun to employ for the most salutary ends the powers which he had obtained by the most atrocious means.

I quote from Macaulay's famous essay, which pushes to its extreme limit the theory that men should be judged by the moral standard prevailing at their time. But Macaulay himself wavers, for after making the rather hazardous assertion that none of Machiavelli's contemporaries were shocked or offended by his writings, he says suddenly at the end of his essay that he " enjoyed a vindictive pleasure in outraging the opinions of a society which he despised."

3

If we are to do justice to Machiavelli we must read his *Discourses on the First Ten Books of Livy* side by side with his *The Prince*. The two books were written about the same time, (1513), and of the two the *Discourses* leaves by far the more agreeable impression of the writer. It glows with admiration of the " ancient valour " of the Roman people ; it admits the value of free institutions and of free governments - if only they know how to maintain themselves in power. It abounds in tributes to the civic virtues. We have to stretch as far forward as Burke to think of any writer who gives us so many pungent aphorisms and comments as he goes along. Some critics have found a difficulty in reconciling the *Discourses* with *The Prince* and express surprise that the two books should have been on the stocks, as they apparently were, during the same months. Yet the doctrine of the two is essentially the same—it may even be said that the *Discourses* extends the sphere to which this doctrine applies. For it now appears that it was intended not only, as his apologists have suggested, for a ruler in the exceptional circumstances of fifteenth and sixteenth-century Italian politics, but for all types of government, free and despotic. The Roman State is praised for the skilful blend of fraud and force, cruelty and leniency with which it won and extended its power.

Indeed, it is quite as much from the *Discourses* as from *The Prince* that those who have sat at the feet of this master have drawn their inspiration. Here, for example, is the text which justifies the modern dictator in taking sole control and refusing to share his authority with anyone :

This should be taken as a general rule—that never or hardly ever has any Republic or Kingdom been well ordered from the beginning or been entirely fashioned anew from its ancient institutions when the work has not been done by one man. Nay, it must be one man alone who prescribes the method and from whose mind must come every subsequent and similar reconstruction. Therefore the founder of a Republic who is wise and is of a mind to benefit not only himself but the public welfare, and who is thinking not only of his own family or dynasty but of his country, must strive to obtain the sole authority. Nor will a wise man blame anyone for extraordinary action taken in the course of founding a Kingdom or establishing a Republic. It must be agreed that, though he may be blamed for doing certain things, he will be justified by their results, and when this result is good, as in the case of Romulus, he will always be justified, since he is to be blamed who does violence with intent to injure, not he who does it in order to pacify.[1]

This idea of the good motive plays a large part in Machiavelli's philosophy, but in practice it comes to mean only that the ruler persuades himself that his end is good. When once he has done that, he is justified in taking any means to achieve it.

4

We may turn now to *The Prince* with an assurance that its teaching is not modified by anything that is said in the *Discourses*. Familiar as it is supposed to be, a reminder of what it actually contains may not be out of place at a time when it plays so large a part in the fashionable

---

[1] *Discourses*, Book I, Chap. 9.

the necessities of the moment that he who deceives will always find those who will let themselves be deceived. Alexander VI never did or thought of doing anything but deceive people, and found plenty of material to work upon ; there was never a man who was greater in asserting or accompanied his assertion with bigger oaths and observed them less ; nevertheless his deceptions invariably succeeded, for he thoroughly understood this side of human nature.

**It is, therefore, not necessary that a Prince should have all the above-mentioned (virtuous) qualities, but it is necessary that he should appear to have them. Nay, more, I will venture to say that if he really had them and observed them always, they would be positively dangerous, whereas if he only appears to have them, they are useful. Thus it is useful to appear, and even to be, pious, faithful, humane, religious, and honest, provided your mind is so fortified that you can and know how to be the contrary.

A last touch to this picture of the perfect Prince is that he

ought to pretend more than ordinarily to religion, because more men do judge by the eye than by the touch ; for everybody sees but few understand ; everybody sees how you appear, but few know what in reality you are, and those few dare not offend the opinion of the multitude, who have the majesty of their Prince to defend them.

A further suggestion is that a Prince, especially if he is a new man, needs to have enemies that he may have the opportunity to conquer them. " Many have thought that a wise Prince, when opportunity offers, ought, but with great cunning and address, to maintain some enemies against himself that, when time serves to destroy them, his own greatness may be increased." A good Prince must be both fox and lion : a fox to wheedle and deceive, a lion to destroy.[1]

5

Some modern readers of The Prince have found it impossible to believe that even an Italian of the sixteenth century could have intended seriously certain of the passages I have quoted. Between the lines they see the savage irony of the outraged moralist ; a cool ferocity deliberately wrought into burlesque. The " Prince " is the Barry Lyndon of a moral romance. After all, it is said, Machiavelli was a wit and he must have foreseen and intended the all but ludicrous effect of some of his cynical inversions of the accepted code. It is

---

[1] The Prince, XVII.

difficult, for example, to suppose that he was unaware of the grimly humorous effect of his description of Cæsar Borgia's treatment of Orco or of his reference to Hiero of Syracuse.

This suggestion may be glanced at, but there is no substance in it. It is impossible to read Chapter VII of *The Prince* without coming to the conclusion that he did sincerely admire both Alexander VI and Cæsar Borgia, and that he means seriously to commend their practices for imitation. If any doubt remained it would be disposed of by his letters to his friend Vettori, which are quite explicit on this point. Moreover, a considerable part of the book is a patriotic pamphlet with a laudable purpose behind it, and it is impossible to think that so skilful a writer would have confused his readers by mixing it up with a hidden exercise in irony. In its general attitude *The Prince* is entirely in line with the despatches in which its author tells the story of his embassies and his efforts on behalf of his employers. According to his code he was a loyal servant of these employers. He was willing to serve the republic while it lasted and he was willing to serve the Medici when they were restored. True that he fell under suspicion in one of the numerous conspiracies against the Medici and was imprisoned and tortured, but there is nothing more against him on this score than that his name was found on one of the lists that the conspirators had drawn up. The truth seems to be that years of continuous association with the assassins, wire-pullers, and conspirators of Italian politics led him to the conclusion that statecraft was the organized cynicism that he represented it to be, and that he was doing a service in attempting to reduce its practice to rule and principle.

But these are side issues. What gives *The Prince* its significance to students of institutions is the completeness of its breach with the past. What, we ask, has happened in the preceding centuries that this man can pass without a glance the entire mediæval theory of Church and State, the idea of a mystical union between the secular and the spiritual for the salvation of body and soul which, in spite of all corruptions and calamities, survived through the Middle Ages, and is still glowing in Dante's *De Monarchia* ? Up to this point, widely as their practices might differ from their professions, European men had paid homage to the idea that the welfare of their subjects was the object of rulers and that their practice as rulers must be judged by the same standards as their practice in their private lives. Now suddenly, without warning or argument, there is launched upon the world, as if it were self-evident and obvious, the idea of government proceeding on principles which actually invert those of the private life, making good in the public sphere what is admitted to be evil in the private, proclaiming the law of the jungle as right and necessary for the ruler who would be successful. Machiavelli seems actually to glory in the inversion, for he carried forward into his new world all the epithets— good, bad, evil, cruel—borrowed from the old morality which are meaningless unless they imply moral condemnation, and thus subtly conveys to his reader that the art of government, in his opinion, owes no account to moral standards as ordinarily understood.

Equally abrupt in its breach with the past is his attitude to the human beings who are the subjects of the prince. He admits that it is more politic for the ruler, if he can, to make them content, but throughout they are treated as raw material which he must subdue to his purpose of keeping himself in power. If they cannot be appeased, they must be intimidated, but in either case his object is not to promote their welfare, but to keep himself in power. Up to the end of the thirteenth century no Emperor, Pope or king, whatever his private thoughts may have been, would have ventured to avow this theory. However shadowy and unreal may have been the idea of the Holy Roman Empire, both Emperor and Pope, in virtue of their partnership, were compelled to do homage to the theory that the welfare of their subjects in this world and the world to come was the object of those who presumed to rule them.

6

It may be said that the gulf between profession and practice was beyond bridging by the beginning of the sixteenth century, and that Machiavelli did a service in sweeping away the old pretences and proclaiming the truth as he saw it. This, we may suppose him saying, is really how men do act in governing their fellow-men, therefore let us not pretend about it, but rather seek to discover the rules of this difficult art, so that it may be practised successfully and with the least risk to those who pursue it. As the exponent of this art Machiavelli has been hailed as the first and greatest of anti-humbugs or debunkers, to use the modern phrase. He is said to have "torn the veil of hypocrisy from the face of truth." The same claim has been made for many lesser men even in our own time, and it raises the question whether the veil is "hypocrisy" and whether the thing unveiled is the "truth." Upon that it may be said that the acknowledgment of any standard or profession of any ideal beyond what is commonly practised is liable to the charge of hypocrisy, but that this kind of pretence, if pretence it is, has been of enormous value in the development of morals. Men do by degrees live up to their own hypocrisies, and in the meantime to be compelled to profess more than they practise is a constant prick to their conscience. It is one thing to do wrong acknowledging it to be wrong, and quite another to do it and believe that it is right. The second of these things is what Plato called the lie in the soul.

Machiavelli's themes were by no means new. The nature of justice and whether States should act justly, as that word is commonly understood, are questions debated between Glaucon and Socrates in the first book of Plato's *Republic*, and between Philus and Scipio in Cicero's *De Republica*. Some of Machiavelli's cynical maxims may be found in the fifth book of Aristotle's *Politics* and others recall the sad wisdom of the Egyptian sage Amenemhet about the year 2000 B.C. Even in the Hebrew story it was certainly not an easy or obvious conclusion that "righteousness exalteth a nation." The importance of Machiavelli is that he was the first to proclaim openly the duality of public and private morals and to assert that to be good in the public sphere which is acknowledged to be the evil in the private. He was not content to let the two principles groan and travail together to some ultimate synthesis or reconciliation in the community life ; he deliberately excluded from the public sphere all scruples and inhibition derived from the private morality. The question he raised has lain at the root of all the philosophies of politics from that time to this. Moderns substitute "State" for "Prince" and thus soften the unabashed egoism of Machiavelli's doctrine. Seen through the coloured mists of Hegelian sophistry it takes on the plausible appearanc of high patriotism. But wherever it appears and in whatever guise, it is a direct challenge to all theories which make the welfare and happiness of the individuals composing a State, and not its own glory or power, the object of those who rule it.

CHAPTER XXIV

THE BIRTH OF PARLIAMENT

I

SELF-CONSCIOUS reflection on political institutions was a gift of the Greeks which passed by the Roman road to the theorists of the Holy Roman Empire and found expression in the *De Civitate Dei* of St. Augustine, the *De Monarchia* of Dante, and *The Prince* of Machiavelli. In England and over the large part of Europe which remained outside or was only temporarily brought under the Roman Empire, government evolved without thought or plan from primitive tribal methods shaped to meet the necessities of defence and the provision of food and shelter. In the primitive State the beginnings were taken for granted ; the purpose, if any, was the business of the gods ; for man it remained to fend for himself here and now. For that he had to put his wits as well as the labour of his hands into the common stock, and though he quickly discovered the necessity of leadership, he seems almost everywhere in northern Europe to have imposed upon his leader the necessity of consulting the tribe. Archæologists conjecture that the conical mounds of the neolithic age are " mounts of assembly," meeting-places on which the tribe gathered to hear the chief or chiefs. This is a guess, but there is abundant evidence to suggest that consultation with the tribe was one of the features which distinguish Northern primitive institutions from those of the Eastern world, where the successful warrior chief was accepted without question as a despot. Democracy is to this extent a characteristic Nordic institution.

The rule of one man unchecked by council or assembly was rare in mediæval Europe. The tribal assembly of the Frank evolved by degrees into the Imperial Diet of the Empire, which, though representatives of Italy and other nominal parts of the Empire might be included in it, became in practice an assembly of German magnates dominated by the more powerful princes. When the Empire broke up, the Diet became a congress of envoys from the different States, each of which claimed to be sovereign. Independent or semi-independent cities, meanwhile, devised various forms of government, such as the Venetian oligarchy with its Doge, Grand Council, Senate, and Council of Ten ; the senates and councils of the Hanseatic cities and their Federal League ; the numerous experiments by which Florence endeavoured but failed to establish a republican constitution strong enough to prevail over the struggles of her factions and the ambitions of her noble families. Hatred of tyranny was everywhere alive, but lacked the organization necessary to withstand powerful individuals, who often found their opportunity in the disorder caused by revolts against oppression and misgovernment. Misgovernment causing disorder and disorder providing an excuse for tyranny was the vicious circle in which many cities and States found themselves inescapably involved.

The Saxons brought their Nordic tribal assembly, or Witan, to all the parts of Europe which they subdued. It seems to have found specially congenial soil in Britain, for it persisted through all the vicissitudes of later times and up to the time of the Norman Conquest was strong enough to require at least lip-service to its theory that it alone had the power to validate the choice of a sovereign. It bowed to necessity when it chose the Danish Canute as king, but it kept its theory alive and compelled the conquering Norman to swear that he would abide by the old Saxon laws. It was these old Saxon laws which prevented the Norman barons from laying their heels on the English as their caste had done on the peoples of continental Europe, and it was the spirit embodied in these laws which the English kings found rising against them when they attempted to make themselves the absolute monarchs that most of their brothers in continental Europe had by this time become.

2

It was the spirit rather than the letter which counted in the later development. Historians are no doubt right when they tell us that with important people would help him to keep contact with his subjects and make it easier to collect taxes and assess them fairly. But for this purpose it was important not only to summon the baronial magnates but to mix with them knights of the shires and representatives of boroughs—a piece of practical wisdom which saved the English aristocracy from becoming the exclusive caste that it was in so many foreign countries. The Liberal spirit, as it may fairly be called, spread to all classes in the years following the black death and the peasant rebellion. Savage as was the suppression of that uprising, the emancipation of the peasant went steadily forward in the subsequent years, and was hastened by the attitude of the King's law courts, which even strained the law in the interests of the humbler classes.[1] It was always a great part of the wisdom of the English to let the beaten cause prevail. The cause of Parliament began to prevail after the defeat and death of Simon de Montfort, that of the peasants after the suppression of John Ball's rebellion.

The story is told in all the text-books and only a brief outline is needed here. In the early days there was no clear distinction between the making of law and its interpretation and administration. Parliament was a "High Court" which heard petitions and passed them on to the King and his council, and which, through its control of the purse, was able to make the redress of grievances the condition of granting supply. It was only by degrees that it asserted its right to be made a party to legislation and it had frequently to complain that the statutes as framed by the judges and entered on the statute rolls were at variance with its petitions and the King's answers to them.[2] As time went on, the knights, citizens, and burgesses decided to sit together as Commons in the Chapter House of the Abbot of Westminster—and, whether intentionally or not, by detaching the knights or small landowners from the great, substantially reduced the power of the higher nobility. From this time onward the consent of the Commons

---

[1] Trevelyan, *History of England,* p. 242.

[2] The statutory rights of Parliament in this respect were laid down in 1322 (15 Edward II) : " The matter to be established for the estate of the King and of his heirs, and for the estate of the realm and of the people, should be treated, accorded, established in Parliament by the King and by the assent of the Prelates, Earls and Barons, and the Commonalty of the Realm according as had been before accustomed."

as well as of the lords spiritual is regularly recorded, but it was not until the reign of Henry VI, after severe struggles in which Speaker de la Mare played a courageous part, that a regular system of legislating by bill and statute was established.

In the intervening years Parliament had engaged in struggles with the Crown, and generally with success, though with some vicissitudes. In 1327 it had compelled Edward II to yield the throne to his son Edward III ; in 1399 it not only deposed Richard II, but named Henry IV as his successor. What might have happened to English institutions if Henry V had lived, or his successor instead of losing his French possessions had come triumphant out of the French war and tried to lord it over England in the French way, is a thought on which some historians have lingered. But the amiable Henry VI, admirable in all other relations and most exemplary as a pious founder, was least of all men cut out for this part. Having looked on while the blundering Beaufort lost the last English territory in France and the unpopular Suffolk alienated the people at home, he found himself at the mercy of factions which drove him from his throne and finally cast him into the Tower and there murdered him. The returning army found vent for its activities in the Wars of the Roses, which for the time being held up all Parliamentary and constitutional development and produced such confusion and anarchy that the country welcomed the strong rule of the Tudor monarchs who followed. Even then Parliament maintained its theory that it was the ultimate king-maker, but after the accession of Henry VII it was in leading-strings to monarchs, who summoned it or not at their discretion. There were eight years in the reign of Henry VIII in which it did not meet at all. If Elizabeth had any trouble with her Parliaments, it was only to prevent them from being more loyal, patriotic, and Elizabethan than she was herself. But then set in the new course of events which was to revive the powers and importance of Parliament and finally to make it impregnable against the royal assaults. During the next century the history of Parliament is largely that of the religious movement.

4

From Anglo-Saxon times onwards the association of religion and the State had nowhere been more intimate than in England. If ever affecting the government of the country and the daily life of all its citizens, questions raising ultimately points of conflict which could only be settled by the sword.

5

Before the middle of the seventeenth century England may well have seemed to be the last refuge of the cause of liberty and free institutions. In the greater part of Europe it had either been extinguished by absolutism or fallen into exhaustion after the struggle of the Thirty Years' War. Except on English soil Parliamentarism had never struck deep root in any of the larger countries, and in England it had still to fight for its life against reactions, white and red—to give them their modern labels—through a period in which the follies of its friends were nearly as dangerous as the assaults of its opponents. Whether it would hold its own against the supreme necessity of keeping order, whether it would fall a victim to a Charles or a Cromwell, was very much in doubt all through the seventeenth century. The King had challenged what by long tradition the Englishman had regarded as the guarantees of their liberties, and he had paid the forfeit, but it had still to be decided whether Parliament could put itself in his place.

The first chief setback was the failure of Parliament to establish itself after the execution of the King. The eternal lesson which faces all revolutionaries, that it is one thing to disestablish an old order and quite another to establish a new, had still to be learnt. The men now in power were as selfish and limited in their ideas as the Cavalier squires. They had no touch with the masses, whose hopes had foundered in the failure of the Levellers ; they failed where they have been expected to succeed, in doing the business of the country in a business-like way. The Long Parliament in which they sat had proved a quite efficient instrument in fighting the King, but it was all at sea when it was charged with governing the country in time of peace. This is not as surprising as it may seem. The main business of Parliament up to that time had not been to govern the country in the administrative sense, but to protect it against the encroachments of the Crown. The King could not levy taxes without the consent of Parliament or legislate if he failed to carry Parliament with him.

It had fallen to Parliament to see that in his conduct of the administration he kept within the law, and that he was made aware by petitions or otherwise of the grievances of his subjects. But in all else the work of government had remained in the hands of the King and his council, and Parliament had had no experience in this highly complicated business. The elaborate technique evolved in the eighteenth and nineteenth century to adjust its activities to those of the other organs of government and to impart order and relevance to its debates had yet to be ; and though there were many factions, there was nothing corresponding to the organized party system of modern times. In such circumstances any large assembly tended to become an unruly mob.

According to modern Parliamentary standards Cromwell was perfectly justified in telling the Long Parliament in 1653 that it was " no Parliament," if by Parliament is meant a representative assembly. The first law of such an assembly is that it shall renew its mandate from the electors at certain intervals, and in 1653 the Long Parliament had passed through all its stages a Bill providing for the retention of their seats by the existing members without re-election, thus constituting itself a permanent and irresponsible governing junta. The " horridest arbitrariness," said Cromwell, " that ever was exercised in the world," to which the Parliament men replied that in forcibly dissolving it Cromwell and his soldiers had exercised a similar arbitrariness. The retort was justified in logic, but when two arbitrarinesses are opposed to one another, that which has an army behind it is bound to prevail. Whatever may be said about Cromwell's method, the Long Parliament deserved its fate.

It is impossible to enter here into detail about Cromwell's subsequent efforts to restore Parliamentary Government—his indirectly elected Barebones Parliament ; his written constitution called The Instrument of Government ; the 1654 Parliament elected under its provisions, but dissolved after four months. It is possible that in the mood in which Cromwell now was and with his Major-Generals panting for power, the best Parliament could not have survived. But Cromwell again had his excuse in the extreme incompetence of these bodies. The 1654 Parliament, instead of applying itself in what a modern would call public business, debated interminably about the fundamentals of they should be " lions under the throne " an opinion heartily shared by James I.

There is no passage in any writing which breathes more of the spirit of English law than the epilogue to Coke's great commentary. It is too little known, and I give it here in full :

When I had finished this worke of the first part of the Institutes, and looked backe and considered the multitude of the conclusions in law, the manifold diversities between cases and points of learning ; the varietie almost infinite of authorities, antient, constant and moderne, and withall their amiable and admirable consent in so many successions of ages ; the many changes and alterations of the common law, and additions to the same, even since our author wrote, by many acts of parliament, and that the like worke of Institutes had not been attempted by any of our profession whom I might imitate, I thought it safe for me to follow the grave and prudent example of our worthy author, not to take upon me or presume that the reader should thinke that all that I have said herein to be law ; yet this I may safely affirme, that there is nothing herein but may either open some windowes of the law, or to move him to doubt, and withall to inable him to inquire and learne of the sages, what the law, together with the true reason thereof, in these cases is ; or lastly, upon consideration had of our old bookes, lawes, and records, (which are full of venerable dignitie and antiquitie) to finde out where any alteration hath beene, upon what ground the law hath beene since changed ; knowing for certaine, that the law is unknowne to him that knoweth not the reason thereof, and that the knowne certaintie of the law is the safetie of all. I had once intended, for the ease of our student, to have made a Table to these Institutes ; but when I considered that Tables and Abridgments are most profitable to them that make them, I have left that worke to every studious reader. And for a farewell to our jurisprudent, I wish unto him the gladsome light of jurisprudence, the lovelinesse of temperance, the stabilitie of fortitude, and the soliditie of justice.[1]

There was another side to this part of English history, which must not be left out of the account. Law, reverenced, developed, and interpreted in the manner in which the great *Commentary* bears witness, might be called " Common Law," but it was more and more out of touch with the common mind. A hundred years later the complaint was universal that justice was denied to poor men by the complexity

---

[1] Coke, *Commentary upon Littleton*, II, p. 395, Epilogue.

of the law and the cost of putting it in motion. "Pleadings were technical, prolix, and conducted in a language not spoken or even comprehended by any but lawyers, and the very writing of the documents was in a hand disused by all but scriveners." [1] Law too, after resisting the tyranny of kings, might impose a tyranny of its own.

---

[1] Godfrey Davies, *The Early Stuarts,* p. 170.

CHAPTER XXV

THE PORTRAIT OF AN ENGLISHMAN

I

WE may pause here to consider what manner of men the English were in the sixteenth and early part of the seventeenth centuries. The Wars of the Roses had gone far to destroy the great nobility and led to a large increase in the number of small land-owners. The dissolution of the monasteries and the redistribution of their lands gave a further impetus to this movement, and by the beginning of the seventeenth century England was largely peopled with squire-farmers, subsequently to become Cromwell's "russet-coated captains," stubborn people planted on the land and determined that neither King nor nobles should lord it over them. Before the end of the sixteenth century the English were thought by foreigners to be the most war-like race of Europe and the most redoubtable in battle. Benvenuto Cellini calls them " English savages " and says that " the great shins of beef" with which they filled themselves "nourish the force and ferocity of their instincts." Europe itself was not mild in the penalties it inflicted on criminals, traitors, and heretics, but it saw something peculiarly uncivilized in the way the English treated one another. Taine, the French historian of English literature, is horrified as he looks back on it. " The axe ready for every suspicion of treason : great men, bishops, a chancellor, princes, the king's relatives, queens, a protector, kneeling in the straw, sprinkled the Tower with their blood ; one after another they marched past, stretched their necks ; the Duke of Buckingham, Queen Anne Boleyn, Queen Catherine Howard, the Earl of Surrey, Admiral Seymour, the Duke of Somerset, Lady Jane Grey and her husband, the Duke of Northumberland, Mary Stuart, the Earl of Essex, all on the throne or on the steps of the throne, in highest rank of honours, beauty, youth, and genius ; of the bright procession nothing is left but senseless trunks, marred by the tender mercies of the executioner." [1] It was thus, when all has been said about Parliamentary and constitutional developments, that the great game of high politics was played in England in the sixteenth, seventeenth, and up to the middle of the eighteenth century. When in the cells at Westminster in 1746 after the three Scottish lords had been sentenced to be beheaded, old Balmerino advises his fellow-sufferer, Kilmarnock, how to behave on the scaffold, we feel that he is handing on a tradition of centuries : " He showed him how he must lay his head ; bid him not wince lest the stroke should cut his skull or his shoulders, and advised him to bite his lips." [2] In considering the factors which made the British Constitution we can never forget the axe. Fear of it was still alive among eighteenth century ministers.

2

The defeat of the Spanish Armada established the position and prestige of England as a sea-power, and in the subsequent years her daring seamen—pioneers, buccaneers, merchant adventurers, or whatever we may choose to call them—were claiming her share of the places in the sun and of the booty coming from the newly discovered countries. A new commercial and merchant class grew up at home in pursuance of this foreign trade, making a sort of third estate beside the great nobility and the small landowners. The whole made an intensely virile, patriotic, restless, self-conscious community with much new wine in old bottles which were to burst before the middle of the seventeenth century. But in the meantime all the simmering emotions of these years had found expression in the greatest literature that ever came out of one country in one generation, not even excepting the Periclean age in Greece.

That is outside the scope of this book, but it is worth glancing at the French writer's estimate of this literature, for he sees it reflecting the English character at an angle which is not ours. Taine, while unstinted in his admiration of the Elizabethan dramatists and poets, finds them violent and disorderly to a degree which is a serious impediment to a

---

[1] Taine, *History of English Literature*, II, Ch. 2.
[2] Horace Walpole to George Montagu, Aug. 5, 1746.

Frenchman brought up in the classical tradition.[1] They acknowledge no rules, they have no moderation, they think heatedly and violently on all subjects, they leap from point to point, they "have no idea of progressive and unique action." Torrents of splendid eloquence pour from their lips on all subjects ; they pass without the smallest sense of incongruity from farce to tragedy, from the coarse and brutal to the lovely and sublime. But what a range these people have— Shakespeare, the author of the Sonnets and *King Lear*, of *Hamlet* and *The Merry Wives of Windsor* ; how profound is his psychology, how almost childish his delight in buffoonery, horseplay, killing, and violence ! Raised to the point of supreme genius, Shakespeare is the personification of the Englishman, with his queer combination of idealism and brutality, his vehemence in action, his lawless and uncertain thoughts. In Shakespeare we recover the atmosphere of his time, the dangerous life of its kings and its tragic nobility, the ignorance, coarseness, and good humour of the common folk, the mingling of cupidity and generosity in all classes.

We may answer that in most of these respects European man appears to have differed little, if at all, from English man, but the latter does seem to have struck his foreign contemporaries as being peculiarly lacking in what they called culture. They note his delight in bull-baiting, bear-baiting, and cock-fighting, the lack of courtly manners at the English court and in English high society, the more than ordinary pleasure which, when on the political and religious war-path, the Englishman seemed to take in seeing heretics and witches burn and traitors have their heads chopped off. He seeemed to gloat over things from which the educated European averted his gaze. Then, again, what ferocious penalties the Englishman needed to keep order in his own country—every man confined to his own district ; every stranger a criminal unless he can prove the contrary ; any man living idly or loitering for the space of three days liable to be branded with a hot iron on his breast and adjudged a slave to the man who shall inform against him ; thieves hung by the score on the same gibbet, as More records in his *Utopia* ! This was "Merrie England," and the fact that it could so regard itself tells us something about its character which it is important

---

[1] Taine, *op. cit.*, Book II, Chs. 2 and 3.

to bear in mind, but the foreign observer who considered it a backward and semi-civilized country in the sixteenth and early years of the seventeenth century could make his case. The Puritan reaction which followed appears to have done much to promote the sober, godly, and righteous life among the English middle class, but a high degree of criminality with a savage penal code which failed to suppress it remained an English characteristic until well on into the nineteenth century. If we may trust Hogarth and the caricaturists Rowlandson and Gillray, the English mob was coarse and drunken in the last half of the eighteenth century ; and even in the nineteenth century fear of it was the chief obstacle to the democratic movement for increasing the franchise.

3

Of all the writings of these two centuries the *Utopia* of Sir Thomas More (*circa* 1514) strikes the twentieth-century reader as the most modern. In this we see contemporary English society indicted for most of the sins which have been thought peculiar to the modern industrial or capitalist age. Though the illustrations are mainly from an agricultural or pastoral life, the " sickness of an acquisitive society " has seldom been more vividly described. Looking at his own time More breaks out angrily at the luxury of the rich and noble and the sufferings of the poor. He sees a " conspiracy of the rich procuring their own commodities under the name and title of Commonwealth " ; he sees landlords " polling and shaving tenants to the quick " by raising their rents, driving countrymen from the land to increase the number of sheep or create game preserves, buying the " young ones of great cattle " very cheap abroad, and then when they have fattened them on their own pastures " selling them exceedingly dear at home." He sees poverty driving men to theft and theft punished by the gallows, yet thieving everywhere " rife and rank" and the law behaving like an evil schoolmaster who is readier to beat than to teach his scholars.

He favours Communism in the strict sense that " all men should have and enjoy equal portions of riches and commodities." This he thought to be in accordance with Christian doctrine, so that the citizens of his Utopia, being (unlike the Communists of a later date) course) atheists to be outside the pale within which the "free encounter" was permitted. In certain ways Sir Thomas More, in his *Utopia* published more than a hundred years earlier, got to a more advanced point of religious and philosophical tolerance than any seventeenth-century writer.

Smaller men fought with the same obstinacy and courage in the same cause. The fussy and cranky little Puritan, William Prynne, who could never agree with anybody, submitted to stand in the pillory and have his ears cropped not once but a second time rather than withdraw a word of what he had written in his fanatical pamphlets. He too played his part in the "free encounter" and is rightly included in the roll of honour which records the names of those who fought for British liberty. It was even more what these men did than what they wrote or said which was to dwell in memory and bring their example again to active life and influence after the reaction which for a time was to submerge their doctrine.

4

The extent to which England was still in these days a country of small farmers and owners may be judged from Harrington's *Oceana, the picture of an ideal Commonwealth*, obviously intended to be England. Its themes are "ownership for all" through the break-up of large estates—the largest were not to yield a revenue of more than £3000 —and the distribution of executive power through rotation by ballot so that the same men should not hold office too long. Thus a third part of the executive body or senate was to be voted out every year and to be ineligible for re-election for three years. Government would thus have behind it the men with a stake in the country and yet be protected from the tyranny of one group or class of men. He drew his ideas both from Aristotle and from Machiavelli, and agreed with both that a certain art and craft was necessary to prevent the poor from becoming dangerous and the nobility from extinguishing liberty. His book is long and boring,[1] but in tracing the Civil War

---

[1] *Oceana* is one of the books which are worth mining for the occasional nuggets of ore to be found in it. Thus :
" The wisdom of the few may be the light of mankind, but the interest of the few is not the profit of mankind nor of a Commonwealth."

to social and economic causes and not to the conflict of abstract rights and wrongs, he was a pioneer in the modern way of writing history. He believed in a republic as the form of government which best corresponded to the distribution of property which he recommended. It was in keeping with the irony which attended political writing in these times that his book was published (1656) when events were tending rapidly to the restoration of monarchy.

We are now at the beginning of this reaction, and this needs separate study.

" You will be told that where the laws be few, they leave much to arbitrary power, but where they be many, they leave more : the laws in this case, according to Justinian and the best lawyers, being as litigious as the suitors."

(Elizabeth) "converted her reign through the perpetual love-tricks that passed between her and her people into a kind of romanze."

to the State." [1] Always and everywhere the State depends on its capacity to keep itself in power, and there is no other test of the rightness or wrongness of its actions.

This, according to the theory, results inevitably from the nature of man. Man is governed by his appetites and desires and by his hates and aversions. The objects of his appetite or desire he calls good and the object of his hate and aversion he calls evil. He alone, in the state of nature, is the measure of both. For the words " good " and " evil " are " ever used with relation to the person that useth them ; there being nothing simply and absolutely so ; nor any common rule of good and evil to be taken from the nature of the objects themselves." [2] Since men are by nature practically equal in bodily and physical qualities, every man in the state of nature is in a position to threaten every other man, when his appetites or desires, hates and aversions conflict with those of other men. Finding this to be an intolerable situation, these violent beings have a sudden access of reason in which they conclude that mutual forbearance is better than mutual extermination. How they reached a conclusion which had escaped all other animals living in the state of nature Hobbes nowhere explains. Apparently there came a moment when they suddenly perceived the need of a " common power " to " defend them from the invasion of foreigners and the injuries of one another, and thereby to secure them in such sort, as that by their own industry, and by the fruits of the earth they might nourish themselves and live contentedly "—rather advanced thoughts, one would have supposed, for the kind of animals which Hobbes describes men as having been in the state of nature.

However, having somehow reached this conclusion, they decided to

conferre all their power and strength upon one Man, or upon one Assembly of men, that may reduce all their Wills, by plurality of voices, unto one Will ; which is as much as to say, to appoint one Man, or Assembly of men, to beare their Person ; and every one to owne, and acknowledge himself to be the Author of whatsoever he that so·beareth their Person, shall Act, or cause to be Acted, in those things which concerne the Common Peace and Safetie ; and therein to submit their Wills, every one to his Will, and their Judgments, to his Judgment. This is more than Consent, or Concord ; it is a reall Unitie

---

[1] Leo Strauss, *Hobbes's Political Philosophy*.
[2] *Leviathan*, Chap. VI.

of them all, in one and the same Person, made by Covenant of every man with every man, in such manner, as if every man should say to every man, *I Authorise and give up my Right of Governing my self, to this Man, or to this Assembly of Men, on this condition, that thou give up thy Right to him, and Authorise all his Actions in like manner.* This done, the Multitude so united in one Person, is called a COMMON-WEALTH, in latin CIVITAS. This is the generation of that great LEVIATHAN, or rather (to speake more reverently) of that *Immortall God*, our peace and defence. For by this Authoritie, given him by every particular man in the Common-Wealth, he hath the use of so much Power and Strength conferred on him, that by terror thereof, he is inabled to forme the wills of them all, to Peace at home, and mutuall ayd against their enemies abroad. And in him consisteth the Essence of the Common-wealth ; which (to define it) is *One Person, of whose Acts a great Multitude, by Mutuall Covenants one with another, have made themselves every one the Author, to the end that he may use the strength and means of them all, as he shall think expedient, for their Peace and Common Defence.*

And he that carryeth this Person, is called SOVERAIGNE, and said to have *Soveraigne Power* ; and every one besides, his SUBJECT.[1]

Familiar as this passage is, it needs to be quoted in full, for its phraseology has been the subject of a debate which still continues. I think it may be said with truth that no passage of 400 words in any book from that time to this has had a greater or more far-reaching influence than this one. German Nazism is its modern counterpart.

2

But we are by no means at the end of the argument. It will be seen that the passage quoted above leaves it in doubt whether the " great Leviathan " is to be " one man or Assembly of men." In the year 1651, when Parliament was still in full being, this was a prudent ambiguity. There is little doubt that Hobbes himself was in favour of monarchy and absolute monarchy. But he left the door open. His theory did no more than favour dictatorships, which might be the dictatorship of an assembly (proletariat) or of a monarch, and if a monarch, of a monarch by acquisition, *i.e.* conquest, or by institution, *i.e.* the choice of his subjects. In no case but one to be mentioned presently, has the subject any rights, for he is involved in

---

[1] *Leviathan*, Chap. XVIII.

an inescapable vicious circle.   Until he has made his contract with the sovereign power, whichever it may be, he is only an individual with no power to speak for anyone but himself, and when he has made it he has given away all his rights and has no longer any power to make any conditions.   His consent may be openly expressed or it may be " tacit," *i.e.* it is to be assumed if he has kept silence or failed to resist, or if his resistance has been overborne :

That he which is made Soveraigne maketh no Covenant with his subjects beforehand, is manifest ; because either he must make it with the whole multitude, as one party to the Covenant ; or he must make a severall Covenant with every man.   With the whole, as one party, it is impossible ; because as yet they are not one Person ; and if he make so many severall Covenants as there be men, those Covenants after he has the Soverainty are voyd, because what act soever can be pretended by any one of them for breach thereof, is the act both of himselfe, and of all the rest, because done in the Person, and by the Right of every one of them in particular.[1]

Thus the power of bargaining with the sovereign power, insisting that he or it shall abide by law or constitution, is precluded by the nature of the case.   The subject cannot do it as an individual ; he has forfeited the right to do it when he has become a member of a State.

In this way the identification of the individual with the sovereign is complete.   The sovereign and subject are one.   By submitting to the sovereign in the supposed social contract the subject has made the sovereign his spokesman and given a tacit consent to everything a sovereign may do :

Every particular man is Author of all the Soveraigne doth ; and consequently he that complaineth of injury from his Soveraigne, complaineth of that whereof he himselfe is Author ; and therefore ought not to accuse any man but himselfe ; no nor himself of injury, because to do injury to oneselfe is impossible.   It is true that they that have Soveraigne power, may commit Iniquity ; but not Injustice, or Injury in the proper signification.

Consequently to that which was sayd last, no man that hath Soveraigne power can justly be put to death, or otherwise in any manner by his Subjects punished.   For seeing every Subject is Author of the actions of his Soveraigne ; he punisheth another, for the actions committed by himselfe.[2]

---

[1] *Leviathan*, Chap. XVIII.   [2] *Ibid.*

So there would seem to be no escape when a man or assembly of men have once made themselves sovereign. They may go on for ever committing the iniquities which are " not injustice or injury in the proper significance " and no one can say them nay.

But at this point comes in Hobbes's great reservation. There is one natural right of which a man cannot divest himself when he makes the supposed contract with the sovereign power. This is the right to defend himself when threatened with violent death. In that respect, if no other, the contract is mutual. He waives his right of defending himself by his own violence on condition that the sovereign affords him protection. If the sovereign fails, he resumes his right to protect himself in his own way, and to seek another sovereign.

Thus qualified, the theory would have permitted submission (1) to Charles I so long as he was on the throne ; (2) to Parliament when it had deposed and executed Charles ; (3) to Cromwell when he was Lord Protector ; and (4) to Charles II after the Restoration. Indeed, Clarendon has left on record that Hobbes used to boast that by this argument he had persuaded many to submit to the " usurper " Cromwell. The possibility of a benevolent tyranny is not excluded under this theory, but no legitimate way is provided of getting rid of a bad or wicked one, so long as it is strong enough to suppress rebellion. Power and legitimacy are one and the same thing ; if power fails, rebellion is justified. You may kick a sovereign, but only when he is down.

3

Hobbes's theory depends on his judgment of human nature. It is important, therefore, to be clear what exactly this judgment is. Man as produced by nature is, in his view, without morals. His state is not so much beyond good and evil as antecedent to it. But he has emotions and passions, and the chief of them is fear, the fear especially of violent death. The way to govern him is to play on this fear ; to make him accept some higher power for the sake of security, and then compel him to walk in fear of this authority. Unless he is under this discipline, the life of man would be " solitary, poore, nasty, brutish, and short." A man has no worth in himself. His value is " as of all other things, his price," that is, what others will give for the use of his power. It is the buyer and not the seller who determines the price, whence it follows that a man's true value is no more than it is esteemed by others. For this reason everything is honourable which is an " argument and signe of power." To be " honoured, loved or feared is honourable as arguments of power " ; good fortune and riches are honourable " for they are power " ; ill fortune, losses, poverty dishonourable since they diminish power. The virtues are measured in the same way. " Magnanimity, liberality, hope, courage, confidence " are honourable, for they proceed from the consciousness of power. Pusillanimity, parsimony, fear, diffidence, or, a modern might say, an inferiority complex, are dishonourable, as implying lack of power. For the same reason to be conspicuous is honourable and obscure dishonourable ; to be descended from conspicuous parents is honourable, to spring from obscure ones dishonourable, since the one helps you to get on in the world (to " obtain the aydes and friends of your ancestors ") and the other keeps you back. If you covet, you should covet big things, not small. " Covetousness of great riches and ambition of great honours as signes of power to obtain them are honourable. Covetousness and ambition of little gaines or preferments is dishonourable." Titles such as duke, count, marquis, and baron are honourable as signifying the value set upon them by the holders of sovereign power.

The " general inclination of all mankind " is " a perpetual and restless desire of power after power which ceaseth only in death." Those who have only moderate power are bound to go on, for fear of losing what they have, unless they acquire more. Kings must go on from conquest to conquest, unless they are diverted by love of ease and sensual pleasure, or by being flattered for excellence in some art or other ability of the mind. In subjects love of ease combined with fear of death and wounds disposes to obedience. Vainglorious men are inclined to be rash in engaging, but retire on the approach of danger, since they " will rather hazard their honour, which may be salved with an excuse, than their lives, for which no salve is sufficient."

Men secretly hate those who do them greater benefits than they can requite. They are like desperate debtors who on seeing their creditors tacitly wish them where they may never see them more. Those who oblige us must be so superior to us that the

sense of obligation is not felt as a " new depression." Religion is the
opiate of subjects. It may be presented by rulers either according to
their own invention or by God's commandment and direction, but
" both sorts have done it with a purpose to make those men that rely
on them the more apt to obedience, laws, charity, and civil society."
Men are by nature false and faithless. " Nothing is more easily broken
than a man's word." " Before the names of Just and Unjust can have
place, there must be some coercive Power to compel men equally in
their covenants by the terror of some punishment greater than the
benefit they expect by the breach of this Covenant." Love of power
and fear of death are the two ruling motives of human kind ; the
first can only be controlled by the second, and those who have power
must instil fear.

4

Since Hobbes's theory rests on his idea of the nature of man, it can only
be challenged on the same ground. If man is the dangerous animal
that Hobbes believes him to be—if, left to himself, he has nothing but
self-regarding instincts and will vent them without mercy upon his
fellow human animals—then he must be governed as the lion is by his
tamer, subject to the right (which the lion occasionally exercises) of
killing his tamer. It is the business of the tamer to be on guard
against that, but this is his own affair and it is not limited by any
contract which he has made with the animal, whose consent to the
process of being tamed and ruled is to be taken for granted, in so far
and so long as he is unable to resist it.

Even on its own assumptions the theory bristles with difficulties.
How comes it that in this human-animal world there are individuals
endowed with the capacity of taming and ruling their fellow-animals ?
A faint analogy may be found in the pack-leaders recognized by
wolves and other gregarious animals, but this carries us a very little
way. Animal society has not evolved in the human way. It has
not subdued nature to its needs, made laws, founded cities, built
cathedrals, produced art, literature, and philosophy. If certain of the
breed of man are capable of doing these things, why should it be
assumed that all the others are without the capacity or at least the
potentiality ? The theory really requires the supposition that there

are two kinds of human beings, superior and inferior, the one made to rule and the other to be ruled, but how the superior came into existence, how the inferior were led to make a contract with them, at what point the superior curbed their own destructive appetites and decided to take up the tiresome, difficult, and dangerous business of keeping order among the inferior and saving them from mutual destruction remains an impenetrable mystery.

Theology too has a doctrine of original sin, differing little in substance from the doctrine of Hobbes, but on it theology built an elaborate structure of belief, professing to show how either by his own efforts or the vicarious sacrifice of a Redeemer the humblest could obtain salvation. Hobbes, on the contrary, leaves the great mass of mankind no prospect of ascent from the lower to the higher level. By submission to tyranny they are saved from mutual destruction ; if the tyrant presses them too hard they may kill him and appoint another, but the gulf between ruler and ruled remains unbridged, and so long as the ruler is on his throne he exacts complete obedience from his subjects in virtue of the supposed fact that, if left to their own devices, they will relapse into mutual destruction.

5

Man may, as is often said, live in a state of perplexing doubt whether he was intended to be beast or angel, but all theories which suppose him to be either wholly the one or wholly the other fly in the face of fact and history. By judicious selections from his record he may be presented as a self-sacrificing hero or as a self-regarding monster, and the business of governing him would be immensely simplified if either version were the whole truth. In the one case the city of God would be established by universal consent ; in the other unquestioning obedience to a superior power would be a recognized necessity. Again, if man were the craven creature whose dominant motive is fear of death that Hobbes supposes, he would not risk his life on crime or war, and the minimum of police would suffice to keep him in order. But all history testifies that he is as reckless in giving his own life for causes that have touched his heart as in taking the lives of others for the satisfaction of his ambitions and appetites. He goes on dangerous crusades for the sake of his soul ; he dies cheerfully for his country ; he is faithful to the death in the service of impostors and poltroons ; he risks his life to save life, even to win a prize, to break a record. And when he kills it is not generally from any passion for destruction, but in the belief that he is doing his duty or acting under necessity. Man's judgment of himself tends, as Disraeli said, to be on the side of the angels, and among the great figures that history presents to us, there are very few who have not something of the sublime in them. There are moments when philosophers and moralists seem suddenly to despair of human nature and unite in telling us that it is a lost cause ; there are other moments when they rush to the opposite extreme and hail some false dawn as the beginning of a moral millennium, but, if we judge from actual experience, the problem of government remains always the same, and it is that of finding a mixed polity which will correspond to the mixed nature of man—hold the bad in restraint and give the good the opportunity of expanding.

CHAPTER XXVII

FROM HOBBES TO LOCKE

I

FROM one point of view Hobbes broke new ground. He might take a low view of the animal called man, but it was in this animal that he discovered the source of power. His sovereign is not sovereign by his own appointment or by divine right ; his authority is " given him by every particular man in the Commonwealth," and by this authority " he hath the use of so much power and strength conferred on him that by terror thereof, he is enabled to form the wills of them all." Here was something which was to be of use to all parties and to lead to the revival of democratic theory after nearly 2000 years. Whatever else he may have done, Hobbes had proclaimed that not kings and governments but the people as conceived in contractual relations with their rulers are the sources of power. The development of this idea in ways unsuspected by Hobbes was from this time forward to be the special contribution of the English both to political philosophy and to the art of government.

The extreme adaptability of Hobbes's theory is seen at once in its handling by Spinoza, who accepts all that part of it which deals with the supposed state of nature, but makes it the foundation not of absolutism but of democracy. He supposes men in the state of nature to transfer their interests not to an absolute monarch, as Hobbes evidently intended, but to themselves conceived as a *societas* which in the last resort will have superior power, but which will govern by means that need not necessarily be tyrannical. Since Spinoza admits, what Hobbes denies, that even in the state of nature men have sociable and sympathetic as well as fierce and hostile characteristics, this is a tenable position. English theorists, in the meantime, were, as usual, adjusting themselves to English politics. Apparently no party could afford to profess the unadulterated Hobbesian doctrine, and least of all the monarchists, who were much more concerned to show that the hereditary monarch was king by divine right than that he was justified by natural law in exercising absolute power over his subjects. The former doctrine was invested in an aura of religious and romantic sentiment ; the latter was hard and unlovely. It was possible to profess loyalty and devotion to a sovereign who held his commission from God, but very difficult to entertain any such feeling towards a tyrant who held you down so long as you were unable to resist him. Clarendon expressed the sentiment of Restoration Royalists when in a " Brief View and Survey " he exposed the " dangerous and pernicious errors to Church and State in Mr. Hobbes's book entitled Leviathan."

2

Orgies of servility followed the Restoration. The Rye House Plot threw the University of Oxford into a paroxysm of loyalty. On the day of the execution of Lord Russell (July 1, 1683) Convocation passed a solemn decree which it presented to the King, " against certain pernicious books and damnable doctrines, destructive to the sacred Persons of Princes, their State and Government and of all human society." In this they formally condemned certain modern authors including " Buchanan, Bellarmine, Milton, Dolman, Hobbes, Goodwin, Owen, Baxter, Jenkins, Goodman, Julian, Protestant Reconciler," and singled out twenty-seven propositions for special reprobation. The first four of these are :

1. All civil authority is derived originally from the people.
2. There is a mutual compact, tacit or express, between a prince and his subjects and that if he perform not his duty, they are discharged from theirs.
3. That if lawful governors become tyrants, or govern otherwise than by the laws, of God and man they ought to do, they forfeit the right they had unto their Government.
4. The sovereignty of England is in the three estates, Kings, Lords and Commons. The King hath but a co-ordinate power and may be over-ruled by the other two.

A day or two later the condemned books and propositions were burnt in the public court of the Schools in the presence of " scholars of all degrees and qualities," who watched the fire and " gave severall hums whilst they were burning." [1]

The condemned propositions are worth recalling, for they show us the form in which the social contract theory was held by the opponents of absolutism at this period and enable us to measure the depth of the reaction against it in courtly circles. In these circles *Patriarcha*, a work by Sir Robert Filmer published after his death in 1680, became the accepted creed in the last years before the crash of 1688. This pushed the doctrine of divine right to its extremest limits. The king, according to Filmer, could literally do no wrong. He was not bound by the acts of his predecessors nor even by his own, for " impossible it is in nature that a man should give a law unto himself. The King alone is the maker of laws which proceed purely from his will." *Regis voluntas suprema lex.* If the Stuarts had had their way, the entire history of England from the days of King John would have counted for nothing from this time onwards.

3

Englishmen being what they are; kings and courtiers who held this doctrine were preparing their own doom, and the " glorious Revolution " of 1688 was the rather tame result of their flight from the scene of their folly. But the new revolutionaries, like their predecessors, required a literature and a philosophy to justify what they had done, and they were supremely fortunate in finding a spokesman in John Locke. Locke was quick on the mark. He had taken refuge in Holland in the last days of James II, but returned in the ship that brought Princess Mary to England in February 1689, and was ready with his *Treatises on Civil Government* within five months after James had fled. In these he shows how " the throne of our great Restorer, the present King William " may be established, and " his title made good in the consent of the people." While he accepts the doctrine of Hobbes that the people are the ultimate source of power, he rejects all the deductions whereby Hobbes twisted that doctrine into a justification of successful tyranny. The people, in his view, constitute government trustees on their behalf and put it under an obligation to

---

[1] *Somers Tracts*, VIII, p. 420.

seek the public good and to defend their rights and liberties which are part of the law of nature. Since the government or legislative acts only in a fiduciary capacity, there remains, according to Locke, supreme power in the hands of the people to remove or alter it when they find it acting contrary to its trust. In such a case an Act of Parliament suffices to alter the succession.

Whether Locke believed in a social contract or only in a social trust between rulers and subjects has been much debated, but the question is of no great importance. The practical point was whether the contract or trust, whichever it was, could peacefully and lawfully be revised to meet changing circumstances. Hobbes left the door open to the one possibility that the sovereign might be unable to maintain himself in power, in which case his violent deposition or supersession would follow as a matter of course ; Filmer and the divine-right royalists closed all doors by making rebellion against the Lord's Anointed sin and treason which no circumstances could justify ; Locke opened the door to peaceful change by putting government and monarchy on a legal basis which it was lawful to amend or modify.

4

But in two respects Locke breaks new ground : (1) He regards a right to property as prior to the State, and therefore one of the rights which the State is bound to protect ; and (2) he is in favour of the toleration of all religious beliefs which are " not inconsistent with civil society." He draws the line only at atheists, " since social obligations can have no hold over them. The taking away of God dissolves all."

The appeal to God or to the authority of Scripture is common to Hobbes, Filmer, Locke, and all the political writers of this time. Some of them are under suspicion of holding extremely unorthodox views about religious truth, but they are as free with the religious argument as the most devout. For them it marks the boundary at which the chase after the human origins of society or social obligations comes to an end. By stopping here and consigning the rest to God they are absolved from entering the mystical and metaphysical region explored by Plato and the Greeks. In Locke's chapter on property,[1]

---

[1] *Civil Government*, Book III, Ch. 5.

the appeal to God is on'every page. "It is very clear that God, as King David says (psal. CXV. 16), has given the earth to the children of men"; given it to "mankind in common." But God who gave them the earth in common "hath also given men reason to make use of it to the best advantage of life and convenience," and the exercise of this reason leads to the conclusion that God meant the individual to possess as his own as much as he "tills, plants, improves, cultivates, and can use the product of." God

when He gave the world in common to all mankind, commanded man also to labour. God and His reason commanded to subdue the earth, *i.e.* improve it for the benefit of life, and therein lay out something upon it that was his own, his labour. He that in obedience to this command of God subdued, tilled and sowed any part of it, thereby annexed to it something that was his property, which another had no title to, nor could without injury take from him.

5

In these and many similar passages we see God and reason constantly identified and leading to the rather perilous conclusion that what the writer thought reasonable, in virtue of the exercise of his God-given capacity, was also the will of God. The same argument was capable of singularly different conclusions; we may see it used by the physio-crats and Henry George in later days to support the exactly opposite inference from that which Locke drew, viz. that private property in land was illegitimate and contrary to the will of God, Who "gave the world in common to all mankind." But merely by raising the question of property Locke gives his argument a range and scope which was prophetic of things to come. He sees that the question in debate is not merely or even perhaps chiefly whether King or people have the right to govern; it is also whether within the government of either there is an acceptable understanding of the conditions on which men work and are secured the fruits of their labour. It is, I think, not at all fanciful to read into Locke's chapters some presenti-ment of the economic theories and controversies which were to qualify and even at times to swamp the constitutional part of the argument in the coming centuries.

Locke perceives that his doctrine of property, if unqualified, might leave the property-less or landless man in the position of an outlaw. He therefore adds an important qualification : " By property I must be understood to mean that property which men have in their persons as well as goods." This, in the end, becomes the foundation of the rights which all men, whether they possess property or not, enjoy in a civil society. No man, he tells us, can alienate the rights which he possesses in his own person except by placing himself in a state of war or aggression against the society in which he lives. Then he becomes a criminal and is liable to the measures which society takes to protect itself. The reader of the *Treatises* needs constantly to be reminded of this qualification, for too often Locke himself seems to speak as if he regarded the guardianship of property as the first object of civil government. Thus :

> The reason why men enter into society is the preservation of their property ; and the end why they choose and authorise a legislative is that there may be laws made and rules set as guards and fences to the properties of all members of the society.

In order to bring this passage into conformity with Locke's general doctrine we have to read into it the aforesaid reminder that the right to property in a man's own person is an essential part of all property. Yet somehow we feel this to be an afterthought which is rather awkwardly tacked on to the original idea. Evidently in Locke's mind, the yeoman farmers, the little men of property, the plain " russet-coated captains " who gave such a good account of themselves when " left to the common refuge which God hath provided for all men," were the main components of an English civil society. But what of the landless man ? It is almost as if we saw someone plucking at his sleeve to remind him that his original formula left all these without rights, and then after much cogitation the ingenious idea occurring to him of a man's possessing property in his own person, and thus the necessity being avoided of reconsidering the whole situation and rewriting these chapters.

6

The authors of the " Glorious Revolution " and their successors who profited by it now had what they wanted—a theory which justified rebellion as the "common refuge which God hath provided"; which taught that men were not savages at war with one another, but even in the state of nature reasonable beings of a social disposition who were entitled to resume their original liberty and to revise the contract or trust-deed which they had concluded with their rulers, whenever these rulers had committed a breach of their contract or trust by endeavouring to grasp for themselves "an absolute power over the lives, liberties and estates of the people." Fine distinctions may be drawn between Locke's theory and the contractarian doctrine commonly held by the Whigs of this period, but they are of little importance if we regard his writings as a whole—writings among which must be included not only the *Treatises on Civil Government*, but also his *Letters on Toleration* and no small part of his philosophical work. What was important was that he cleared the atmosphere of all sophistries justifying tyranny and placed government on a basis on which it was seen to be the common concern of reasonable men. This theory might justify rebellion as a last resort against incurable tyranny or misrule, but for all normal purposes it contemplated peaceful change to meet changing circumstances—change effected by the consent of men who acknowledged that the welfare of the people was the object of government.

Though the doctrine of Locke might be cited by democrats of a later period as the foundation of their belief, it would be a complete misunderstanding to think of him or of any theorist of this period as advocating democracy. His treatises were easily digested by the aristocratic Whig families, which for the next 130 years appointed themselves to keep the King within bounds and to pursue what they believed to be the welfare of the people. Their acceptance of his doctrine may be said to have marked them off from the European and especially the French aristocracies which clung tenaciously to absolutist theories until they were overwhelmed by revolution; but it did not in any sense make them democrats or incline them to share their privileges with the unenfranchised masses.

Yet in certain respects Locke was in advance of his time. His plea for toleration was too liberal not only for his own generation but for nearly all generations up to the present time. His *Letters on Toleration*, though platitudinous to the point of boredom to a modern English reader, were as paradoxical to most of his contemporaries as presumably they would still be to a German, Russian, or Italian dictator. Locke himself, as we have seen, left atheists outside the pale on the ground that denial of God " dissolves all," but many of his contemporaries were of opinion that the admission of Nonconformists and still more of Papists to full civil rights would have as dissolvent an effect as that of atheists. Until a few years ago it was taken for granted that tolerance of all opinion, political or religious, not threatening public order was one of the marks of a civilized people, but experience has proved that complacency on this subject is premature. The doctrine of Locke, like that of Sir Thomas More, is greatly in advance of the practice of many European countries in the twentieth century.

CHAPTER XXVIII

THE PATRIOT KING

I

THE next *ad hoc* literature, if I may so speak—literature springing from the politics of the hour—is Bolingbroke's *Patriot King*, written in 1738 but not published until 1749. This has received a rather misleading advertisement from the fact that it is supposed to have inspired Disraeli's nineteenth-century Toryism. It is largely a polemic against the politics of his own day by an adventurous and disappointed politician who had played in turn with each of the parties, Tory, Whig, and Jacobite, and was disgusted with them all. By the time his book was published Bolingbroke had barely escaped impeachment for high treason and had spent a considerable part of his working life in exile in France, where he offered his services to the Young Pretender. Historians are agreed that he did the country good service by concluding the Peace of Utrecht, and this must be placed to his credit as a wise and courageous act. But as leader of the Tory party in the last years of Queen Anne he was an unscrupulous and violent partisan, earning an inglorious distinction as a persecutor of Nonconformity, albeit that he was himself a religious sceptic. He was both an eloquent speaker and a brilliant writer, and he certainly knew what he was talking about when he was exposing the corruption of parties in his own time. But his record necessarily brings him under suspicion of speaking as a partisan when he denounces party and raises the question in what sense he regarded loyalty to a sovereign as a binding obligation.

Nevertheless, when the necessary discount has been made, the *Idea of a Patriot King* is a brilliant and interesting work, which would be important if only because it raises a question which is still in the balance—how far parties are necessary to the working of Parliament. It may be said, and I think truly, that Bolingbroke does not realize all the implications of the question he raises, or at all events the question as it was to present itself in the subsequent years, but it is undoubtedly one of the questions which even to-day belongs to the standing or falling of Parliamentary institutions.

To understand him we must follow his own line of approach. He is not a metaphysician or even a philosopher. He will not enter into any " nice inquiry " into the origin of monarchical institutions. The shortest and surest method of arriving at real knowledge is " to unlearn the lessons we have been taught, to remount to first principles, and take nobody's word about *them* ; for it is about *them* that almost all the juggling and legerdemain, employed by men whose trade it is to deceive us, are set to work." The truth may be ascertained by " so clear and so simple an use of our intellectual faculties that it may be said properly enough to be revealed to us by God." The exercise of these faculties leads to certain conclusions. If there is a " divine right " in kings, it is only a right to " govern well and conformably to the constitution at the head of which they are placed." A " divine right to govern *ill* is an absurdity ; to assert it is blasphemy. A people may choose, or a hereditary succession may raise, a *bad* Prince to the throne ; but a good King alone can derive his right to govern from God "—whose intention it is that government should be good. Again we observe the appeal to God and once more in the mouth of a man reputed to be a sceptic.

But " good " is a relative term in the conditions of human life. We must

tell ourselves once for all that perfect schemes are not adapted to our imperfect state ; that *Stoical* morals and *Platonic* politics are nothing better than amusements for those who have had little experience in the affairs of the world and who have much leisure. In truth all that human prudence can do is to furnish expedients and to compound as it were with general vice and folly ; employing reason to act even against her own principles ; and teaching us, if I may say so, *insanire cum ratione*, which appears on many occasions not to be the paradox it has been thought.

In other words emotion is a large part of politics. Taking due regard of men's feelings and passions, we must consider what is good on the whole and not expect the impossible. A hereditary monarchy is better than an elective one, for it avoids struggles over the succession. There is one source of evil the less open ; and one source of evil the less in human affairs, where there are so many, is sufficient to decide.

Bolingbroke makes the subtle remark that " when monarchy is the essential form, it may be more easily and more usefully tempered with aristocracy or democracy or both than either of them, when they are the essential forms, can be tempered with monarchy." The reason is that the introduction of a real permanent monarchical power, or anything more than the pageantry of it, into either of these must destroy them and extinguish them, as a greater light extinguishes a less.

Thus a hereditary limited monarchy in which prince and people take in effect a sort of engagement with one another—the prince to govern well and the people to obey him—is most to be desired. In governing his people the prince or king is " under the most sacred obligations that human law can create and divine law authorise to defend and maintain, in the first place, and preferably to every other consideration," the freedom of the constitution :

Now the greatest good of a people is their liberty. . . . Liberty is to the collective body what health is to every individual body. Without health no pleasure can be tasted by man ; without liberty no happiness can be enjoyed by society.[1]

2

Between the various controversialists about the nature of monarchy Bolingbroke takes his stand as a moderate man :

I neither *dress up* kings like so many *burlesque Jupiters*, weighing the fortunes of mankind in the scales of fate, and darting thunderbolts at the head of rebellious giants ; nor do I strip them *naked*, as it were, and leave them at most a few *tattered rags* to clothe their *majesty*, but such as can serve really as little for use as for ornament. My aim is to fix this principle, that *limitations* on a crown ought to be carried as far as it is necessary to secure the liberties of a people ; and that all *such limitations* may subsist, without weakening or endangering monarchy.[2]

---

[1] *Patriot King*, Clarendon Press Edition, p. 74.   [2] *Ibid.*, p. 60.

Having thus guarded himself against the reproach of advocating absolutism, Bolingbroke is in a position to claim large powers for the "patriot king" who keeps within the limits laid down by a free constitution. He will not be merely a figure-head ; he will definitely oppose the spirit of faction or party ; if he finds his people divided when he comes to the throne, he will seek to reunite and reconcile them, proscribing no party but espousing none. Parties or factions —Bolingbroke uses these terms as synonyms—invade and rob one another ; and while each pursues a separate interest, the common interest is sacrificed by them all. The "patriot king" will "defeat the designs and break the spirit of faction, instead of partaking in one and assuming in the other."

The indictment of party can always be stated in terms which make it seem a platitude. Everyone must agree that faction and the spirit of faction are evil things and that national unity and the spirit of unity are things to be desired. The trouble only begins when we attempt to define these words and apply them to particular cases. As a rule no one considers his own party a "faction" ; it is only the party opposite to which the word applies. To its own members a party is a combination for the support of certain principles or the promotion of certain causes supposed to be in the national interest. Not only zealots and fanatics but a multitude of simple and honest men have quite sincerely held this view of both the Tory and the Whig parties and the Liberal and Conservative parties in the two centuries since Bolingbroke wrote. But to him and to men living among the cabals and intrigues of the years before and after the "Glorious Revolution" it may well have seemed that parties were a great public mischief.

Yet even then the alternative of a patriot king above party sweeping away the corrupt and factious with his own strong hand, choosing his own ministers among good men of high integrity, making a judicious use of Parliament as an advisory body and finding a Parliament willing to confine itself to this role, can scarcely have seemed very promising. Bolingbroke says somewhere himself that those who set out to find a king generally reverse the process of Saul the son of Kish, who, going to find his father's asses, found a kingdom. They go in search of a king and bring back an ass. A man who had lived in the reign of James II and afterwards in those of the first two Georges could scarcely have encouraged optimism on this subject. In fact, Boling-broke does not. He seems to say that getting a good king occasionally is at all events a point gained and that while he is on the throne his subjects can prepare themselves against the accession of a bad one which will almost certainly follow.

3

The modern idea of party as an organization of Parliamentary forces which ensures that all opinions shall be heard before a decision is taken, which, by training men to act together in majorities and minorities, ensures that when one government breaks down another shall be ready to take its place, which regards Opposition as an essential part of the machinery of government, and even votes its leader a salary out of the public purse—all this was still in the future when Boling-broke wrote. Right up to modern times coalitions have toyed with the idea of calling themselves " national," and the name has served to bring them a certain amount of temporary support at times when strong government was an evident necessity. But the old saying that England does not love coalitions has by no means lost its force, and to-day there is a general consensus of opinion that Parliament best serves its purpose as the " grand inquest of the nation " when there is a strong and well-organized Opposition able to provide an alternative government, and in the meantime sustaining points of view which would otherwise be without spokesmen. But the party system as it has operated in Great Britain since the middle of the eighteenth century is a peculiarly British invention and few other nations have been able to adopt it or even to understand it. It is threatened by two opposite dangers—on the one hand by a multiplicity of parties, which makes government unstable, on the other by a too long continuance in office of one party, which cuts its opponents off from contact with practical affairs and sends them wandering in a wilderness of lost causes and impracticable ideals.

But in Bolingbroke's time the country was only just starting on the development of Parliament through party, and he cannot fairly be judged by later experience. Quite apart from their contributions to political theory his writings abound in shrewd and penetrating observations about the behaviour of kings and princes. He " asserts in general that the indifference of mankind about the education of Princes especially in a Government constituted like ours is monstrous." He constantly returns to this theme :

Let not princes flatter themselves. They will be examined closely, in private as well as in public life ; and those, who cannot pierce further, will judge of them by the appearances they give in both. To obtain true popularity, that which is founded in esteem and affection, they must, therefore, maintain their characters in both ; and to that end neglect appearances in neither, but observe the decorum necessary to preserve the esteem, whilst they win the affections of mankind. *Kings,* they must never forget that they are *men* ; *men,* they must never forget that they are *Kings.* . . .

A prince should chuse his *companions* with as great care as his *ministers.* If he trusts the *business* of his to these, he trusts his *character* to those ; and his character will depend on theirs much more than is commonly thought. General experience will lead men to judge that a similitude of character determined the choice ; even when chance, indulgence to assiduity, good nature, or want of reflection had their share in the introduction of men unworthy of such favour. But, in such cases, certain it is that they, who judged wrong at first concerning him, will judge right at last. He is not a trifler, for instance. Be it so ; but if he takes trifling futile creatures, men of mean characters, or of no character, into his intimacy, he shows a disposition to become such ; and will become such, unless he breaks these habits early, and before puerile amusements are grown up to be the business of his life. I mean that the minds of princes, like the minds of other men, will be *brought down* insensibly to the *tone* of the company they keep.[1]

Judged by their practice, Bolingbroke and his friends were not over-scrupulous politicians, but it is worth noting that he goes out of his way to condemn Machiavelli. It is not enough for him that the Italian should occasionally recommend honesty and mercy as good policy for his Prince, he insists that his motive must be disinterested. Now and again he startles us with a passage which has a prophetic ring, as in the subtle analysis of the process by which a ruling class may slip into tyranny while pretending to be serving liberty. For a time they may impose on themselves, but not for long :

Their consciences will soon be seared, by *habit* and by *example* ; and they, who wanted an *excuse to begin*, will want *none* to *continue* and to *compleat,*

---

[1] *Patriot King*, Clarendon Press Edition, pp. 135–8.

the tragedy of their country. Old men will outlive the shame of losing liberty, and young men will arise who know not that it ever existed. A spirit of slavery will oppose and oppress the spirit of liberty, and seem at last to be the genius of the nation. Such too it will become in time, when corruption has once grown to this height, unless the progress of it can be interrupted.[1]

The passage might have been written by Aristotle. It is strange, however, that the man who can write thus about liberty should have been the principal author of the "Occasional Conformity Act" of 1711 and the even more drastic Schism Act of 1714, with the ruinous penalties and disabilities that they inflicted on Nonconformists. Apparently, like most of his contemporaries, he failed to see that freedom to worship in his own way and to bring up his children in the religion of his choice was a large part of the liberty of a free citizen. Or was he in these respects a pure cynic giving the Tory party what it wanted?

I have dwelt at this length on Bolingbroke because his writings raise questions touching the art of government which are still alive. There were other great writers in the last years of the seventeenth and first half of the eighteenth century who plunged into the politics of their time and scourged the ruling politicians and prevailing political manners with merciless pens. In his *Absalom and Achitophel* and in *The Hind and the Panther* Dryden has left an imperishable portrait-gallery, which is also a rogues-gallery, of the men of his time ; and many passages in these works, such as his portrait of Zimri (the Duke of Buckingham),[2] have become familiar classics of this kind of writing. Swift in the next fifty years performed the same service or disservice to the politicians of his time, bringing an incomparable talent for invective to bear on all and sundry. But all this is journalism *in excelsis* addressed to the men of the hour in the circumstances of the hour, of enormous interest to historians but with little bearing on the development of institutions. The immortal *Tale of a Tub* and *Gulliver's Travels* stand in a different category, but

---

1 *Patriot King*, Clarendon Press Edition, p. 81.
2 A man so various that he seemed to be
Not one, but all mankind's epitome :
Stiff in opinions, always in the wrong,
Was everything by starts and nothing long, etc.

these are parables of what is universal and not specifically political in human nature. For specifically political writing with a direct bearing on the working and growth of political institutions we have—in England—to wait for Burke. Among philosophers Hume contributed usefully to the beginnings of political economy, but he was sceptical about anything that might be called a theory of politics. In this respect, as in so much else, he considered custom to be the great guide of life, and any form of government to be justified in so far as it worked. Hume was the pragmatist of political theory.

CHAPTER XXIX

THE SOCIAL CONTRACT

I

STUDENTS of institutions may be warned against getting bogged in the interminable disputes about the social contract. So far as the contract is supposed to be a historical account of the origins of society, it cannot be stated in any form which is not in large part either mythical or imaginary ; so far as it is supposed to explain the actual relations of men to one another or of subjects to rulers, there is no version of it which is not open to correction, qualification, and recrimination. Between Hobbes and Rousseau the varieties of the theory are endless, and here I can do no more than glance at a few of them.

At the outset a distinction has to be made between the contract which men are supposed to make with one another, and that which they are supposed to make with a sovereign, but most omit the first stage and come straight to the second. From this point everything depends on the view which the contractarian takes of human nature. To Hobbes, as we have seen,'man is a dangerous and irrational animal who, in a sudden access of semi-rationality, put himself in the hands of a keeper or committee of keepers, reserving only his right to slay or depose them if they failed to keep him in order and thus exposed themselves to his retaliation. To most other contractarians men even in the state of nature are comparatively rational and sociable beings, who nevertheless need discipline, and have decided to entrust the task of keeping order to a sovereign who undertakes to govern them, but to observe certain limits to his power, such as to respect law, to consult them from time to time and so forth. Most of these regard the contract as variable with the consent of the parties to meet changing circumstances or the changing need of successive generations ; but some who are not strictly contractarians at all, though they are often classified among them, conceive the relation of subjects to rulers to be that of submission in perpetuity to a sovereign by divine right, who has no responsibility except to God, and against whom rebellion is as the sin of witchcraft. Here, if there is any contract, it is between the king and God, and subjects can in no circumstances contract themselves out of their obligation to obey the king, who, being appointed by God, can " do no wrong."

All manner of questions arise as to the manner in which the supposed contract was concluded and its legal consequences. Does the individual lose his rights when he coalesces with the community which submits to the contract ? Is his consent express or tacit ? Is it to be presumed, as Hobbes seems to say, to any tyranny which he is unable to resist ? What is the position of minorities who object to the contract ? Can the generation which makes the contract bind succeeding generations to observe it ?

If the authorities were agreed about the contract there would still be a wide field open to different legal opinions about its construction, but since no two contractarians agree about the nature of the contract which they profess to be interpreting, the opportunities for recrimination are unlimited. Contractarians are not only searching in a dark room for a black hat which (probably) is not there, but are all the time engaged in a lively debate about its style and shape. In the end the gist of the matter seems to be that it is totally impossible to express in any static formula the truth about the ever changing and evolving processes of human life and government. It is probable that human origins were of many different kinds, but whatever they were, they throw little light on later developments. " Nothing in progression," says Burke, " can rest on its original plan. We might as well think of rocking a grown man in the cradle of an infant ! " [1]

2

Nevertheless this phantom, if phantom it is, played so large a part in the history of the seventeenth and eighteenth century that it is well

---

[1] *Letter to Samuel Span of Bristol.*

worth the careful study given to it by Mr. J. W. Gough,[1] who enables us to chase it from Hobbes to Locke and from Locke to Rousseau, Fichte, Kant, and a large number of learned but mostly forgotten writers down to our own times. Its importance in practical affairs during the last part of this period was that it divided men into two camps according as they believed the human process to be on the whole a benevolent co-operation of rulers and ruled, subject to revision in changing circumstances, or a sinister conspiracy of evil and tyrannical men whereby men who were born free have everywhere been put in chains. The first hypothesis admirably suited the Whigs of the English Glorious Revolution of 1688 ; the second acquired the high-explosive force which issued in the French Revolution.

Rousseau though late in the field is the most important name in the list of contractarians. It is very much in doubt whether he in the least foresaw or intended the consequences which followed from his writings, and academic critics have had no difficulty in convicting them of all manner of inconsistencies and even absurdities. But he was a man of genius, and when he said " Man is born free, and everywhere he is in chains " he shook a world which had slept through a century of debate between lawyers and metaphysicians. He did not, as is generally supposed, either in the *Contrat Social* or in any of his writings, paint the original state of mankind as one of idyllic innocence and happiness,[2] nor did he prescribe revolution as a remedy for the evils of his day. But his whole argument assumed that the original state, *i.e.* the civil state which was substituted for the state of nature, was far better than the existing state ; and since he supposed the change for the worse to be due to the selfishness and depravity of rulers, who had departed from their original compact to observe law and pursue the interests of the ruled, it was extremely probable that his doctrine would kindle the revolutionary spirit. The eloquent language in which he swept aside the intellectual theorisers of his time and pilloried governments as having betrayed their original undertaking to procure the good life for men who in the state of

---

[1] *The Social Contract. A Critical Study of its Development.* Oxford Clarendon Press.

[2] On the contrary, he followed Hobbes in thinking the state of nature to be one of instinct and fear in which self-preservation was the first law.

nature were at the mercy of the strongest, and as having perverted their mandate to the seizure of arbitrary power, was well calculated to have this effect. This was the "depravation," the "extreme term of government" bringing it back finally " to just the law of the strongest which it was originally designed to remedy."

The predecessors of Rousseau had mostly written to justify an existing order—Hobbes to justify either a Stuart or Cromwellian absolutism, Filmer to justify the claims of Charles II and James II to rule by divine right, Locke to justify the bloodless Revolution of 1688. Rousseau alone seemed in the eyes of his countrymen to be indicting an existing government, holding it up to ignominy as a conspiracy of the rich and powerful to enslave the poor, showing how " despotism, gradually raising up its hideous head and devouring everything that remained sound and untainted in any part of the State," had " trampled on both the laws and the people and established itself on the ruins of the Republic." He might throw his thesis into a philosophical form which made it appear to be a disquisition upon all governments without application to any government in par-ticular, but it afforded exactly the material which the men of action needed in the rising storm against the miseries and corruptions of the French monarchy, and seventeen years after his death it produced its first results in the storming of the Bastille. The *Contrat Social* was thus a high explosive with a delaying time-fuse.

3

What Rousseau himself would have said about it, if he had lived, is beyond guessing. His own ideas about the improvement of society were gentle and romantic. He talks of the State in mystical language which all but anticipates Hegel. He believed in a community of virtuous people agreeing to abide by the golden rule and subduing their individual wills to a " general will " which he assumed to be good. Though unshakable in his belief in liberty, he was no demo-crat. He held that the " great multitude " in large States were incap-able of self-government and proposed a " mutual covenant " whereby they should place themselves in the hands of an aristocracy of the wisest and best. It was very like Plato's dream of the philosopher-kings. But what should happen if they failed to appoint the wisest and best

18   273

he left an open question which the revolutionaries who imbibed his doctrine almost everywhere answered by nominating themselves. Then the wheel came full circle, and there followed exactly what Rousseau himself had supposed to have happened when man in the state of nature had innocently placed himself in the hands of select beings whom he had expected to respect his rights and liberties. The new rulers, like the old, had a very low opinion of man's nature and capacity. They said that the "men in chains" required a period of probation to enable them to recover the natural virtues of which centuries of oppression had robbed them. The "transition of an oppressed nation to a democracy," said one of the Revolutionary Committees after the great upheaval, "is like the effort by which nature rose from nothingness to existence. You must entirely refashion a people whom you wish to make free—destroy its prejudices, limit its necessities, root up its vices, purify its desires." [1] Thus, via Rousseau's theory of the wisest and best, we reach the dictatorship of the proletariat, a tyranny which, like all the tyrannies that preceded it, justified itself by a belief in its own superior wisdom and righteousness.

Once more the contract theory is seen as a double-edged weapon. Hobbes's version of it did as well for Cromwell as for Charles II ; Rousseau's was equally serviceable to the fathers of the American Constitution and the terrorists of the French Revolution ; and the great Napoleon could declare his deep attachment to it. Yet some parts of it had abiding value and influence. Rousseau gave new meaning to the idea of the "rights of man" which was a logical development of contractarian theory. If man, as this theory supposed, made contracts with a sovereign power, he must, even in a state of nature, have had certain claims or interests which might reasonably be called his "rights" and for the protection of which he was able to stipulate. By presenting him as the victim of tyrants and oppressors who had betrayed their trust, Rousseau, so to speak, laid the foundation of an action for the restoration of these rights. In Rousseau's hands he was no longer a complainant suing for the mitigation of his lot, he was plaintiff demanding his dues from those who had defrauded

---

[1] Quoted by Morley, *Rousseau*, Vol. II, pp. 132-3.

him. In France this was the new white light which blazed about the throne. Government was suddenly seen as the interest of the whole people and not as the private concern of King and courtiers who held the monopoly of it.

" When men say that they have rights they usually mean that they are suffering from wrongs. . . . Rights are ideals in terms of action man first becomes formidable in action when he claims his ideals as his rights." These two sentences, written more than thirty years ago, still seem to me to contain what is important in the doctrine of the rights of man. Rousseau's picture of men suffering wrongs set his countrymen on fire because immense numbers of them felt themselves to be in that position. They had submitted to it as to inevitable fate until they were suddenly made aware that they were in chains which they had the power, if they had the will, to strike off.

4

A word may be added here about the general tendency of French thought in the eighteenth century. That was essentially the thought of men in opposition—opposition to the corruption and tyranny of the ruling monarchy. The French philosophers might quarrel among themselves, but they were all in different ways undermining the monarchy—some, like Voltaire, by a corroding irony, which proved a deadly weapon against priestly and courtly persecutors in the hands of this great libertarian ; others, like the Encyclopædists, by a rational criticism substituting facts and solid principles for the mystical unreason with which the satellites of the monarchy disguised its evil realities ; others, like Rousseau, comparing the evils and miseries of the actual world with a romantic ideal. Being detached from all experience in the art of government, most of them were driven back on the general and the abstract ; and being liable to the pains and penalties attending freedom of speech, their approach to practical affairs is cautious and indirect. But in general they give the impression of a great battery of wit and humanitarian zeal directed upon a corrupt and decadent tyranny.

So far as they had a consistent philosophy, it was borrowed from the Englishman, Locke. But Locke suffered a significant change in being translated into French. In England he was one of the pillars of the Glorious Revolution accomplished in 1688, and supplied it with a philosophical justification of the successfully asserted right of subjects to change their rulers if these had proved unfaithful to the trust which they were supposed to have undertaken. Before the eighteenth century was far advanced, his writings had become the bible of the *status quo*. Imported into France, they were propaganda for revolution. For in spite of the theoretical existence of States General and Parlement, the French monarchy in these years was the unqualified tyranny that Louis XIV had made it, and a doctrine which struck at the foundations of absolutism was rank treason in the eyes of the Court. The writers who expressed the critical spirit of their time kept open their retreat to Switzerland and England ; and it is perhaps surprising that so much of their work was published and circulated in France. But the Court was stupid and they were very skilful at the game of *double-entendre* whereby they were enabled to undermine authority while seeming to defer to it.

From Bodin, the sixteenth-century writer whose *Republic*, in six volumes, is probably the most unreadable book ever written on politics, down to the writers and pamphleteers of the Revolution, there is an immense mass of French literature on political theory. But whatever may be the literary or historical interest of others, only two, Montesquieu and Rousseau, have abiding importance for the English student of institutions. I have spoken of Rousseau, and next to him Montesquieu deserves the highest consideration. His *Esprit des Lois* has fallen under condemnation for having conveyed to the makers of the American Constitution the false idea that the separation of the legislative, executive, and judicial powers which they finally adopted was the central characteristic of the English constitution. But at the time when Montesquieu wrote (1748) the final form of this constitution was very much in doubt, and the supremacy of Parliament over the executive was not firmly established until the close of the long struggle with George III. To an observer in 1748 it may well have seemed that English institutions were moving in the direction that Montesquieu indicated ; but in any case, if the fathers of the American constitution wished to follow the English model, it was their business to inform themselves as to its true nature, instead of consulting a French authority writing thirty years earlier.

It is unfair to the *Esprit des Lois* to treat it merely as a bridge-builder between English and American institutions. For though a puzzling and ill-arranged book, it is full of penetrating observations and has a humane and charitable outlook rare in the writing of this time. Montesquieu is a pioneer in the modern kind of history, for he sees the importance of soil, climate, and general environment in the making of laws and institutions. He anticipates Burke in holding that a constitution must be based on the character and virtue of a people instead of the people being subdued to fit a constitution imposed on them. He distinguishes " monarchy " from despotism and observes that in monarchies education tends to raise and ennoble the mind, whereas in despotisms its only aim is to debase it. In despotisms education begins with making a bad subject in order to make a false slave. The despot himself is at the same time a slave and understands only the slavish disposition.

Conquest Montesquieu regards as " a necessary, lawful, but unhappy power which leaves the conqueror under a heavy obligation of repairing the injuries done to humanity." The general law governing war and conquest is " to do as little harm as possible to the conquered." Acquisition carries with it " the spirit of preservation and use, not of destruction." Taxation ought to be in direct proportion to public liberty. In democracies " taxes may be greater than elsewhere without being burdensome, because every citizen looks upon them as a tribute which he pays for himself and which secures the tranquillity and fortune of every member of it." In reading Montesquieu we have the sense of being in good company—the company of a humane and cultured gentleman who looked out on the world with a benevolent eye.

But in the end we return to Rousseau, the man of feeling, the romantic idealist, whose appeal to the emotions made him as a propagandist worth a whole team of historians, Encyclopædists, and rationalists. His quarrel with the intellectuals of his time and his change of the issue from reason to emotion mark the beginning of modern emotional revolutionary propaganda.

CHAPTER XXX

BURKE

I

THE French philosophers and theorists, and especially Voltaire, found readier listeners among enlightened despots in other countries—Frederick the Great, Catharine II of Russia, Joseph II or Austria, Charles III of Spain, Gustavus III of Sweden—than at the Court of their own country, which neither heeded their advice nor succeeded in suppressing them. Learning nothing and forgetting everything, the unreformed French monarchy stumbled on to its doom.

In England the theorists and propounders of constitutions had had their say by the middle of the eighteenth century, and English institutions now developed from experience and practice. After 1688 no English sovereign, not even George III in his most wilful mood, attempted again to govern without Parliament. But in all other respects the sequel was shaped, not in accordance with any deliberate design, but—it may almost be said—by a series of accidents. The fact that George I was ignorant of the English language made it difficult or uncongenial to him to preside over a council of ministers, and left the ministerial chair to be occupied by a minister of strong will, who was as resolved to be first among his colleagues as not to be dependent on the King. But if the collocation of George I and Sir Robert Walpole led to the establishment of the Cabinet system and the supremacy of the Prime Minister, subject to Parliamentary control, it was the loss of the American colonies which, more than anything else, put its quietus on the effort of the crown to recapture the control. If George III and Lord North had succeeded in suppressing the American Rebellion, it is rather more than a guess that they would

have reduced Parliament and representative institutions generally to
a shadow both here and across the Atlantic.

For a large part of the eighteenth century parliamentary control
was mainly that of a hundred and fifty Whig families, who through their
proprietorship of close boroughs or purchase of " rotten " boroughs,
were able to ensure a majority in the House of Commons and prevent
the return of the Stuarts. The representative system which had had
a real existence in early times had been partly vitiated by the efforts
of Tudor sovereigns to establish a Court party by a profuse creation of
boroughs and partly rendered obsolete by the shifts of population.
At the end of the eighteenth century out of a population of eight
millions only 165,000 possessed a vote.   Not only were constituencies
for sale, but many of the politicians who were nominated to them
could be bought for a price.   For years together King and government were competing with one another to obtain supporters either
by patronage or the distribution of bribes.   Corruption was stan-
dardized, recognized, and condoned by all the factions.   In practice
the government was that of a small, landed oligarchy for whom the
world outside scarcely existed.   The people, said a bishop of the
Established Church, " had no concern with the laws except to obey
them." [1]   As late as 1793 a judge could say from the Bench that
" the landed interest alone had the right to be represented " and speak
contemptuously of the " rabble who have nothing but personal
property." [2]

2

The best minds in England were aware of the scandals and defects
of the eighteenth-century Parliamentary system and Burke's scheme
for economical reform which Rockingham adopted in 1782 was a
substantial beginning of a change for the better.   But none of these
blemishes seemed to abate the admiration with which English institu-

---

[1] Bishop Horsley, quoted by Buckle, *History of Civilisation*.   " In this
State only the State itself could govern and only one could lead.   It was
the task of all to follow the State in absolute discipline and submission,"
—Herr Kerrl, the Reich Minister of Church Affairs, reported by *The Times*
Berlin correspondent, Nov. 25, 1937.

[2] Lord Justice Clerk summing up in the trial of Margarot and Gerrald.

tions were regarded by liberal-minded men abroad and especially in France. England to them was the home of the free, the country which had learnt to curb the power of kings, the country, says Voltaire in his *Lettres sur les Anglais*, " where the nobility is great without insolence and without lording it over vassals and where the people partake in the Government without confusion." This seems an indulgent judgment of a system under which only 165,000 out of a population of eight millions were enfranchised. Yet it is not quite the paradox that it seems. For, as the century proceeds we find the unenfranchised people more and more recognized as a power to which all parties need to pay deference. Lord Rosebery speaks of Chatham as " the man who almost discovered popular feeling in England," and there is much contemporary evidence in support of this view. Chatham, says Dr. Johnson, " was not, like Walpole, a Minister given by the King to the people, but a Minister given by the people to the King." He was " carried," said Gibbon, " on the people's shoulders." The people, says Burke, " are the masters and the employers of Parliament and its natural lords. . . . Let us identify, let us incorporate ourselves with the people." This was more and more the language of the Whig reformers as the corruption of the House of Commons became notorious and the voice of the multitude was heard complaining that they were being betrayed by an assembly which had in former days been their champion and protector.

Nor was this a mere bandying of words. The organized mobs of the large towns played a large part in the politics of the later eighteenth century. They were extremely independent and no one could predict exactly what they would do. In London, if I may repeat what I have written in another book, the famous Middlesex elections brought them on to the scene as a new power, and the City knew well how to manipulate them in their subsequent struggles with King and Parliament. They alone seemed to make any serious impression on George III and his satellites. The London mob was both Jingo and Radical. Chatham was its hero as well as Wilkes. If it smashed the windows which were not illuminated for the return of Wilkes, it also burnt down the house of the Constable of Westminster because, in his absence from town, it was not lit up for the second-rate victory of

Cartagena. Its resources were varied and picturesque. It burnt a petticoat in effigy on a hint that the Queen Dowager was exerting undue influence on the new King, and a big boot to point its displeasure at Bute. Unpopular politicians went in fear of their lives not from assassination, but from mob fury. When Crosby and Oliver were ordered to Westminster, an enormous crowd blocked the approaches to Parliament, Lord North's carriage was wrecked and even the brothers of Charles and Stephen Fox were pelted and roughly handled. When Wilberforce borrowed Pitt's carriage in 1795, he was warned that, if it were recognized, its occupant would run a good chance of being murdered.[1]

Other causes contributed. Under pressure from the people the oligarchy had to yield point after point in the battle for free speech. Wilkes, Crosby, and Oliver, with the mobs behind them, wrung from Parliament the right of reporting its proceedings ; the right of petitioning Parliament carried with it the right of the petitioners to assemble to organize their petitions, and thus slipped insensibly into the right of public meeting. Political associations multiplied, correspondence committees were established all over the country ; the foundations of the free political life afterwards to be pursued by an enfranchised people were laid in these years. A strong reaction set in after the French Revolution which held up the movement for a generation, but on the whole it may be said that in fighting their battle with the King, the Whigs of the eighteenth century prepared the way for the democratic development of the age that followed.

3

We look in vain for any pattern or plan in this development. It passed from one stage to another by a logic of its own which often took its agents and instruments by surprise. Philosophers like Bentham or William Godwin, doctrinaires like Tom Paine played upon it from different angles, but, so far as they tried to subdue it to any ordered system, without result. It had innumerable pamphleteers and satirists who wrote and spoke with an extraordinary scurrility about events which have lost their interest and even their meaning

---

[1] *The Public Life*, I, pp. 12–13.

with the lapse of time. But it had one great prophet and luminary in Edmund Burke, who, Irishman as he was, seems even now, after nearly 150 years, to embody more of the quintessential English mind with its mingling of liberalism and conservatism, its hopes and its fears, its ideals and its nightmares, than any great figure before or since. Burke is no Utopian ; he has no plan for the reconstruction of an imperfect society or mental image of the perfect statesman or prince. He is just the indefatigable commentator on the public life in which he himself plays a part, who tests everything by its results and is much more concerned to discover the laws and principles of what he sees before him than to speculate on what might be. He was, like David Hume, a political pragmatist.

Burke visited Paris in 1773 and found there a brilliant crowd of intellectual doctrinaires who seemed to him to be talking away the foundations of society and religion without preparing anything to put in their place.[1] It has been supposed that the horror of revolutionary violence to which he gave such eloquent and lurid expression in later life grew out of this visit. But seventeen years earlier, in his *Vindication of Natural Society*, he had written that the world would fall in ruins " if the practice of all moral duties and the foundations of society rested upon having their reasons made clear and demonstrative to every individual." To the end of his life he seemed to believe that there was something not merely venerable but even mystical in human society and institutions which was beyond analysis by clever sceptics. Burke, as Lord Morley put it, " foresaw from the first what, if rationalism were allowed to run an unimpeded course, would be the really great business of the second half of his century." [2] He had, indeed, an almost prophetic sense of the havoc which might be wrought by political dogmas fermenting in shallow brains, and speaks impatiently

---

[1] It is interesting to observe that a very different man, Rousseau, shared Burke's dislike of French left-wing intellectuals. " These vain and futile declaimers go forth on all sides armed with their fatal paradoxes, to sap the foundations of our faith and nullify virtue. They smile contemptuously at such old names as patriotism and religion and consecrate their talents and philosophy to the destruction and defamation of all that men hold sacred "— Rousseau, quoted by Sabine. *Political Theory*, p. 578.

[2] Morley's *Burke*, p. 15.

of the " petulant, assuming, short-sighted coxcombs of philosophy who imagine that they have discovered the secrets of the standing and falling of states." For him it is

a cardinal truth that if you encourage every individual to let his imagination loose upon all subjects, without any restraint from a sense of his own weakness and his subordinate rank in the long scheme of things, then there is nothing of all that the opinion of all the ages has agreed to regard as excellent and venerable which would not be exposed to destruction at the hands of rationalistic criticism.

Undoubtedly his Paris visit confirmed him in his suspicion of rationalism. He returned from it denouncing atheism which, like Locke, he regarded as outside the pale of the toleration which he advocated for all other beliefs or unbeliefs. " The most horrid and cruel blow that can be offered to civil society," he said in a speech on the relief of Protestant Dissenters in the year 1773, "is through atheism . . . the infidels are outlaws of the constitution, not of this country but of the human race. They are never, never to be supported, never to be tolerated. Under the systematic attacks of these people, I see some of the props of good government already begin to fail ; I see propagated principles which will not leave religion even a toleration. I see myself sinking every day under the attacks of these wretched people." It was the language which Calvin had used about Servetus, the *homo blasphemus* who had questioned the doctrine of the Trinity. Students of the growth of toleration may be advised to compare Burke's diatribes with Gladstone's speeches on the Bradlaugh question.

4

It is small wonder if with speeches of this kind to his credit and the still fiercer denunciations in his closing years of the French regicides, Burke got himself classed as a reactionary, but that is a judgment which does him serious injustice. With Charles James Fox and the Rockingham Whigs he fought valiantly against King and court for what in these times would be called Liberal principles. He was a Liberal in the matter of Wilkes, on the question of the American Colonies, on the administration of India. He burned with the fierce indignation which blazes in his indictment of Warren Hastings, at the stifle their consciences in submitting to tyranny than may be found in the same context :

Few are the partisans of departed tyranny, and to be a Whig on the business of an hundred years ago is very consistent with every advantage of present servility. This retrospective wisdom, and historical patriotism, are things of wonderful convenience ; and serve admirably to reconcile the old quarrel between speculation and practice. Many a stern republican, after gorging himself with a full feast of admiration of the Grecian commonwealths and of our true Saxon constitution, and discharging all the splendid bile of his virtuous indignation on King John and King James, sits down perfectly satisfied to the coarsest work and homeliest job of the day he lives in. I believe there was no professed admirer of Henry the Eighth among the instruments of the last King James ; nor in the court of Henry the Eighth was there, I dare say, to be found a single advocate for the favourites of Richard the Second.

No complaisance to our Court, or to our age, can make me believe nature to be so changed, but that public liberty will be among us, as among our ancestors, obnoxious to some person or other ; and that opportunities will be furnished for attempting, at least, some alteration to the prejudice of our constitution. These attempts will naturally vary in their mode, according to times and circumstances. For ambition, though it has ever the same views, has not at all times the same means, nor the same particular objects. A great deal of the furniture of ancient tyranny is worn to rags ; the rest is entirely out of fashion. Besides, there are few Statesmen so very clumsy and awkward in their business, as to fall into the identical snare which has proved fatal to their predecessors. When an arbitrary imposition is attempted upon the subject, undoubtedly it will not bear on its forehead the name of *Ship-money*. There is no danger that an extension of the *Forest laws* should be the chosen mode of oppression in this age.

With great energy Burke sets himself to combat the view of the Court party that " we have a very good Ministry but that we are a very bad people," and asserts that people are not riotous and discontent unless they have good cause for their discontents. He quotes the opinion of a Frenchman : " Pour la populace, ce n'est jamais par envie d'attaquer qu'elle se soulève, mais par impatience de souffrir," a maxim which he himself strangely forgot in the vehemence of his reaction twenty years later against the French Revolution.

In the same treatise Burke develops his theory of *practical* politics. " The question," he says, " is not concerning absolute discontent or perfect satisfaction in Government ; neither of which can be pure and unmixed at any time or upon any system." Again, " it is no inconsiderable part of wisdom to know how much of an evil ought to be tolerated, lest by attempting a degree of purity impracticable in degenerate times and manners, instead of cutting off the subsisting ill practices, new corruptions might be produced for the concealment and security of the old." Finally it is a dereliction of duty for superior persons to stand aloof from public affairs on the ground that they possess angelic qualities which entitle them to sit above the battle :

We are born only to be men. We shall do enough if we form ourselves to be good ones. It is therefore our business carefully to cultivate in our minds, to rear to the most perfect vigour and maturity, every sort of generous and honest feeling that belongs to our nature. To bring the dispositions that are lovely in private life into the service and conduct of the commonwealth ; so to be patriots, as not to forget we are gentlemen. To cultivate friendships, and to incur enmities. To have both strong, but both selected ; in the one to be placable ; in the other, immoveable. To model our principles to our duties and our situation. To be fully persuaded, that all virtue which is impracticable is spurious ; and rather to run the risque of falling into faults in a course which leads us to act with effect and energy, than to loiter out our days without blame, and without use. Public life is a situation of power and energy ; he trespasses against his duty who sleeps upon his watch, as well as he that goes over to the enemy. [1]

6

If one begins quoting Burke, it is difficult to stop. Many of his speeches and writing are on spent issues and lost causes, but there is scarcely one of them, not even those on the Regicide Peace, which do not yield passages that are alive and vivid to-day. This massive, solemn, seemingly unhumorous man is not only a great rhetorician whose purple passages adorn the anthologies of oratory, he is one of the subtlest and most penetrating analysts of political human nature and its hidden motives. In that respect he is equalled only by Machiavelli, but the difference between the two men is between the sceptic and the believer, the sceptic who thought meanly of human nature, the believer who valued it highly but knew its limitations. If one tried to define Burke's master-thought it would be found, I

---

[1] Cf. Cicero on the same subject, *supra*, p. 121.

CHAPTER XXXI

THE AMERICAN CONSTITUTION

I

THE scene shifts now to the far side of the Atlantic, and we see all the winds of doctrine blowing from Europe to the Colonists who were fighting their battle against King George and his ministers. It is the fashion of modern American historians to tell the story in a manner more merciful to the English than English historians have done. They point out that after the Seven Years War had transferred Canada to England and broken the French power in the West, the Colonists were able both to dispense with and finally to defy the English on whom till then they had relied to defend them, or to help them defend themselves, from the foreigner. Even so, the sequel might have been different, at least for a time, if King George and his ministers had had the sense to understand that methods of government and taxation which might be imposed upon a people who were in this sense in a state of necessity were unlikely to be accepted for long when they felt able to stand alone. It was at this stage, as Burke kept insisting, not so much what the English ministers did as the way in which they did it which gave offence. They might be entirely within their rights, wholly justified in strict law and justice, and yet it might be the grossest impolicy to insist upon these rights in the teeth of the American feeling that they had become a form of oppression.

There is more than a stroke of irony in what followed. The French, whose eviction from the North American continent had twenty years earlier been a blessed relief to the Colonists, were now to be their main support in evicting the English. There has been a long-lasting legend that the Americans were spurred on to their revolt by reports of what was happening in France and by studies of the French philosophers, especially Rousseau, who reached them through the medium of Benjamin Franklin and Thomas Paine. The high generalizations of the Declaration of Independence and its appeal to the " self-evident truth " that " all men are created equal, and that they are endowed by their Creator with certain inalienable rights, and that among these are life, liberty, and the pursuit of happiness. . . . That to secure these rights, Governments are instituted, deriving their just powers from the consent of the governed," etc., etc., have lent colour to this idea. Jefferson, who was the principal author of this document, no doubt gathered much of his material from French sources, and used it to season his rhetoric. But the Colonists were extremely practical people, and it is pretty clear that in taking the extreme step of casting off their allegiance to the British Crown they were less influenced by Gallic ideology, as it would now be called, than by the intimations given them that they might look for material support from the French Government if they would go to this length. It was, in fact, not the doctrine of Rousseau nor even the writings of Tom Paine (who was with difficulty dissuaded from launching his anti-religious ideas upon the Puritans of New England) which was the decisive factor at this stage, but the extremely shrewd practical diplomacy of Benjamin Franklin, who was said to have " twisted King Louis XVI and his ministers round his little finger " at Paris.

Which of the two kings hurt himself more by his handling of the American question—the English king by estranging, or the French king by befriending, the Colonists—was afterwards very much in doubt. Louis's feelings on reading the Declaration of Independence in the year 1776 must have been somewhat mixed, but he was under the severe temptation of getting even with the old enemy of his country, and it would have needed more foresight than kings and ministers generally possessed, then or later, to perceive that a monarch who helped other people to throw off a monarchy might be playing with fire. The success of the American Revolution in 1783 undoubtedly gave a new impetus to the Revolutionary parties in France, and it would be no great exaggeration to say that the American people repaid their debt to Louis by encouraging his subjects to cut off his head. It is one of the sardonic little facts in which history abounds

British model, had by no means become established, and would scarcely have been recognized as their normal practice by the British themselves. We should be near the truth if we said that the separation of the three powers *would have been* the British system if King George had had his way ; for in that case the King would have been in control of the executive, and he and his friends would almost certainly have reduced Parliament to an advisory or at the best a purely legislative body. This was the constitution contemplated by Bolingbroke, with the " patriot king " at the head of it. That a system which was bad and tyrannical when a hereditary monarch held the reins could be made good and democractic by placing an elective President at its head seems to have been the American thought.

3

But even if the analogy was a false one, it had useful results. The British model was well adapted to a homogeneous people living in a compact area in which opinion can be compressed into a few dominant types, and a party system resting on a foundation of certain general ideas held in common be made the basis of stable government responsible to Parliament. But where there are many different States scattered over a wide area, and local opinion is various and disconnected, parties are unlikely to consolidate in this simple form which makes it safe to leave Governments at their mercy. The English themselves failed to bring Ireland within their system, and a fatal kind of discord is too easily set up when a large bloc differing in race and religion is included in a Parliament which controls the Executive. It is extremely improbable that responsible government in the English sense would have worked in the federal Parliament of so populous and varied a country as the United States. If the fathers of the American constitution stumbled accidentally on this conclusion, it must be counted to them for good luck ; if they perceived or foresaw it, it is a tribute the more to their foresight and wisdom. British administrators will think themselves fortunate if they succeed in explaining to Indians that the American model is better suited than the British to the federal government of a continent.

But the real miracle is that even with the subsequent amendments this constitution drawn up at the end of the eighteenth century for four million mainly agricultural people should have sufficed for the immense and varied population of the United States 150 years later. This continuity has been an immense advantage, but there is inevitably a contra-account. The fathers of the constitution shirked the question of slavery and left the right of secession an open question, thereby laying the seeds of a terrible civil war. They left the States so fortified and entrenched in their separate systems that when they grew into one community, it was difficult, and sometimes impossible to provide them with the common legislation which a modern community ought to have. Most serious of all, in some respects, they left the different States to provide their own judiciary and police, thus depriving the country of a uniform system of law and justice removed from corruption and political influence. Finally the steps which they took to guard the constitution from rash changes have so effectively tied it up as to block the road to what in other countries is called progressive legislation. An unintended consequence of some of these provisions is that the Supreme Court, which was intended only to be the interpreter of law, has become in the popular eye a sort of additional Second Chamber placing its veto on legislation which the country desires. The Judges may reply that they can do no other. It is not their fault if the interpretation of a hundred-and-fifty-year-old constitution entails this consequence Any written constitution is a kind of social contract which begins to expire as soon as it is adopted, and its validity will then depend on the success of subsequent generations in revising it.

To the work of the Convention which drafted and agreed upon the American constitution succeeded that of procuring its acceptance by educating the American public in its principles. To this Alexander Hamilton, John Jay, and James Madison—especially Hamilton—contributed heroically with their pens. Their articles, which came hot from the press number by number in New York between October, 1787 and April, 1788, and were afterwards reprinted in the *Federalist*, are among the best examples of serious political propaganda, and their effectiveness may be judged from the fact that Hamilton won ratification from the doubting State of New York against what had seemed to be overwhelming odds. They are without rival as continuous and detailed expositions of great constitutional issues. They draw widely from Greek and Roman as well as modern history, and not seldom remind us of Burke in their spacious generalizations :

Justice is the end of government. It is the end of civil society. It ever has been and ever will be pursued until it be obtained, or until liberty be lost in the pursuit. In a society under the forms of which the stronger faction can readily unite and oppress the weaker, anarchy may as truly be said to reign as in a state of nature, where the weaker individual is not secured against the violence of the stronger ; and as, in the latter state, even the stronger individuals are prompted, by the uncertainty of their condition, to submit to a government which may protect the weak as well as themselves ; so, in the former state, will the more powerful factions or parties be gradually induced, by a like motive, to wish for a government which will protect all parties, the weaker as well as the more powerful. It can be little doubted that if the State of Rhode Island was separated from the Confederacy and left to itself, the insecurity of rights under the popular form of government within such narrow limits would be displayed by such reiterated oppressions of factious majorities that some power altogether independent of the people would soon be called for by the voice of the very factions whose misrule had proved the necessity of it. In the extended republic of the United States, and among the great variety of interests, parties, and sects which it embraces, a coalition of a majority of the whole society could seldom take place on any other principles than those of justice and the general good.[1]

They who have turned their attention to the affairs of men, must have perceived that there are tides in them ; tides very irregular in their duration, strength, and direction, and seldom found to run twice exactly in the same manner or measure. To discern and to profit by these tides in national affairs is the business of those who preside over them ; and they who have had much experience on this head inform us, that there are frequently occasions when days, nay, even when hours, are precious. The loss of a battle, the death of a prince, the removal of a minister, or other circumstances intervening to change the present posture and aspect of affairs, may turn the most favourable tide into a course opposite to our wishes. As in the field, so in the cabinet, there are moments to be seized as they pass, and they who preside in either should be left in capacity to improve them.[2]

Like Burke, Hamilton towards the tragic close of his life became more and more alive to the danger of popular government, and more and more insisted on the need of bulwarks against the democratic tide.

---

[1] *The Federalist*, No. 51. (Hamilton or Madison).   [2] *Ibid.*, No. 64. (Jay).

CHAPTER XXXII

THE OLD RADICALS

I

IN the last thirty years of the eighteenth century extra-Parliamentary agitation was rapidly developed in all parts of England. Political associations and correspondence committees were now being set up in the provincial cities as well as in London, and all were learning how to set their mobs in motion. A special class of "friends of the people," men of advanced views who had no chance of being elected to Parliament, now began to make their influence felt as agitators, journalists, and pamphleteers. Of such were the old radicals, John Cartwright, Joseph Priestley, Richard Price, John Jebb, Horne Tooke. Behind these again were the Liberal and Radical philosophers Jeremy Bentham, William Godwin, James Mill, to mention only the most important.

2

Most of these men had the peculiarly British quality of puritanical rationalism. Their thoughts and (in most cases) their lives were austere ; the enormous belief that they had in reason as the guide to human affairs kept them aloof from the masses and disarmed them as revolutionaries. Though some of their doctrines were French in origin, they were quite incapable of the romantic mob oratory of the French revolutionaries. With few exceptions their writings were extremely dull, their thoughts being concentrated on a purely abstract kind of political theory in which Parliamentary reform, as understood by the middle classes, played the leading part. If they glanced at what a modern world calls the social question as manifested in the daily struggle of the masses for food and shelter, it was generally to dismiss it as outside the sphere of government. William Godwin, the author of *Political Justice*, was said to have kindled a passionate emotion in emancipated youth (including his son-in-law, Shelley) with his advanced views about property and the marriage laws, but he disliked the practice of these views in his own family circle, and a contemporary says that in society he either fell asleep or was the cause of sleep in others. Man, in his view, was a machine and his behaviour, which was called morality, might be calculated with mathematical exactness, if it was worth while to do so, which he gravely doubted in his less sanguine moments.

Godwin was all but an anarchist; men, he said, should submit to truth and justice only; submission to governments was largely immoral. Most of the others thought the franchise to be the door of entry to the political millennium. They demanded universal suffrage and annual Parliaments. "The English nation," said Rousseau, "thinks that it is free, but it is greatly mistaken, for it is so only during the election of members of Parliament; as soon as they are elected, it is enslaved and counts for nothing." [1] If this were the true theory of freedom, the life of a free man would be one of unceasing elections. The English radicals were content to ask for annual elections. The Septennial Act, said Cartwright, suspends the liberty of the nation for six parts in seven of human life. That a member of Parliament should be elected for only one year, and that during that year he should be a delegate carrying out the instructions of his constituents was the radical doctrine. In this way, and in this way only, could the electors be assured that they were not being enslaved by their own representatives.

3

It has been said that the greatest Englishman of the eighteenth century was not the great Lord Chatham, nor his son, nor Burke, but John Wesley, the heroic little man who went from village to village on his tired horse braving insult and ridicule to preach his gospel of salvation to a multitude which had either not known or had forgotten Christianity. Certainly of no other can it be said that after 200 years his followers in the English-speaking world number at least twenty

---

[1] *Social Contract*, Book III, Sect. 15.

million, and of very few that their influence was so far-r̶e̶ many directions. Communists who believe religion to be " opium of the people " have cited Wesley as one of the leading, if unconscious, agents in administering this narcotic, and have attributed to his influence the fact that the English ruling class were able to carry their poor without serious trouble through the dangerous period of the French Revolution. Those who believe in the gospel of class-hatred or who think that the English poor would have gained by a violent upheaval on the French model may be left in possession of this idea. There is no doubt at all that Wesley did bring the Christian spirit into thousands of humble homes, and that in so doing he softened manners and encouraged charity and forbearance. His influence was by no means confined to his own followers and converts. It awoke the Anglican Church, which at the end of the eighteenth century seemed to be sunk in sloth and worldliness, to a new life ; it helped to revive a spirit of piety and dutifulness in all classes, and prepared the way for the great philanthropic movements of the nineteenth century. Certainly it cannot be left out of account if we are considering either the social or the political life of the nineteenth century. The spirit of Wesley was still alive in the Nonconformist conscience at the end of that century.

Exemplary as most of the old radicals were in their private lives, they prided themselves on being proof against all religious emotions. They were, in fact, sternly and conscientiously irreligious. Coleridge said in after years, " It was God's mercy to our age that Jacobins were infidels and a scandal to all sober Christians. Had they been like the old Puritans they would have trodden Church and King to dust." More than anything else it was their atheism which exposed them to the reaction which followed the French Revolution. The tide now ran violently against them, and not least among the middle class, whose revolt against the ruling oligarchy had till then been their principal support. The Revolution scared this class and drove powerful champions of popular rights, like Burke, into the Conservative camp. After the Revolution came the war, which enabled the Government to brand all opposition as treason while it lasted and to cling tenaciously to power when it was over. Pitt hastily withdrew his scheme of Parliamentary reform, which would have created a hundred free country constituencies, and stringent coercion now became the weapon of the ruling class.

Now and for the next twenty-five years radicalism became a dangerous trade to be pursued under threat of imprisonment, transportation, and even the gallows. John Frost was sentenced to six months' imprisonment and to stand for an hour in the pillory at Charing Cross because he had been overhead to say in a coffee-house that he was "for equality and no King." Watt and Downie were actually sentenced at Edinburgh to be hanged, drawn, and quartered. Cobbett, who was only half a radical—the rest of him being pure agricultural Tory—was sentenced to two years' imprisonment in 1810, and thought himself extremely lucky to be permitted to feed himself from his own farm and to edit his *Register* from prison. In 1830 the so-called "peasant rising," an agitation of labourers to obtain a wage of 2s. 6d. a day, led to the hanging of several and the transportation of no less than 450 to Australia. During the same years indiscriminate Enclosure Acts, justified as the means to a more scientific agriculture, extinguished the yeoman class and reduced the number of property-owners to a minimum.

When at length the tide turned, what chiefly survived of the radical doctrine was a deep distrust and suspicion of government. Serious-minded and disinterested men who had watched the proceedings of Governments in the last years of the eighteenth and early nineteenth centuries concluded almost of necessity that government was an evil. They had seen a half-mad king and a corrupt Parliament plundering the taxpayer and exalting particular interest at the expense of the public. They had seen perpetual encroachments on liberty in the name of Governments which cloaked the pretensions of cliques and powerful families with the forms of authorized power. The experience seemed to prove it impossible that human beings could be trusted with power over their fellow-creatures and not abuse it. To keep government, therefore, within the narrow limits in which its operations could be checked by a vigilant public opinion and the processes of law seemed the natural remedy. With few exceptions this note is struck by all the Radicals, practical and philosophical. Cobbett is against the "thing," the "system," which when analysed turns out to be the ruling caste entrenched in government. Bentham's busy and benevolent brain spins many schemes for human betterment, but they are all schemes in which the people are encouraged to help themselves without the intervention of government. Socialist Utopias in which a benevolent Government orders the life of a model community are either passed unnoticed by these thinkers or dismissed as amiable dreams. " Owen," says Bentham, " begins in vapour and ends in smoke." " All legislative interference," says Place, " must be pernicious. Men must be left to themselves to make their own bargains ; the law must compel the observance of compacts, the fulfilment of contracts. There it should end."

If we wish to trace to its source the individualism which characterized British Liberalism and Radicalism for the first three-quarters of the nineteenth century we may find it here.

3

Subsequent critics have dwelt so much on the defects and limitations of the old Radicals that we are in danger of forgetting the services that they rendered in their time. It may therefore be worth while to dwell for a little on their positive contribution to the course of British politics.

Judged by results, by far the most important of the English theorists of the late eighteenth and early nineteenth century is Jeremy Bentham. With his innumerable crotchets and his passion for improving things, he is the White Knight of these times. There is no question which he is not ready to answer, no emergency for which he has not made some provision. He is beyond all question benevolent and disinterested, but he seems at great pains to give his virtues a forbidding aspect. He believed, like Godwin, that conduct and morals could be reduced to mathematical formulas, he had no patience with poetry,[1] colours, romance, emotion. To music alone he permitted a place, and it is one of the oddities of his singular character that he was steeped in Bach and played the organ more than passably well. Nevertheless he had moments of high excitement in the development of his political theories. Taking up an essay by the Birmingham radical Priestley, he

---

[1] His definition of prose and poetry was : " Prose is that which goes on to the margin except at the end of a paragraph ; poetry is that which stops short of it."

chanced upon this sentence : "The good and happiness of the members of any State is the great standard by which everything relating to that State must finally be determined." It seems an obvious platitude to a modern reader, but it did not seem so to Bentham. "I cried out," he says, "as it were in an inward ecstasy, like Archimedes on the discovery of the fundamental principles of hydrostatics : εὕρηκα." Thus was born the famous formula "the greatest happiness of the greatest number." From this moment the utilitarian philosophy was started on its career.

In treating man as a self-regarding animal, Bentham and his school did not fundamentally differ from Hobbes and the other theorists who traced him back to the jungle and held his subsequent develop-ments to be manifestations of an enlightened self-interest. All alike were in difficulties in trying to explain why man alone of the animals was capable of these developments and what put it into his head to seek security either by submitting to his superiors or taming his own savage breast. But the special success of the utilitarians lay in the sublimation—to use the modern word—of the primitive instincts. At their touch the herds of jostling, self-assertive, mutually destructive animals were transformed into societies of peaceful, dutiful, conscien-tious citizens, each of whom suppressed his own appetites in order to seek the happiness of the greatest number, being impelled thereto by the exercise of his reasoning faculty, which told him that in so acting he was serving his own highest interest. Acceptance of this theory might not produce in all the inward ecstasy which it excited in Ben-tham, but it brought peace of mind to the rationalist, who had been ill at ease, while right-conduct, as he acknowledged it to be, seemed to have no intellectual justification. The golden rule no longer needed a mystical background ; it could be practised by a conscien-tious rationalist without compromising his intellectual integrity. A positivist could join it on to the religion of humanity and make it one of his principal articles of belief.

Hegelian tutors and lecturers were still riddling the utilitarian theory and its formulas with the small shot of class-room criticism when I was an undergraduate at Oxford. "Utilitarian," they said, was a grand word for "useful," but useful for what, they wanted to know. If the answer was "the greatest happiness of the greatest number," then what was meant by happiness ? Was it material or intellectual, could the happiness of a poet or a musician be measured against that of a banker or a jockey ? If everybody was to sacrifice himself for the sake of somebody else, would not all suffer a diminution of happiness and the object be defeated in the effort to attain it ? The picture of the individual life being swamped in this aimless altruism was painted in lively colours and duly repeated by students in answer to questions in examination papers.

And yet, looking back on it after fifty years, I am convinced that all these little points were of no importance compared with the immense value of this formula in the development of English politics. To numbers of serious and high-minded men it was a new light, revealing a hitherto unexplored world of disinterested endeavour for the common good. If one asks how the English Parliament, which all through the eighteenth century had been a by-word for corruption and venality, became in the first forty years of the nineteenth century an example to all the world of purity and integrity, the answer must, I think, be that in these years the philosophical Radicals, professing the utilitarian theory, had preached respect and reverence for the something which they called " the public interest " and made its betrayal seem treason and crime. Their contemporaries thought them a shade too self-conscious of their own virtue in suppressing their own selfish instincts for the benefit of the greatest number, but the deification of the greatest number was a great step forward in the exaltation of the public interest over the private.

Herein they were unconsciously joining hands with John Wesley and the Christians. It is in the combination of the two that we find the secret of Victorian England.

4

John Stuart Mill, who by his character no less than his writings was a great and beneficent influence in the middle years of the nineteenth century, saw in later days the limitations of individualist radicalism and the unforeseen consequences to which it was tending. A conception of freedom which left the little child free to sell his " labour " for ten hours a day at seven years of age and looked askance at " collective bargaining " as an encroachment on the liberty of the workman to make his own bargain with the votaries of freedom who were developing the industries of the towns, was manifestly in conflict with the humanity which the individualist Liberal had himself made the basis of his doctrine. The turning point came with the agitation for the repeal of the Corn Laws. John Bright might be opposed to factory acts, but he could not melt great audiences to tears about the pinch of poverty in humble homes without stirring them to think about other things that caused suffering besides the taxation of bread. The retaliation of the country party upon the laisser-faire capitalism of free-trade manufacturers was just and salutary and started both parties upon a more humane view of political action.

Considering the high demands of the old Radicals at the end of the eighteenth century, it is strange that democracy should have made so little progress in England in the nineteenth century. The Reform Bill of 1832 abolished the rotten boroughs at a stroke, and was to that extent a heavy blow at the ascendency of the landed class, but it left the workers wholly unenfranchised and admitted only about half the middle class. Nevertheless, the most influential of the radical leaders, especially Cobbett and Place, were active in its support as the best possible to be expected in the then circumstances. Forty-five years were still to pass before the town workers were brought in by a measure of household suffrage in the boroughs which was carried by a Conservative Government in the teeth of Whig Opposition. Followed fifteen years later the enfranchisement of the agricultural labourers or as many of them as had a household qualification. But it was not until 1918, when the Great War was still raging, that England became a democracy in the sense in which that word was understood by the eighteenth-century radicals, all property qualifications being swept away and the suffrage given as a right to all adults of both sexes. The movement for Women Suffrage owed its first impulse to John Stuart Mill and a group of old Liberals but its success was due to the shrill and formidable agitation of the young women of the twentieth century.

It would be an entire mistake to treat Liberal and Democratic as equivalent terms during the nineteenth century. For the greater part of it all the Whigs and most of the old Liberals drew a sharp line between Liberalism and Democracy. In his book *Parliamentary*

Reform, Walter Bagehot, who better than any other writer expressed the view of these men, rebukes Liberals for having " a vague kind of abstract idea that the franchise must be extended some time or other." They " would have been shocked," he says, " to hear themselves called democrats, but when they talked about reform, their language, so far as it had meaning at all, had a democratic meaning." Bagehot speaks approvingly of the " balance of 1832," the balance which gave the predominant influence in the State to " the general aggregate of fairly instructed men." All that he thought necessary to do was " to enlarge the influence of the growing parts of the nation as compared with the stationary " ; to " augment the influence of the capitalist classes," but " to withstand the pernicious theories which some of them " (*e.g.* John Bright) " for the moment advocate, to organize an expression for the desires of the lower order, but to withstand even the commencement of a democratic revolution."

The ideal politician of these times was an elderly man of moderate opinions with a stake in the country and some experience in the management of affairs either as a magistrate or in business. Victorian England came near the Aristotelian idea of a ruling middle class, except that Aristotle would have excluded nearly all the men of business as pursuing unworthy and demeaning occupations. Cleverness, originality, too much thinking were to be deprecated in public men. A statesmen, said Bagehot, should be a man of first-class capacity and second-rate ideas. The objection to workers as politicians was that, being self-taught, they were liable to suffer from " fervid ideas of unseasonable originality." In a well-balanced community such ideas needed some expression, but care must be taken that it was not too much. It would be sufficient to give the working class the run of a few selected constituencies, while reserving all the rest to the " fairly intelligent and reasonably educated part of the community." Aristotle had admitted that there was a certain kind of wisdom in the masses which was denied to the wise and prudent, but if there was such a wisdom, the intellectual Liberal of the Victorian age thought that a very slight tincture of it would be sufficient. Even John Stuart Mill, who, I think, would not have been alarmed to hear himself called a democrat, favoured proportional representation and various kinds of fancy franchise to prevent " instructed opinion " from being swamped by the mass vote. Checks and balances were the order of the day.

5

Never were British politics so dominated by theory as in the first fifty years of the nineteenth century. The old Liberals had a theory for everything. Bentham, Adam Smith, James Mill, Malthus—above all Malthus—covered the whole ground with theories, most of which were negative. Government must not interfere with trade ; it must not stand between the poor and the consequences of a thriftless multiplication beyond the limits of subsistence ; it must not restrict free bargaining between employers and employed. The unforeseen consequences of legislation, which with the best intentions generally had pernicious results, was a frequent theme of nineteenth-century writers and speakers. Before the end of the century, Herbert Spencer had pushed the doctrine to the verge of anarchy. Yet, stern as they looked, theorists of this school were generally benevolent and disinterested ; if they seemed cruel, it was, as they explained, only to be kind. It was no kindness to fight against the law of nature which had decreed the struggle for existence and prescribed the penalties for those who failed.

The doctrine bore good fruit in its time, and under its influence Parliament did notable work in abating privilege and removing disabilities. But what most of the theorists had failed to perceive was that their theory carried far beyond the limits that they themselves had imposed upon it. If the appeal was to nature, and governments were to stand aside from the rewards which she offered to the fit and the penalties which she prescribed for the unfit, then the whole structure of society and almost all that was called civilization might be arraigned as presumptuous interferences with her laws. Nature knows nothing of a system which puts all the forces of law and order at the disposal of those who own property. The question now arose how that was to be reconciled with the equal opportunity for all and the careers open to talents at which the Liberal theorist professed to aim. For an immense number there was evidently no such career within the limits of their existence. Something might be said for a system which protected the property which a man had acquired by his own efforts, but how, on the principles of Herbert Spencer, justify the accumulation of hereditary wealth, ensuring the sons and daughters of the wealthy a pampered and sheltered life, while all the others were thrown on the world to engage in the struggle for existence ?

Joseph Chamberlain let a most alarming cat out of its bag when he said in his " unauthorized " speeches before the election of 1885 that the rich owed "ransom" to the poor. The word raised angry protests from Whigs and Conservatives, but the theorists saw the necessity of revising their doctrine. They now said that the real unit of society was not the individual, as Herbert Spencer supposed, but the family, and that if the family was not permitted to make provision for its offspring by handing on its wealth, the most creditable motive for industry and that which sweetened toil for the breadwinner would be removed. It was precisely on this incentive that the greater part of civilization had been built up. If founding a family was to be forbidden, and everything that a man made was to perish with him or be confiscated at his death, then life would become a confused struggle in which each generation would seek to consume what it produced and hand nothing on to its successor.

On this side, also, there was undoubted truth, but nothing was the same after Chamberlain had spoken. The Liberal now realized that he could not go on talking about " equality of opportunity " unless he made a serious effort to equalize conditions between rich and poor. The great and still unfinished struggles over taxation, the advocacy by both parties of social reform, and the institution of the social services date from this point. The Liberal party worked unremittingly on the new lines until its career was ended by the war.

6

In international affairs Victorian Liberals sympathized with all the young European nationalities struggling into existence or endeavouring to throw off the yoke of foreign potentates. Within the bounds of prudence they threw the influence of British Governments on the side of Italy, Hungary, Bulgaria, and the various Balkan peoples who were in revolt against Turkish or Austrian rule. They even preferred Prussia to the France of Napoleon III, and were generally on her side in the war of 1870. But they failed to foresee the rivalries and animosities which would be set up between the nations or the havoc which would be wrought by the excesses of national sovereignty. The Europe of their dreams was a family of free States, undisturbed in their self-determination, and brought more and more into peaceful relations by the extension of trade and the acceptance of the doctrine of Adam Smith. Gladstone, in advance of his time, expounded the idea of a Concert of Europe in terms which might have been used to describe the League of Nations.

Can a democracy govern an Empire ? This question, raised by the Greeks, was answered in a characteristically British manner by the Governments and Parliaments of the nineteenth century. If governing an Empire meant governing men of European race and equal civilization from the capital of Great Britain, the American War of Independence had taught British statesmen that it was dangerous, costly, and unprofitable. Pericles said that in spite of her devotion to democracy and free institutions, Athens had earned the title of the " Tyrant City " when she attempted to turn her city-state into an empire. Similarly, Great Britain found that, however benevolent and disinterested her intentions might be, she too was in danger of being dubbed a tyrant when she endeavoured to impose her rule upon men of her own race who had founded colonies and communities in distant parts of the world. The lesson was not learnt without tears, but long before the end of the century it had become an acknowledged principle that for all these self-government, extending even to fiscal freedom, was the condition of their loyal adhesion to the British Commonwealth. The principle was severely tested after the South African War, when many thought it the height of rashness to extend this freedom to the Dutch who had recently been in arms against Great Britain. But this too was splendidly justified by the results.

" The British Empire considered as a whole, defies classification and bears no real resemblance to any other political organization which now exists or has yet been tried." So runs the memorandum adopted by the Conference on Inter-Imperial relations in 1926, and the " Statute of Westminster," passed five years later, fully justifies his description of it. This abounds in unsolved legal problems, touching the position of the Sovereign, the right to secede, and so forth.[1] Under it, the British Commonwealth is a League of Nations without sanctions. It is inherent in its Constitution that no members of it shall coerce any other. The addition of Article XVI of the League Covenant to the Statute of Westminster would have caused it to be rejected by all its members. They stand or fall as a voluntary association bound together by tradition, sentiment, and self-interest. No compulsion could make it succeed if good will were lacking ; any attempt to apply compulsion would be fatal to good will.

But the Statute of Westminster is only a part of the story—the part which applies to the self-governing Dominions. There remain India and the vast tropical dependencies of the British Crown. The Greek who drew a sharp line between the civilized Greek and uncivilized or " barbarian " outer world would probably have said —if he could have imagined such an Empire—that " tyranny " was the right kind of rule for all the non-British or non-European elements. Great Britain can make no such distinction. In India she finds herself dealing with a great and ancient civilization which has powerfully influenced religion and thought in the Western world and which, under her own tutelage and unifying control, has developed a vivid national self-consciousness. For her too it has become necessary to provide a self-governing constitution which will not relegate her to an inferior status, compared with the self-governing Dominions. She presents a unique problem with many complications which cannot be solved at one step, but ability to solve it aright is one of the great tests of the art of free government.

Nor, if we look ahead, is that likely to be the end of the story. The coloured races under the British flag are more and more putting in their claim to a voice in their own government, to a life of their own, and to guarantees against unfair exploitation. The questions they raise are varied and difficult, and require a corresponding variety of skill and knowledge. I have suggested in a previous chapter that one at least of the causes of the decline and fall of the Roman Empire was a failure to keep its output of administrative talent up to the needs of its enormous territory. A similar problem faces the British Empire in relation to its dependencies. The increase in the

---

[1] See the author's *Great Britain, Empire and Commonwealth*, pp. 739-42.

numbers of the bureaucracy required for domestic purposes is all the time drawing heavily on a necessarily limited reservoir of administrative ability.

Here again we are in the presence of a vast experiment in the art of government. I think it should be brought home to the nations and dependencies under the British flag that their hope of preserving and maintaining free institutions depends in these days immensely on the success of this experiment. If that fails, we should probably see the same swing-back towards tyranny in other parts of the world that we are now witnessing in Europe. Those who are discontented with the British system may be asked to consider whether they are likely to be able to stand alone, and if not, whether any other partnership than that of the British Commonwealth offers them a better prospect of realizing their hopes and desires.

The Great War by extinguishing Liberalism and substituting Socialism as the regular opposition and the alternative government brought a new school of theorists on to the scene. This raised questions about the future of Parliament which must be considered in another chapter.

CHAPTER XXXIII

MODERN PARLIAMENTARISM

I

IT was the middle-class men enfranchised by the Reform Bill of 1832 who laid the foundations of the modern Parliamentary system. Bringing their keen sense of duty and business-like methods to bear on the affairs of the nation, they cleared Parliament of corruption, made it orderly in its habits, and established for it the respect and reverence which continued throughout the nineteenth century. These men might be narrow in their outlook about the sphere of government, hard in their conduct of their own businesses, and timid in their reception of new ideas ; but they were extremely efficient within their own limits, and they made the English Parliament a highly efficient business assembly. Until the Irish came on the scene and invented the art of obstruction, requiring new and stringent rules of procedure, they needed nothing but their own instinct for fair play and orderly procedure to keep debate within bounds and ensure that business should be completed in reasonable time. Parliaments in these days produced a succession of leaders, of whom Gladstone was the supreme example, who were first-rate and highly scrupulous men of business as well as skilful Parliamentarians and eloquent leaders of men.[1]

It was in these years specially that the rules governing finance became as laws of the Medes and Persians for the British Parliament. These were first of all that Governments and Governments alone should be responsible for the annual budgets, and that they should

---

[1] *The Public Life*, I, p. 24. In this chapter I have repeated one or two phrases or short passages from the same source.

stand or fall on any financial proposal of importance. Next, and corresponding to this, that Finance Bills should be debated in " Committee of the whole House " ; and third that no private member should be permitted to propose new taxes or measures increasing public expenditure without obtaining the authority of the House in a special resolution which needed to be backed by the Secretary to the Treasury, *i.e.* to obtain the consent of the Government. These rules have been the sheet-anchors of public solvency in Great Britain and have saved the nation from the periodic financial crises which afflict other Parliamentary countries. But this system could scarcely have stood the test of time unless British Governments had been assured a relatively long life. For they assume, generally speaking, that the same Government will be in office when a Budget is introduced and when it passes into law, and they would almost certainly be disregarded if Governments were liable in Britain, as in certain other Parliamentary countries, to pass from the scene between the introduction and completion of their finance bills. That may happen in Great Britain, but it happens too seldom to affect the system. When it does happen a new Government must either make itself wholly responsible for the Budget of its predecessors or introduce a new one for which it will take the same responsibility.

Englishmen have been so accustomed to take this system for granted that they are in some danger of forgetting its importance. That is best seen by comparing it with the French system, under which a Government with a precarious existence introduces its financial scheme and hands it over for scrutiny or amendment to Committees of the Chamber and Senate. After weeks or months, in which the Government proposing it may have passed out of office, it is returned in a form in which its original authors scarcely recognize it and could not be expected to take responsibility for it. So the year ends with the Budget unbalanced, and a deficit caused by the disallowance of taxes or new proposals for expenditure has to be met by borrowing. The borrowings mount up and produce periodic crises, flights of capital abroad, and depreciation of currency. A succession of these crises produces disorder and is extremely threatening to Parliamentary government.

2

It may be said, then, that a large part of the success of Parliamentary government in Great Britain has depended on two factors : (1) the stability of Governments through the retention of the power of dissolution in the hands of the executive ; and (2) the strict management of finance.   But, important as these things may be, they would not alone ensure the success and permanence of Parliamentary institutions. There are other imponderable factors of great importance in which, so far, Great Britain has shown a good example, and which are equally necessary to give full meaning to the expression *government by consent.* Can we rely on their continuance at a time when the scope of Parliamentary action has been immensely extended, and the controversies between parties and classes have been correspondingly intensified ?

The substitution of the Labour or Socialist party for the Liberal as the regular Opposition in the British Parliament raises this question in new forms on which past experience offers little guidance.   The old parties came near breaking the Parliamentary machine on the Irish question in 1913 and 1914, but there was no other question in sight which threatened any fundamental schism.   Both had in view the same type of economic society, both were opportunist and flexible in deciding the next step in domestic policy, neither exacted any positive test from its members.   Up to the war British Labour was (according to Continental standards) deeply tainted with " bourgeois Liberalism " ; it had worked in complete harmony with the Liberal party in the 1906 Parliament, and had apparently had no object in view but to quicken the pace of Liberal and Radical legislation. After the war, however, it adopted the title of " Socialist " and its more ardent members sought to bring it into line with Continental Socialists by adopting their theory of the " class-war " and their idea of the party as an exclusive and highly disciplined body refusing compromise and declining co-operation with any other party or group.

Can British Parliamentary methods be adjusted to the new doctrine or to a party constituted on these lines ?   Can they survive if the give and take, the consideration for minorities, the gradualism and the moderation which have hitherto been the essence of the Parliamentary system are rejected by the impatient idealists of a new order ?   To attempt to answer that question in detail would take me into the region of prophecy, which is still the most gratuitous form of error. But a few general observations may be risked.

The Socialist doctrine is totalitarian : it contemplates the substitution of bureaucrats and experts for private persons over the chief part of the national activities, and in the countries in which it is practised in any systematic way it is found to be quite incompatible with free criticism or Parliamentary government as we understand it. Its more advanced advocates in this country have already told us that its establishment in the manner that they desire would require the suspension of Parliamentary methods, at all events for the time being, and it does not seem probable that, when once suspended, they would easily be restored. Whatever the merits of the Socialist doctrine, I think it must be recognized that one of the most serious problems it raises is that of combining it with free Parliamentary methods.

It is improbable that British politicians will push any doctrine to the logical and fanatical extremes that may be seen in other countries, but experience since the war suggests that the new kind of politics is not easily digested by the British Parliament. Instead of choosing their parties in accordance with their former Conservative or Liberal principles, a large number of voters have in these years had no politics except to keep out of office a party which they think threatens them with revolutionary change. Accordingly, the Labour party, though it has succeeded in extinguishing the Liberal party, has failed to establish itself as an alternative Government for more than two brief periods in a minority ; and for sixteen years the country has been governed almost exclusively by the Conservative party and the few members of the Labour and Liberal parties who have been willing to make terms with it.[1] Whether the political results of that have been good or bad is a subject on which many opinions are possible, but they have certainly not been favourable to the development of the Parliamentary system on the lines laid down in the nineteenth century. The " swing

---

[1] There were two short intervals in 1924 and 1929–31 respectively in which a minority Labour Government was in power, and eighteen months, in 1931–32, in which Liberals of all schools co-operated with the Conservatives. After that only those Liberals who were able to accept the Conservative policy of Protection continued this co-operation.

of the pendulum," which gave each party its opportunity and educated both in the business of administration has all but ceased. As the years pass the number of Opposition leaders who have had any experience in government constantly diminishes ; doubts as to the competence of this Opposition to provide an alternative Government and fears of what it may do if it were given the opportunity become an argument for keeping the existing Government in power, which acts powerfully at General Elections. At the same time the opportunities of advancement in a political career and even of entrance into Parliament are more and more concentrated in a few hands. The young Liberal has practically no chance of obtaining a seat in the House of Commons ; the young Conservative, being one among so many, has few chances of advancement and is expected to efface himself in the interests of the Government's business. Whether in these conditions the public life will continue to attract the ablest men and women has become a serious question.

3

Still more is it a question whether Parliament would continue to hold public attention if government were always to be safely entrenched behind an unchallengeable majority, if there were to be no more exciting divisions, no uncertainty as to what might happen next month or next week. In this respect the fate of Parliament is largely in the hands of the press, which may report its proceedings seriously and intelligently or, in default of other legitimate sporting interest, lower its prestige and authority by dwelling inordinately on its occasional brawls and scandals. A certain stage management is required to maintain this prestige in the eyes of the public. This is not only a desirable, but in these days of propaganda, a necessary part of the art of Parliamentary government, and it can only be provided by a conscious effort on the part of leaders and whips with the collaboration of the press.

Parliament working in a free atmosphere adds immensely to the interests of life and the political education of the people. In this respect the countries working under the system of "responsible government" have, or should have, a great advantage over those in which the elective assembly is detached from the executive. When the fate of a

Government may depend on one division and one day's debate, the interest in Parliament must be greater than when the Executive has a secure life beyond its reach. Where it is possible to interpellate a Government day by day on any question of importance, even on any question touching the life of an individual citizen, the nation gets the sense that it is engaged in a perpetual grand inquest into its own affairs. Question time in the British House of Commons is still the most illuminating hour in any Assembly in the world to-day.

We are learning, meanwhile, that an enlargement of the franchise does not correspondingly open the doors of entry into Parliament. To widen and increase the number of these doors is becoming almost as important for this generation as to extend the franchise was for former generations. A system under which large blocs of safe seats are in the gift of whips on one side and of trade unions on the other may, under democratic disguises, slip back into something perilously resembling the closed or rotten borough system of the eighteenth century. If Parliament will not have proportional representation, it must find other ways of opening its doors. Municipal government with its aldermen may offer an analogy, but a system under which a large number both of the most experienced elderly statesmen and of the most promising young men are unable to find seats in the House of Commons cannot be the last word in modern representative institutions.

The rule of one party will not last for ever. It may end suddenly in some unforeseen crisis or gradually fade out from sheer boredom on the part of the electors. There comes a time when even Aristides must depart. If we wish to be easy in our minds about what may happen when that time comes, we can do nothing better than seek to place Parliament on a footing in which it will be recognized as a truly representative democratic Assembly. Given that condition, a British Parliament may be trusted to pursue its ancient work of remedying grievances while declining policies and programmes which exceed its capacity for legislating in an orderly way or crush minorities after the manner of the dictators. The laws of Parliamentary well-being are mainly two : first that Parliament shall prove capable of finding remedies for social injustice, and next that its members shall agree not to place a greater load on it than it will bear. Failure in either of these respects would be failure in both. If liberty and authority, Liberalism and Socialism, are ever to be reconciled it must be by Parliamentary means. Revolutionary and class-war methods are fatal to liberty, and turn Socialism into terrorism.

4

Subsequent opinion has discovered a certain condescension, as of self-consciously superior beings looking down on their inferiors, in the attitude of the early Victorian Liberals. This unamiable characteristic has given them a bad name, but it should not blind us to what was reasonable in their doubts and fears. The literature of this period raises in a manner that is almost prophetic a whole group of questions which democracy in Europe has failed to solve in the subsequent years. How many of the "fervid ideas of unseasonable originality," which Bagehot feared, can be translated into action by the Parliamentary method of suasion and argument ? Up to what point will minorities submit to be overriden ? What will happen if they fly to violence to resist the supposedly Sovereign Parliament ? It is failure to answer these questions which has been the ruin of Parliamentary institutions in a large part of Europe. Struggles between extremists have paralysed Parliaments and produced the disorders which have given tyranny its opportunity. The British people came dangerously near the limits of Parliamentary action in their dealing with the Irish question in 1912–13 ; the failure of Parliaments has been the excuse for Fascist Revolutions in Germany and Italy. In Great Britain some advanced politicians have accepted the "inevitability of gradualness" as a condition of Parliamentary government, but in Europe the great majority, both of Fascists and Communists, have brushed Parliaments aside with impatient contempt as a quite inadequate instrument for the drastic changes which they deem necessary in the structure of society.

Undoubtedly these extremists are right from their own point of view. In no country would it have been possible under Parliamentary institutions to abolish private property at a stroke, as in Russia, or even to bring it under the complete control instituted by the totalitarian States. In no country would it have been possible under Parliamentary institutions for a Government to undertake the suppression of religion, as in Russia, or its transformation to suit the purpose of the State, as in Germany. If any State requires these violent breaches with the past, it has to begin by abolishing Parliament and extinguishing the free institutions of which Parliament is the trustee and guardian. The two things stand or fall together, for if Parliament goes down, free speech, the free press, and all other guarantees for liberty go with it. A State may in course of time evolve under Parliamentary government into new forms which judged by present standards will be as revolutionary as any Socialist Utopia, but it cannot jump to them without breaking Parliament.

To this extent the Victorians were right. Holding the doctrine of the sovereignty of Parliament to be of supreme importance, they sought to guard it against sudden incursions of the unseasonable to which their instincts told them it would be unequal. " In its season bring the law," was their watchword. Their standards are not ours. A modern Parliament can accept at the hands of Conservatives legislation which could only have been carried by revolutionary methods through the Parliaments of the mid-nineteenth century. Nevertheless, the principle remains the same. Now, as then, there are limits which Parliament cannot pass ; now, as then, the continuance of Parliament depends on the willingness of Parliamentarians to keep within the line at which radicalism passes into revolutionism or Conservatism into Fascism. To respect this unmapped boundary has so far been a large part of the Parliamentary instinct built up in the British people from long practice and experience. Except so far as it is in this sense instinctive, the management of Parliament is a difficult and delicate art of which only a few great nations appear to possess the secret.

In truth it requires a far higher degree of political education and a far greater sense of responsibility in the individual citizen than any other form of government. The Greeks said that tyranny, which they detested for themselves, was the right form of government for barbarians, since they partook of the nature of slaves. It is at all events an immense simplification of the process of government when one man is in a position to impose his will on others who do not need to be persuaded or argued with. The slower method may well be justified in the long run, for as both Germans and Russians have discovered in past times, it is an enormous hazard for any country to stake its all on one man or one dynasty. But in the short run there is no gainsaying the advantages which dictatorship appears to offer on critical occasions when swift action is necessary. Even the democracies find it essential to part with their liberties in time of war, and if the life of nations is to be a perpetual hovering on the brink of war, they are likely to need a special kind of Parliamentary technique to save their free institutions from challenge on the ground of immediate efficiency.

5

I was born into a world which took Parliament for granted as an eternal institution with deep roots in history and human nature. But, if we go back in its history, we find that only in England among the great Powers has it any long history, and there until quite recently it was qualified by a limited suffrage. At this moment there are only two great nations, Great Britain and France, which practise it in the characteristically English form known as "responsible government," *i.e.* the dependence of government on a majority in the elective House. Even in these two the same principle gives widely different results, since in France the Chamber is practically indissoluble [1] for a period of four years, whereas in England the executive retains the right of dissolving Parliament at any moment. Being assured of his seat for four years, the French deputy has little scruple about replacing one combination of Ministers by another, whereas the English member of Parliament is all the time aware that a vote against a Government may involve him in a general election, possibly within a few weeks or months of the previous election. For this reason the British system ensures much greater stability for Governments than the French. Subject to its right of criticism, the British House of Commons leaves the general control of affairs to the Government for the term of the Parliament, *i.e.* as a rule for about four years. A French Government seldom has a safe tenure for more than a few months. Since 1871

---

[1] The French Chamber can be dissolved by the President with the consent of the Senate, but only once, on the exceptional occasion of the Boulanger crisis in 1888, has it been dissolved by this process. For all normal purposes dissolution is regarded as unconstitutional.

the average duration of French Governments has been only eight months, and there have been considerable periods when it was not more than three.

The American system which ensures the executive an existence independent of the legislature, though democratic, is not Parliamentary in the European sense of the word or comparable with either the British or French system. It is part of a Federal Constitution and adapted to the conditions of a widely scattered community divided into a multiplicity of States with Governments of their own and largely independent legal systems. It is therefore scarcely an exaggeration to say that the British system of responsible Parliamentary government is unique in the world to-day, unique at all events among great nations.[1] By general consent it has so far been the most successful of all the experiments in free institutions recorded in history. It is therefore of great importance both for our own guidance and for the help of others, especially members of the British Commonwealth who follow the British model, to be clear about the causes of this success and to make sure, so far as we can, that we do not imperil them, as we go forward into a new period of experimental politics.

---

[1] The British Dominions and the smaller northern and Scandinavian countries in Europe have generally followed the British model, and with great success.

CHAPTER XXXIV

THE AGE OF THE IDEOLOGUES—HEGEL

" It has not pleased God to save his people by dialectic."—St. Ambrose.

I

THE last phase in the history of government in Europe may be shortly described as " the age of the ideologues." The word is not an elegant one, but it has gathered about it meanings and associations peculiar to the period following the Great War, and it signifies something for which there is no other word. There are now three great Governments definitely founded on theories or ideologies,[1] formulated not by statesmen or men of affairs but by philosophers and writers ruminating in their studies, who claim to have discovered truths to which political practice must conform.

The begetter and ensuer of all these is Hegel, whose discovery of the process which he called " dialectic " is at the back of both the leading ideologies, the Fascist and the Communist. Hegel supposed that the human mind was furnished with an analytical apparatus which enabled it to discover the nature of the universe and its *modus operandi*. This he called " dialectic," and it seemed to him to reveal an eternal contrariety at the heart of things. According to this view, every positive was dogged by its negative until the two were reconciled in a higher unity which immediately gave rise to another negative requiring a similar reconciliation, and so on *ad infinitum*.[2] History

---

[1] This word seems to be a base-born synonym for " ideas," but if " ideologue" is admitted, it is convenient to follow it up with " ideology."

[2] To this must be attached the qualification that in the mind of the Absolute the universe existed as a " whole " determining the pattern to which the historic spirit was working, as it pieced together the fragments of which this " whole " was composed.

thus conceived is an unending succession of the Hegelian triads—theses, antitheses, syntheses—in which institutions and forms of government provoke their own undoing and the substitution of their opposites just in proportion as they reach or approach perfection. The idea is difficult enough as used by Hegel, but if one keeps tight hold of the fact that in his philosophy there is practically no distinction between thoughts and things, his assumption that a principle which, if true, seems to belong solely to the region of metaphysical logic, is equivalent to a law governing practical affairs becomes relatively intelligible. Detached from this context, it is one of the most obscure and confusing that has ever entered into political controversy.

2

A glance at Hegel's *Philosophy of History*,[1] a series of lectures delivered in Berlin about 1823, which are still widely read as containing the essence of the Hegelian system, so far as it touched history and politics, may be useful at this point.

Something called " freedom " plays a large part in the argument of this book, but as we read on we find that this Hegelian " freedom " is widely removed from what is ordinarily understood by that word. " Spirit," says Hegel, is " self-contained existence " (Bei-sich-selbst-sein) ; and " this is Freedom exactly. For I am dependent, my being is referred to something else which I am not ; I cannot exist independently on something external ; I am free on the contrary when my existence depends on myself." The history of the world is " the progress of the consciousness of freedom." But this freedom cannot be realized by the individual in his own life. In that there is only freedom of a low and limited order which finds its exercise in the sphere of particular and limited desires. It is only in " the moral whole, the State, that the individual has and enjoys his freedom, on the condition of his recognizing and believing in and willing that which is common to the whole." [2] The State is thus " the actually existing realized moral life. For it is the unity of the universal essential will with that of the individual ; and this is morality. . . .

---

[1] English translation by J. Sibree, p. 18.
[2] *Ibid.*, p. 40.

Truth is the unity of the universal and subjective will, and the universal is to be found in the State, in its laws, its universal and national arrangements. The State is the Divine idea as it exists on earth."

The Hegelian " freedom " is thus very nearly the opposite of freedom as its champions had hitherto conceived it. The individual attains to it not by living his own life but by submitting to, conforming to, and ultimately being absorbed by the State. As the picture is filled in, he more and more dwindles to a pale shadow and finally vanishes in the all-embracing whole. Religion, art, and philosophy are inseparably united with the spirit of the State. " Only in connection with this particular religion can this particular political constitution exist, just as in such a State such or such a philosophy or order of art." Being " the Divine idea as it exists on earth," the State is a fit object of worship, and it is a gross presumption for us to criticize the history that has gone to its making.

Since they are agents of the " divine idea " prescribed by the " world spirit," the makers of States receive plenary absolution for anything they have done or may do in their sacred cause.

World historical men—the heroes of an epoch—must, therefore, be recognized as its clear-sighted ones ; their deeds are the best of that time. . . . Great men are egoistical ; they form purposes to satisfy themselves, not others . . . it is possible that such men may treat other great, even sacred, interests inconsiderately ; conduct which is indeed obnoxious to moral reprehension. But so mighty a form must trample down many an innocent flower —crush to pieces many an object in its path. . . . What the absolute aim of the spirit requires and accomplishes—what Providence does—transcends the obligations and the liability to imputation and the ascription of good or bad motives, which attach to individuality in virtue of its social relations. . . . The deeds of great men, who are the individuals of the world's history, appear not only justified in view of that intrinsic result of which they were not conscious, but also from the point of view occupied by the secular moralist. . . . Moral claims that are irrelevant must not be brought into collision with world-historical deeds and their accomplishment. The litany of private virtues—modesty, humility, philanthropy, and forbearance—must not be raised against them.

The heroes of history are beyond good and evil.

A word more must be said about the part which religion—as

distinguished from this general conception of the world-historical spirit—plays in the Hegelian State. Hegel hates the idea of something called religion being invoked to purify and moralize the State. A recall to religion, as it has recently been termed, " an utterance of anguish and a call for help, as it often seems to be, expressing the danger of religion having vanished or being about to vanish entirely from the State—that," he says, " would be fearful indeed," since it implies that the " implantation and inculcation of religion " would be a remedy against the evil alleged, whereas religion is self-produced and cannot be invoked, and has no such function. It is there already in the State and has determined the nature of the State and its constitution. The State is justified by religion, and each State has the religion which is appropriate to it. The Athenian or Roman State was based on the specific form of heathenism existing among their respective peoples ; a Catholic State has a spirit and a constitution different from that of a Protestant. All religions have their times and seasons ; the one thing necessary is a pre-established harmony—to borrow Leibnitz's phrase—between the State and religion.

Lenin said that all revolutions must have a theory, and in the writings of Hegel the German Nazis had a ready-made theory to their hand. The deification of the State, the ascendency of the world-historical hero, his superiority to the home-spun morality of everyday life, the subordination of the individual, and the idea that he gains a higher freedom by absorption in the State, the annexation of art, philosophy, and science by the State ; the intoxicating idea that the divine spirit has decreed a great destiny in a particular State and will give absolution for anything they may do to its leaders and heroes —everything is there down to the smallest details. Nothing that is essential, though much that is silly, has been added to it by subsequent writers. Only in one respect has the doctrine been modified. Hegel seemed to assume a long-existent State which would be the expression of a basic religion ; the Nazi concludes that a special religion must be invented to fit the needs and justify the proceedings of his new-born State.

These ideas are in the strictest sense of the word metaphysical, they are derived not from any contact with what is commonly called experience, but from the philosopher's inner consciousness through a process of self-divination and declared by him to be the truth and the only truth. Nothing could be more dogmatic or less qualified than Hegel's repeated assertion that this is the nature of the cosmic process, and that it has acted, is acting, and will eternally act in this way. The dialectic reveals and proves its necessity, and there is no more to be said about it. His examination of history is not research work leading up to the discovery of historical laws, but a selection of illustrations to show the operation of an already discovered law. Even so, it is extremely difficult reading, as the reader who has struggled with Part IV of his *Philosophy of History*, the part dealing with the " German World," may have discovered.

3

If Hegel had meant only that each stage of history is a resultant of many forces, some of them pulling in opposite directions, his doctrine would have been a mere truism. But he meant a great deal more than this. He meant that by the use of " dialectic " a rhythm or pattern might be discovered which would give form and meaning to history, and within certain limits enable its next stage to be foreseen. Being an idealist with religious instincts, he saw the forces at work as spiritual and history as the unfolding of an immanent spirit. History, thus conceived, was no longer a record of the crimes and follies of man or a tale told by an idiot signifying nothing ; it was far wiser than man ; it had in it the elements both of wisdom and of necessity. Things must have happened as they did happen, and since they happened, they were right. The spirit was infallible, and it owed no account to what mere mortals call " good " and " bad."

We are here in the deep waters of determinism and free-will, and even the greatest are in difficulties when embarked on that sea. The Greeks used the word ἀνάγκη, which in this context may be translated as " brute fact," when thinking of the past. This left the moral judgment in suspense. Having happened, things must be regarded as fated, necessary, inevitable, but whether they ought to have happened or might have been prevented is not brought into question. Dante in seeking to prove, in his *De Monarchia*, that the Roman Empire was ordained by God is driven step by step to the conclusion that, having intended the end, God must have intended the means, the conquests and the extinction of other nations, that it required. But not seldom he seems to be in trouble with this argument ; and when it comes near to making God the author of evil, he speaks of " nature " as the operating factor, nature which must be perfect since it is the work of the Divine intelligence (*natura in nulla perfectione deficit quum sit opus divinæ intelligentiæ*). I think in any case Dante would have drawn a sharp distinction between " intending " and sanctioning or sanctifying the means. He would have said that, though it might be within the divine counsel to let good and evil work together to good conclusions, it was impious to use language which implied that God was the author of evil.

Hegel feels no such difficulty. He seems to deny that the words " good " and " evil " as used by men in their dealings with one another have any meaning in the sphere of statesmanship and state action. In his *Philosophy of History* he goes to the length of saying that *The Prince* of Machiavelli who, as we have seen, was first in the field with the idea of a dual morality—private and public—is " the great and true conception of a real political genius with the highest and noblest intentions." Like Machiavelli, he considers everything justified in the service of the State, not the State conceived as the mere civil government employing police and officials for internal administrative purpose, but as a mystical entity transcending all its parts, raised above its members and claiming their allegiance, service, and so far as that word has meaning, worship. The Greek idea that the purpose of the State is to provide the good life for its citizens is now absolutely reversed. The object of the citizen is to promote the honour and glory of the State. Plato, who said that nothing was to be imputed to God which would be disgraceful to man, would have been shocked at a doctrine which made Nero and Caligula as well as Marcus Aurelius and Diocletian exponents of the " divine idea," but no uneasiness on this point seems to have crossed the mind of this German philosopher.

Hegel at the beginning of the nineteenth century was thinking mainly of Germany—Germany struggling to make some sort of unity out of her numerous states and provinces. The ruling Prussian in those days was not a metaphysician, he was a hard-faced man who cared nothing about the historic spirit or the dialectic. But a doctrine which merged the individual in the State was entirely acceptable to him, and when it descended from the class-room to the camp, he interpreted it as justifying and requiring submission to him and his caste. Those who reflected on the matter must have been puzzled to know what part they were expected to play, for if it was all pre-determined and if whatever happened, historic necessity required it to happen, there seemed on the face of it to be nothing for them to do. But the Hegelian always had it both ways. He ran free will side by side with the absolute, to whom (or which) all events, past, present, and to come, are spread out as on a map ; beside historic determinism he posited an objective will with which he imagined the citizen to be co-operating freely with the historic process. He agreed that this arrangement was puzzling to the understanding, but he brought in another faculty called " reason," which, he said, effected a reconciliation between these opposites.

4

The Hegelian world is as mysterious to the non-metaphysician as is the world of Einstein to those who are innocent of mathematics. It is, nevertheless, an ironical fact that this great mystagogue provided the least imaginative of all ruling castes with exactly the justification they needed for their extremely practical pursuits. The State, as Hegel defined it, raised high above the humble business of keeping order and providing the conveniences of life for its citizens, was bound to be predatory and aggressive. Only in this way could it increase its power and behave in the completely egoistic way that the theory required. A philosophy which provided a moral foundation for organized selfishness and pronounced all things lawful which were supposed to be in the interests of the State found congenial soil in a country which appeared to its neighbours to have made war its national industry. In the works of the philosopher himself a certain mistiness softened the sharp edge of this higher unscrupulousness and made it seem profound and even religious. Presently Darwinism was to be invoked to give it a veneer of scientific support, and war was now said to be a " biological necessity." As it went down the years and was developed by the Treitschkes, the Schlieffens, the

Bernhardis, and in due time by the Mussolinis and Hitlers, it became the background of Nazism and Fascism.

Hegel being mainly concerned with German affairs appears to have given little thought to the kind of world there would be if his doctrine were practised by all the nations. That is inevitably a world of incessant conflict in which the different units acknowledge no law but that of the jungle. Away into space go all the ideas, mystical or practical, for bringing order and unity into the world—City of God, Holy Roman Empire, Napoleonic schemes and dreams. This is the great set-back of modern times. We are now again—or shall be if the Hegelian doctrine prevails—in the state of nature, as Hobbes supposed it to be, with men organized as States playing the same part as individuals in the Hobbesian jungle. In the meantime the development of modern weapons has more than ever made it a question whether under the supposed conditions the life of man can be other than " nasty, brutish, and short."

CHAPTER XXXV

THE AGE OF THE IDEOLOGUES—MARX

I

THE Hegelian *pur sang* having proved that the life of the world was inevitably one of national conflict, it remained for a collateral branch to prove that the life of the nation was inevitably one of class-conflict. The straight descent issued in Nazism and Fascism ; the collateral in Communism and Bolshevism. Between the two all prospects of a life of peace were extinguished. If men were not fighting their enemies abroad, they would have to be fighting their fellow-citizens at home. Hatred, external and internal, would be the law of life and the ruling motive of the human jungle.

Karl Marx, the founder of the collateral branch, took over from Hegel the theory of dialectic ; and the idea of things being involved in an eternal conflict with their opposites seems to have had a peculiar fascination for him. But starting with a strong anti-religious bias, he saw no need for the mystical idea of a spirit at work which Hegel had attached to it ; and by assuming the dialectical process to be a principle embedded in the material nature of things, he swept away all that was spiritual and idealistic in the original philosophy and prepared the way for the attack on religion which has become an essential part of Marxism in practice. The " spirit " which Hegel had imported into history was, in Marx's view, a figment of his imagination, and little better than the God of the orthodox religions. Clear both out of the way, and the true doctrine of economic determinism could be built on a foundation of dialectical materialism, and made self-supporting and self-sufficing without any of the opiates which mystics, capitalists, and priests had invented for the doping of their fellow-beings. If by an inherent necessity, residing in the

329

nature of things, every institution was fated to go on to its doom, there could be no room for God or spirit, or even, one may add, for the mildly benevolent creative evolution of modern philosophy.

Marx is the Calvin of economic theory, and his doctrine raises many of the same problems as the theology of Geneva. The capitalist in the Marxian scheme plays the part of the sinner in the doctrine of Predestination. He is the victim of a fore-ordained process which he is powerless to avert. Neither prayers nor vows nor any virtue on his part will help him. Whatever he does, he must be among the lost on the day of Judgment. One would have thought that this was enough, and that the other classes might look on with a certain sympathy as his doom approached. But just as the Calvinist preachers denounced and castigated the sinners who were so unhappy as to have been excluded from the divine indulgence, so Marx and his disciples visited their wrath on the unregenerate capitalists. Both had the same idea of combining free will and predestination. The Calvinist said that he was co-operating with the divine purpose for the destruction of sinners ; the Marxian that he was promoting the inner nature of things and its preordained purpose by hastening the destruction of capitalists. In this way determinism joined hands with revolutionary activism.

I think it would be possible, if it were worth while, to write a manual of Marxian teleology, eschatology, or whatever it may be called, on parallel lines with the handbooks of Protestant theology which were in vogue in Calvinist circles seventy or eighty years ago. Having eliminated the God of Christian theology, Marx seemed to be driven by some inner compulsion—his daimon, as Socrates would have called it—to discover a principle which would perform the same functions of wrath and punishment as had been attributed to the Christian deity. Objective corroboration was as lacking in the one case as in the other. There was no more proof that Marx's idea of the nature of things corresponded to reality than that the ruler of the universe resembled the God of this Protestant theology. But just in proportion as ideas of this kind lack substance or probability, so is the fanaticism with which the doctrinaires of the sects—religious or economic—defend them against doubters and heretics, and even slightly differing interpretations within their own fold. Having regard to the course which the Marxian revolution has run in Russia, it would, I think, be scarcely an exaggeration to say that as much blood has been shed over shades and shadows of this doctrine in the twenty years of the Russian experiment as in many centuries of the Christian persecution of heretics.

2

Loosely hitched on to the theories of dialectical materialism and economic determinism was Marx's idea of surplus value—the notion that the whole value of a product depended on something called " labour," and therefore ought to be paid back to " labour " and no part of it be annexed, or, as he would say, confiscated, in the form of profit or remuneration, by capitalists. By " labour " he meant manual labour, the labour of the proleteriat as distinguished from that of the " bourgeois." So little of this idea, as expounded in Chapter V of *Das Capital*, has survived criticism that it has become the fashion even with socialist writers to treat it as a comparatively unimportant part of the Marxian creed which may be discarded without hurt to the rest. Those who test political theories by their results in practical affairs can by no means consent to this easy dismissal of it. Judged by its results this part of the Marxian doctrine has been of more potency than all the rest of it put together. Upon it have been founded the denunciation and cruel persecution of the bourgeois. A multitude to whom " economic determinism " was pure mystification understood only too well when they were told they had been robbed and despoiled by employers and their satellites described as " bourgeois." Before the theory of " surplus value " is regarded as dead and disposed of, it must be observed that it has sent hundreds of thousands of innocent persons to their graves. Marx proclaiming that men were being robbed by bourgeois exploiters had the same effect in the twentieth century as Rousseau proclaiming that they were enslaved by tyrants and oppressors had had in the eighteenth. Both were high explosives which required a certain rise in the temperature to make them dangerous. But the explosion came as soon as this temperature was reached, and in both cases with devastating results.

The denial of value to the various services—planning, managing, designing, inventing, organizing—which contribute to the making of things, and may even be said to give value to manual labour, is so obviously nonsensical that his apologists have been reduced to arguing that Marx could not have meant what he quite clearly has said. Some of them even complain of his obstinacy on this point, and put themselves to much trouble to discover small qualifications of his main proposition. But his obstinacy, if that is the right word, is easily intelligible, for an immense part of his superstructure depends on the assumption that there is something collectively called " labour ", to which rightly belongs all that capitalists have appropriated as profit. Hence his elaborate attempts to show that all labour can be reduced to something which he calls " simple labour " or " generalized human labour " by reckoning a small quantity of skilled labour as equal to a larger quantity of " simple labour." This simplification was essential to his doctrine. In this way alone was he able to make a clean-cut division between exploiters and exploited and to present his form of revolution as differing from all others that had preceded it, in that it would once and for all make an end of an exploiting class and place in power the proletariat which was the maker and therefore the rightful owner of wealth. If a distinction had to be drawn between the different contributories to the making of wealth and different rewards assigned to them, this grand simplification would be impossible and the " proletariat," like the bourgeois, be divided up into different degrees of wealth and poverty.

Even more than that, the whole ultimate goal of the " class-less society "—a society in which all social distinctions would be abolished and no man consider himself better than his neighbours—would become impossible. For this especially the equal reward on the basis that everyone contributed equally to the making of wealth was essential. It is true that Marx does not commit himself to any particular method of distributing wealth and that some of his disciples, including Stalin, have under stress of circumstances spoken of the equal sharing of wealth as " the ideal of a petty bourgeois," [1] but it follows from the whole materialist conception of society that class-distinctions must follow from inequality of rewards. The doctrine of " surplus value " points clearly to equality of incomes as its logical

---

[1] Sabine, *op. cit.*, p. 712.

corollary, and it is impossible to believe that Marx did not have it in mind in developing his idea of a class-less society. It is at any rate extremely improbable that a class-less society could be built on an inequality of incomes.

The idea of a " class-less society " is worth some attention, for it throws an interesting light on the development of Marxian theory. It assumes that the dialectical struggle, the conflict between opposites, will some day come to an end, and a triumphant proletariat—free of all the passions and infirmities of the sinful men called capitalists—will be at rest and live peacefully together on a footing of absolute equality. Then government, being no longer necessary, will " wither away " and the dictators, having accomplished their work of wrath and terror, retire gracefully from the scene. Marx himself was somewhat vague about it, but Lenin had no doubt that this too is part of the predestined order,[1] and the promise of it is the answer commonly given by Marxists to those who allege that their creed is one of unrelieved gloom and destruction.

Up to this point it had been claimed that the Marxian theory was " scientific," but no such claim can be made for this development of it. That is unadulterated fiction. No evidence from the past can be adduced to suggest the slightest probability that human society will evolve in this way. It is on the face of it highly improbable that the storm and violence of the years of terror will produce a race of sinless beings, or that the dictators, having done their work, will quietly and gracefully wither away. All history shows violence breeding violence and dictators clinging to power until they are displaced by other claimants to power.

Yet I confess to finding in this fiction one of the chief redeeming features of the Marxian doctrine. It is as though the Marxist could not bear the unrelieved gloom of his own story of violence and slaughter. Like a romantic novelist who has dragged his hero and heroine through scenes of death and terror, he *must* have a happy ending. When his lambs have exterminated the lions they will at last lie down together. There is a pleasant touch of irony in the

---

[1] Interesting evidence on this point will be found in *Unto Cæsar*, by F. A. Voigt, Ch. I.

fact that after all his derision of religious ideas, his own millennium should so greatly resemble the Christian apocalypse in which there shall be no more war and a little child shall lead them.

3

Marxian writers go in and out and round and round the writings of their master in a strenuous endeavour to discover what he meant and whether what they suppose him to have meant is logically and metaphysically watertight. But very few of them seem to think it worth while to ask whether these theories have any foundation in fact. Are they, to put it crudely, true or false? In his invaluable history of political theory, Professor Sabine, after devoting the utmost pains to disentangling the various shades and phases of Marxism, comes to the conclusion that its central doctrine is a mystical and unverifiable hypothesis. " The question raised by dialectical materialism," is, he says, " whether dialectic in any form was a real scientific method, and whether an unconditional law of historical development is a tenable conception. At the present time both logic and science seem inclined to answer these questions negatively." [1] One is tempted to say that if logic and science are right, all this trouble about what Marx means is as remote from reality as any scholastic debate about chimæras booming in the void or angels dancing on the points of needles.

But the new fashion which has replaced Marx on the pedestal from which he was deposed by Victorian critics has a strong hold on modern metaphysical economists, and it is only one of the elders who can venture to say that there is not a scintilla of proof for the greater part of his theory, and least of all for the economic fatalism with which it has darkened the mind of the rising generation. Nearly everything that Marx predicted has proved untrue, when tested by the experience of the subsequent years. If the rich have become richer, the poor have not become poorer; wealth has not become concentrated in fewer and fewer hands, but distributed over a wider and wider area; the class conflict has not been an active principle in any nation; it is rather the too-ardent national unity with which modern statesmanship

---

[1] Sabine, *op. cit.*, Ch. XXXII.

has to deal. The one revolution which has taken place has little or no resemblance to the Marxian idea of the revolt of an industrial proletariat against its capitalist masters. It was an imported revolution imposed on a peasant people by a group of professional revolutionaries in the chaos following war.[1] The truth is that capitalism, the name by which we call the prevalent means of production, distribution, and exchange, is not a " system " invented by a few individuals, but a gradual development of constantly changing forms to which all the nations and all classes have contributed. Being a combination of human devices and expedients it is of course open to every sort of criticism, and it may be only the primitive stage of an evolution which will take us eventually to one or other of the Utopias now dreamt of, but the idea that it is doomed to an inevitable revolutionary cataclysm is unsupported by either evidence or probability.

The historian of political theory can go on to trace the differences between Marxism, Leninism, and Stalinism, and the different techniques by which the doctrine has been administered to the Russian people, and pursue his theme in the vacuum which is suited to scientific research. But those who are interested in practical affairs can scarcely be indifferent to the cost in life and suffering that the application of this doctrine has involved or to the merciless extermination of one another practised by the original theorists in their pursuit of the true faith. It would be far beyond the scope of this book to decide between the different versions of the Russian experiment in its present stage, but one thing is evident. It has owed little or nothing to the founder of the sect. Marx, as one of his disciples has said, " omitted to supply the blue-print of reconstruction." He could teach his disciples how to destroy, but he could not tell them how to rebuild. In the absence of instructions, the attempt to build Socialism on the ruins of Tsarism has been an endless improvisation, in which great failures and remarkable achievements have produced a result that has little or no relation to the original Communist theory. So at least it seems to the

---

[1] Engineers tunnelling under a river have sometimes to create the bed through which they drive their tunnel by throwing in masses of clay. Precisely so had Lenin and his co-revolutionaries to industrialize the Russian peasant people before the country could become suitable ground for the Marxian experiment.

observer from without ; but, if we may believe the sympathetic historians of the movement, the result is a "new civilization " devised by scientific experts whose plans it is treason and " defeatism " to question or criticize—or would be if they did not so often question and criticize one another. Political experiments on this scale are assuredly of profound interest, but most of them are by this time extremely remote from the original doctrine.

4

Marx's biographers lay special stress on the fact that he took no interest in the dreams of an ideal order in which socialists of the Robert Owen and William Morris school indulged their fancy. He disliked Utopias and would have it understood that he was no sentimentalist. But this attitude seems to have cloaked the fact that he gave hardly any thought to what would follow the revolution he predicted. Here too he seems to have been obsessed with his idea of necessity. Having once made up his mind that socialism was the opposite to capitalism —in itself by no means a necessary conclusion—determinism decreed that it should follow the overthrow of capitalism, and there was no more to be said about it, except to throw out the nebulous and entirely intuitional idea of a class-less society. As a revolutionary tactician, Marx was well justified in avoiding all details about reconstruction. He knew enough of international revolutionaries to be aware that any attempt to define Socialism would produce the schisms and quarrels which have attended all such attempts in subsequent years. To concentrate on the destruction of capitalism and leave the consequences to be dealt with when they arose was good strategy for the apostle of revolution.

But this has had the unhappy result of leading large numbers of his followers to speak and think of destruction as if it were an end in itself. When to this is added the apocalyptic thought that it is all written in the book of doom, we have the germ of an idea which easily becomes an unreasoning fanaticism in men and women of a certain temperament.

5

The one point on which the Marxian challenge to orthodox economics appears to have substance is its criticism of the belief that supply and demand can be relied upon to effect an automatic balance between production and consumption. Given sufficient time, this belief would probably still be justified, but with foreign markets severely restricted by tariffs and quotas, modern machine production may pile up its output beyond the capacity of consumption at home or sale abroad, and so produce depressions requiring longer time for automatic adjustment than any Government concerned for the welfare of its subjects can contemplate with patience. Whether this situation can be met by unemployment insurance or by taxation transferring spending power to the mass of consumers ; whether, and if so, in what degree it requires State control of industry ; whether there are any monetary measures which might relieve the situation—all these are questions in active debate and experiment, and likely to remain so for many years to come.

But the Marxian theory that capitalist Governments make war in order to find outlets for their excess products has neither fact nor probability behind it. If either buying or selling must be considered as if it were an object in itself, there are many modern nations to which it is even more important to buy from other countries than to sell to them. Their merchant adventurers and foreign traders have by many centuries of activity supplied them with a variety of products which by long custom and use have become necessaries of life. To maintain and expand these supplies has become for all nations highly desirable and for some an absolute necessity, and would remain so whether their form of government was capitalist or socialist, imperialist or pacifist. There is nothing specifically capitalist in activities of this kind, nor even in the desire to discover new markets, for that also might very well be the object of a communist Government, say Russia in the Far East. It may be said with truth that a large number, perhaps the majority, of wars recorded in history had economic objects—the acquisition of wealth or territory supposed to be rich and the like—and it need not at all be denied that the organized Protectionism of modern times increases the causes of friction between nations. But this is very different from the supposition that capitalist Governments deliberately make war to obtain outlets for excess products. In a perfect capitalist world most of the obstacles which have caused products to be in excess would be swept away.

6

No one would deny that Marx's *Das Capital* contains a formidable indictment of English industrialism eighty years ago, or that in so far as it has contributed to the awareness of poverty which is one of the redeeming features of recent time, it has had great and salutary influence. All the middle parts of *Das Capital*—the chapters on the "Working Day," "Labour and Manufacture," "Large Scale Industry"—are a scathing record of a period in which the captains of industry had slithered into the evolution of the machine age with little thought for the human material which they had thrown into it. It is fair, however, to observe that the evidence on which Marx relies is mainly that of British documents prepared by British officials who testify unflinchingly to the evils attending the rush into industrialism. These documents are evidence of an awakening of the public conscience even at this period. But Marx's chapters have a permanent value as a protest on behalf of the dignity and worth of the individual human against those who classed him as a commodity caught up with other commodities in the grinding of the machine and the higgling of the market. Though he would no doubt have repudiated the suggestion, it is nevertheless the truth that the moral, spiritual, and even the religious elements which he has deliberately extruded from his philosophy are at the back of this part of the book, and the chief explanation of the influence it has had.

That Marx had in this sense a good and powerful influence should never be forgotten, but after all it is the great Marxian myth, which, like the great Hegelian myth, has shaken the world. This is the main fact to be faced and we cannot shirk it. Great myths do not obtain a hold over masses of people without reflecting in some sense their moods and aspirations. Both Marxism and Fascism—as in a previous generation Rousseauism—have expressed the combination of discontent with idealism which is always present in human nature, and which flares into active life when misery has become intolerable or war has brought confusion to the normal life. At such a moment the multitude turns on its rulers and demands to know why they have failed in their task, and where it may look for salvation. Then the scriptures are searched for signs and portents and the myth-maker is hailed as the saviour. He may have been long dead. He may, like Rousseau and Hegel and Marx, have evolved his myths from his inner consciousness without contact with government or politics ; he may have died peacefully in his bed with no presentiment of the nature of the explosive which he was bequeathing to a subsequent generation ; his myth might, like scores of other myths, have remained cold and dead, if some rise in the temperature had not brought it to its flash-point. But when that point is reached, it is not its truth or falsity but its emotional appeal which causes it to explode. It was not true that men were born free and were afterwards enslaved, but to assert it as a fact was to kindle a multitude to the belief that they were in chains which they had the power, if they had the will, to strike off. It was not true that capitalism had created poverty, but to proclaim it as unquestionable truth was to arouse millions of poor men to a sense of their poverty, and concentrate their anger on sinful men called capitalists. It was a fantastic notion that the German State or any other embodied the " divine idea," but only by getting it believed could the totalitarian State be presented as an object of worship. It needs both courage and egotism, such as only a few of the great myth-makers have possessed, to take a myth and declare it to be the truth and the only truth. But this is essential if it is to perform its purpose. The author of the myth and his followers must be as men possessed, and the appearance on their territory of a counter-myth must rouse them to a fury of persecution. Then and then only will fanaticism do its perfect work. It may hereafter be said that the first half of the twentieth century was the age of political, just as the first half of the sixteenth century was that of religious, fanaticism.

CHAPTER XXXVI

THE AGE OF THE IDEOLOGUES—FASCISM AND NAZISM

I

I HAVE spoken about the parentage of Fascism and Nazism, but something more remains to be said about their modern developments.

These had a Russian source. Bolshevism was no mere local revolution. It claimed to be a universal doctrine of salvation to be preached by missionaries who, like the Christian Apostles, were to go out into all the world. Openly and deliberately the Soviet Government avowed its intention to undermine the Governments of its capitalist neighbours by stirring up disaffection in their countries and seducing soldiers and sailors from their allegiance. Its organization, the Comintern, was the nearest approach to the Society of Jesus seen in modern times, and it worked by the same combination of secrecy and advertisement as made that famous religious order both feared and hated. Its general intentions were openly proclaimed, its method was the secret inoculation of the various bodies politic with the germ or virus of its revolutionary creed. It was so organized that the central authority could at the same time disavow responsibility for its proceedings and continue to support it by liberal subsidies.

The fear of revolution was widespread in the years following the Great War. Germany had had her own experience of it in the upheaval which dethroned the Hohenzollerns; most of the other defeated countries were in a state of confusion which made a ready soil for agitators and conspirators; even the victorious were in the difficult state of transition from war to peace and had large discontented elements which were embittered by the failure of the promises made to them during the war. The effort to set up Parliamentarism on the British model in countries which had no experience of that form of government encountered unexpected difficulties, especially

340

in the Succession States. In many countries Left-wing politicians found it impossible to agree to the modest extent necessary to enable them to co-operate in the keeping of law and order.

Working on these conditions the Bolshevist propaganda had great success in spreading the fear of revolution, but scarcely any in producing revolution. Almost everywhere it came up against the fear of disorder which in modern Europe, as formerly in ancient Greece, has provided the opportunity for tyranny. Saviours of society began to appear offering peace and security for life and property on condition that the multitude placed itself in their hands and gave up the habit, which had proved so fatal in the Liberal and democratic States, of busying themselves with politics and quarrelling about them. Let them put themselves in the hands of a leader who knew how to keep order and all would be well. It has been much debated whether Mussolini saved Italy from anarchy or whether the Parliamentarians had done that before he appeared on the scene. The point is of no great importance. What is certain is that from the year 1919 onwards he successfully exploited the fear of anarchy and by a series of clever manœuvres obtained control of the armed power of the State, before resistance had time to develop.

Mussolini had the great advantage of being an ex-revolutionary who knew the technique of revolution by heart. He decided that, if having gained power he was to remain in power, he must, like Lenin, have a theory which also could be preached as a gospel of salvation. To the dictatorship of the proletariat he would oppose a reincarnation in the Italian people of the glory that was Rome symbolized by the fasces, the bundle of rods with the axe projecting from them—image of the power whereby criminals were scourged and executed—that the lictors carried, like the mace-bearer preceding the mayor, before the Consul when he walked in procession. Discipline and obedience were now the watchwords equally of Bolshevism and its rival, Fascism, but whereas the Bolshevist conceived of himself as the agent of a world-wide revolution, the Fascist was to be the ardent devotee of his own nation and fired with the ambition to restore what he believed to be its hereditary Empire. Mussolini thus presented himself not as a vulgar adventurer seeking power, but as a man of destiny walking in the footsteps of the Imperial Cæsars, who appeared in the nick of time to save his country from anarchy and lead it through discipline and self-denial to a new glory.

The Greeks had said that tyranny was a suitable form of government only for those who were by nature slaves, but thus dressed up it was made to appear as the leadership of a great people reaching forward to achievements worthy of them. By contrast Mussolini painted in the coarsest colours the plight of the unhappy peoples given over to Parliamentarism and democratic anarchy. Liberalism and liberty were "rotting corpses," Parliamentarism the effete superstition of a brief and rapidly passing phase. Here he joined hands with the Russian dictator of the proletariat, and audaciously borrowed from him the pattern of the modern kind of totalitarian tyranny, that of an executive claiming to control and regulate the whole of life. As in Russia, so in Italy there was to be only one party, the party of the dictator, and all opposition to it and criticism of it was to be branded as treason and defeatism. As in Russia, so in Italy irreconcilable opponents were to be "liquidated"; in both countries alike strikes and labour agitation were to be sternly suppressed, the free press to be exterminated, and the public, as far as possible, protected from the infection of foreign ideas. In both there was set up the immemorial apparatus of despotism, the secret police, the informer, the spy, seizure and imprisonment, even death and exile, at the discretion of the executive. As in Russia, so in Italy children were to be instructed in the new ideology as soon as they began to lisp, and taught how to carry arms before they were out of the nursery. In glowing rhetoric the leader sang the praises of war and poured contempt on dotards and weaklings who prated of peace. Cicero had said that though other nations might endure slavery, liberty was "the inalienable possession of the Roman people." In the modern Rome Mussolini spoke of liberty as an object of ridicule.

To the cool northern peoples it seemed incredible that crowds should be roused to enthusiasm by the rhetoric in which the Italian leader indulged. They said that if any of their own politicians should venture to talk to them in this strain, they would conclude that he had gone out of his mind. But Mussolini understood the southern temperament of his own people and he knew exactly how to appeal to them. There are touches of the nursery and the cinema in his proceedings which claim our indulgence. It is even possible to believe that he sometimes has his tongue in his cheek. But as time passed and he still remained in the saddle, it had to be admitted that he was a man of great ability who had thought out every move in his game. He next appeared as a social reformer with large and ambitious plans for modernizing his ancient country.

Slums were demolished, great roads built, swamps drained, scientific agriculture introduced. Trains were punctual ; beggars were driven off the streets. The country was poor, but with strikes forbidden and labour at his disposal, much could be accomplished at small cost. Travellers coming into the country and speeding along its new motor-roads concluded that miracles had been accomplished ; and if a few shook their heads and lamented the defacement of the Italy they knew, these were easily dismissed as sentimental laggards behind the time. Fascism took the wind out of the sails of democracy by proclaiming itself to be modern and progressive beyond all other progressives. Nor could it be denied that a great deal of genuine patriotism and zeal for the welfare of the country had been enlisted in its service. There was much talk of a new form of government, the " corporative state " providing through guilds and corporations for the self-government of industry and commerce, subject to the supreme control of the Duce. This was said to be the modern substitute for Parliament, but what it did and how far it was permitted to function was always very difficult to ascertain.

The Russians had had to borrow a prophet from Germany ; Mussolini found one in his own countryman, Machiavelli. He was a close student—or so it was reported—not only of *The Prince* but of the *Discourses* and *Dispatches* of the great Italian. From these he learnt the ways of " wheedling or destroying " his opponents, and the necessity of rising above the common morality in the government of States. Machiavelli in his *Discourses* had been specially urgent that the leader who set about to restore a State should be in sole possession of power and be careful that his authority should not be divided or the prestige and glitter associated with it be shared by others. For the sixteen years since he came to power no name but Mussolini's has ever been associated with the Italian movement. The King remains on a nominal throne, but to all outward seeming in much the same position as a Merovingian King when Charles Martel or Pepin was Mayor of the Palace.[1]

In the free countries a critical press affords their neighbours the means of judging whether their forms of government give satisfaction to their peoples. In the dictatorships this judgment has for some years past depended on travellers' tales or the reports of exiles and fugitives. All such reports differ beyond reconciliation. According to some, life in Italy is orderly and happy as never before ; the cheering crowds which follow the Duce and acclaim his speeches feel a genuine emotion ; the pomp and glitter of the regime, the shows so liberally provided for them have enlivened their existence and given them exactly what their southern temperaments need. Their free institutions had never been popular or their politicians respected ; they have felt no sense of loss and a very lively sense of gain. According to other reports, all this was on the surface ; the regime was but a glittering façade. Behind it was poverty and discontent growing in proportion as extravagance and foreign adventures exhausted the wealth of the country and reduced its standard of living. Fear and suspicion, which reduced people to whispering in their own homes for fear of spies and informers, were said to be widespread ; the rich and middle classes wondered whether they could have suffered more from the anarchy from which the regime was supposed to have saved them than from the appropriation of their property and investments practised under various disguises by these saviours. Distinguished men were in exile and grim stories were told of the fate which had befallen critics and suspects, of their sudden disappearance or consignment without trial to the prison islands, even of being kidnapped or killed on foreign soil.

The regime hardly took the trouble to deny these stories. These, according to its theory, were the necessary methods of an efficient executive. To let its authority be questioned or its doctrine criticized was a folly in which Liberals and sentimentalists might indulge, but which no proud nation conscious of its destiny could afford. In the totalitarian State minorities could be tolerated only on condition that they kept their opinions to themselves.

---

[1] An Italian assures me that the King of Italy has much greater influence than is commonly realized in foreign countries.

2

There were now two great States practising the totalitarian doctrine and enforcing the submission of all to one leader and one party. Within ten years a third was added to them, and liberty and democratic government were now extinguished in half Europe.

The German Nazi Revolution had certain points in common with the Italian. Italy had been among the victorious nations in the Great War, but she considered that she had suffered serious injustice in the partition of the spoils. One of Mussolini's most effective grounds of appeal to his countrymen was his promise to obtain for them in other ways what his ineffective Parliamentary predecessors had failed to secure by negotiation at the Peace Conference. Still more appealing was Hitler's promise to restore Germany to her former proud position after the years of disillusion and mortification following her defeat in the war. Her former enemies had spared her no humiliation ; her Parliamentarians had tamely accepted the intolerable idea of " treaty-fulfilment," and cherished vain dreams of reconciliation with enemies to whom they owed nothing but revenge. A proud people needed proud and defiant leadership. After long and skilful underground preparation, Hitler came offering to play the part.

Whether he would have succeeded by the patriotic appeal alone may reasonably be doubted, but he too, like Mussolini, had on his side a widespread and genuine fear of Communism on which he and his followers worked without scruple or remorse. This came to its climax in the firing of the Reichstag, which was immediately proclaimed as having been the signal for a Red revolution which would have destroyed the country if there had not been a strong man at hand to quench the flames. Once more it was said that Parliamentarism had proved unequal to dealing with anarchy, and the destruction of its place of meeting appeared to millions of simple people as a symbolic event which, by an almost miraculous intervention in the nick of time, had cleared the ground for a new edifice.

Finally, Hitler, like Mussolini, had at his hand a head of the State who was ready to play the same part as the King of Italy, and prepare the way for him at the critical moment. Hindenburg, though greatly respected for his military achievements, was advanced in years and wholly without experience of politics conducted in Hitler's way. Being a Junker and an extreme agrarian Conservative, he no doubt genuinely believed in the imminence of a Communist revolution.

The Communists, meanwhile, had contributed largely by making difficulties for the other parties to prevent the success of Parliamentarism in Germany. If in nothing else, Bolshevist, Fascist, and Nazi joined hands in their detestation of Parliamentary government. All alike aimed at dictatorship of one kind or another. Their cry was all or nothing. There was to be no party but their party ; no will but their will. Compromise, adjustment, consideration for opponents and critics were the resources of weaklings in doubt about their own aims and principles. They had no doubts ; they knew the truth, and by virtue of this inspiration claimed to control the entire lives of all their fellow-citizens. Their States were totalitarian ; personal rights, political liberties, representative institutions had no place in any of them.

3

As in Russia and Italy, so again in Germany the new institutions were purely ideological. They owed nothing to custom and usage, time and growth. They were a compound of theories, instincts, and intuitions which have been seething in the brains of German metaphysicians and theorists from the time of Frederick the Great. No other country has produced anything quite like the literature of self-assertion and self-admiration which, starting with Fichte, found expression in a long series of German writers up to the eve of the Great War. In composing his book, *Mein Kampf*, which is to the Nazi what *Das Capital* is to the Communist, Hitler had an enormous mass of material to draw upon, and the resulting product is rather what theologians call a syncretism, borrowings from a great many different sources, than an original inspiration. But in one respect he gives a new trend to the doctrine. He takes up and assigns a central position to anti-Semitism as expounded by the Germanized Englishman, Houston Stewart Chamberlain, in his notorious book, *The Foundations of the Nineteenth Century*, published in 1901. In Hitler's hands hatred of Jews becomes not merely a fanaticism but a positive obsession. The Jews, in Hitler's eyes, are the authors of all evil. They poison the race, they frustrate all honest politics ; even when they seem to be on opposite sides, they are working together in the same underground conspiracy to destroy the Gentile world. The rich Jewish financier is a Bolshevist in disguise ; he is working on parallel lines with the Moscow revolutionaries to substitute a soul-destroying internationalism for the healthy and inspiring life of the race-pure nations. Even when the argument seems to be proceeding to a cool and rational conclusion, it is suddenly broken to drag in the Jew.

Anti-Judaism is thus the major premise of this extraordinary book. From this starting-point Hitler proceeds to build up the hypothesis of a pure race with which the Jew is in eternal enmity, as the powers of darkness with the powers of light. Hence the supposed " Aryan " of whom Hitler gives an extremely confused and inconsistent account. The Aryan, we are told in one of the earlier chapters, " renounced the purity of his own blood, and with it his right to stay in the Eden which he had created for himself. He sank, overwhelmed in the mixing of races, and by degrees lost for ever his capacity for civilization until he began to resemble the subjected aboriginal race more than his father had done, both in mind and body. For a time he could still enjoy the blessings of civilization, but first indifference set in, and finally oblivion." Yet this being who has been overwhelmed in the mixing of races miraculously reappears in the subsequent chapters as the incarnation of human culture reaching perfection in the modern German. By this time the blameless Aryan has become a necessary foil to the evil Jew, and imagination runs riot over the superb physical and moral qualities of this imaginary being and the necessity of defending them by ruthless measures against the racial poison of Judaism.

Once more we see a myth coming suddenly to unexpected and dangerous life. Comte de Gobineau, the Frenchman who was the author of this myth [1] and Houston Stewart Chamberlain, his disciple, who had transformed it into the gospel of an anti-Jewish German Nationalism, had come and gone, and their theories had been treated as curiosities of literature which would not bear the scrutiny of science or any serious examination. Chamberlain's

---

[1] *The Inequality of Human Races,* by Count Arthur Gobineau, English trans. by Oscar Levy.

book especially, with its proof that Jesus Christ was not a Jew,[1] had been derided almost everywhere outside Germany, but there, after an interval, it found the requisite conditions to convert it into a high explosive with shattering results. Under the influence of this fanaticism Hitler effected a subtle change in the Hegelian doctrine which had made the State an object of worship for its own sake. The State was now the frame within which the race-pure nation sought self-expression, and it was this race-pure nation to which all service and devotion were due. Men and women of the German race were to submit themselves to physical culture, like Spartans in ancient times, in order to be worthy of it ; they were to guard the blood from foreign, and above all from Jewish, contamination ; they were to think with their blood and not with their brains—which for practical purposes seemed to mean that they were not to think at all. Contempt for book-learning and intellectualism and unbounded belief in mob-oratory and loud-speaking as the method of the leader are in fact explicit in Hitler's book.

With these emendations Nazism carried forward the old Prussian doctrine of the State. " If," says Hitler, " we ask ourselves what the forces are which make and maintain States, we find that they come under one single denomination : ability and readiness to sacrifice the individual for the sake of the community." It is admitted that in order to imbue the individual with readiness to sacrifice himself for the community economic measures must be taken to improve the lot of the poor, hence in its own peculiar sense Nazism is also Socialism. But subject to this, the stress is laid on force, ruthlessness, intolerance, fanaticism, the absolute ascendency of one man, one party, one doctrine, and the crushing out of any rival personalities or doctrines, especially the deadly heresy of Parliamentarism. There is no need to apologize for using violent expressions in describing this ideology, for they are all used by Hitler himself and are evidently regarded by him as indicating the qualities which distinguish his system from the weak and inferior types of democracy and Parliamentarism. Again and again he returns to the analogy of the Roman Church with its Pope

---

[1] *The Foundations of the Nineteenth Century*, by Houston Stewart Chamberlain, English trans., Vol. I, pp. 201 *et seq.*

and its infallible doctrine beyond argument or compromise. That and nothing short of it is the model for the government of States.

4

It does not appear to have been perceived at the beginning that this doctrine was bound to bring the State into conflict with religion. But that, too, was the logical and necessary result of the totalitarian theory which claimed supremacy for the State in all the activities of life, regardless of the supposed distinction between secular and spiritual. The totalitarian State required a special art, a special science, a special law, and above all a special religion to correspond with its ideology. Within a very few months of the triumph of Nazism, the Hegelian idea that the State should have a religion which expressed its attitude to things in general (Weltanschauung) came to life, and busy brains were at work devising a special " German Christianity " in conformity with the race and blood doctrine and the moral and physical qualities required by the State. The main object was to exclude from this amended creed all that the Nazis regarded as weak and unvirile—the cult of peace, humility, charity, forbearance—in the commonly accepted versions of the Christian religion, and to formulate a new body of doctrine—a virile and patriotic national doctrine—in which children were to be brought up. Christianity, like Communism, had been an international doctrine ; and if it was to survive in Germany it had to be a specifically German creed.

This brought the State into conflict not only with the Roman Church but with a small and stubborn body of the Protestant Confessional Churches which refused to accept the revised creed or to pledge themselves to " refrain from politics," which meant to keep silence about the persecution of the Jews and other un-Christian activities, as they held them to be, of the German State. For the rest of the world, this controversy was symbolized in the persecution of Pastor Niemöller. Millions in other countries saw being fought out in the concentration camp in which this brave man was confined the supreme question whether States were to be absolved from what had hitherto been regarded as " common Christianity," that is from the ideas of right and wrong, justice and mercy which are held binding between man and man.

5

My purpose here is to examine the ideas behind the prevailing European systems rather than to enter into details about their methods of government. These are liable to so many changes and improvisations that almost anything that could be written at one moment is likely to be out of date before it is printed. In general it may be said that we see Fascism and Communism starting from different bases but gradually converging on the same methods and conclusions. Russia having exterminated her bourgeois is obliged to set up an official and managing class which in virtue of its better pay and position gradually fills the position of the old middle class. At the same time the necessity of paying differential wages and bonuses to workmen in proportion to their skill and output leads to a new grading of the proletariat which relegates the idea of a class-less society to a dimmer and dimmer future. The control of the greater industries, formerly in the hands of capitalists, remains in the hands of the State, but whether this can resist the tendency which elsewhere turns men into capitalists in proportion as they are able to save is an unsettled question.

In Italy and Germany revolutions which were intended to save capitalists from the assaults of the proletariat resulted in placing them more and more under the control of the State. In all these countries " planning " became the watchword, planning spread over periods of years, originally with the intention of bringing order into the supposed chaotic life of individual enterprise by instituting great public works, but gradually under stress of circumstances becoming more and more concentrated on military purposes and the manufacture of armaments. The extreme stress which the Fascist ideologues laid on valour and power as the measure of national greatness, their fear of Communism, and the fear which they inspired in Communists led inevitably to this result and eventually involved all the great Powers in a ruinous competition in armaments. State control grew tighter and less and less scope was left to individual enterprise and private profit-seeking as this situation developed. Capitalists were heard saying that it made little difference to them whether the system under which they were working was called Communist or Fascist. At the same time the idea of autarky or self-sufficiency, to render States self-supporting in time of war and proof against the "sanctions" of the League of Nations at other times, gained ground among the Fascist Powers. In Germany especially immense ingenuity was spent in finding home-made substitutes for imported products, and exchange control gave the Government a tight grip upon foreign trade.

In these and other ways Europe in these years was moving farther away from the idea of a family of nations helping to supply each other's needs and co-operating for each other's benefit. National sovereignty was now pushed to lengths which forbade this reciprocity.

6

The ideas on which Nazism is based are comparatively simple, but since the new regime came to power a group of German jurists and philosophers have elaborated them into a body of doctrine which is as mystical and obscure as the corresponding German product, the doc-trines of Marx. This also needs a brief examination, but that is no easy matter, since many of the words used by these writers have no exact equivalents in the English language, and some of their thoughts seem to be beyond the reach of the English mind.

The Germans, like the Russians, claim to have a "constitution" (Verfassung), though everything contained in it seems to be the negation of what an Englishman regards as "constitutional." The Russian with its apparatus of Councils and Parliaments,[1] presents the same paradox, for the qualifications attached to it that there shall be only one party and that opposition to it is a "counter-revolutionary" crime which may be punished with death, seem to nullify everything that an Englishman regards as Parliamentary and deliberative. But whereas it is conceivable that if debates arise within the one party the Russian apparatus may provide a bridge by which Russia may return to Parliamentary government, no such possibility is left open in the German "Constitution." That is said to close the door once and for all upon any return to Liberalism or Parliamentarism. It is declared without qualification that any sharing of his responsibility

---

[1] The constitution promulgated in 1936.

by the Führer with any deliberative body or any other authority whatever is contrary to the National Socialist idea.

But the Führer, we are asked to believe, is no ordinary despot using his subjects as his footstool. He is leader and spokesman of the *Volk*—a German word which embraces both people and race, the Germans outside as well as within Germany, and may be stretched to cover all the peoples of Teutonic stock. The *Volk* is supposed to have a subconscious collective soul or will which in a mystical way has become embodied in the Führer, who interprets it and gives it infallible expression, just as the Pope interprets the doctrine of the Catholic Church. The English words "leader" and "leadership" fail to express this idea. Hitler is not, like Stalin, a dictator, nor like Mussolini, the chief official of his State, and still less is he in our sense of the word the mere leader of a National party. He is the incarnation of the Volk will and the Volk soul ; all the individuals composing the Volk attain a mystical unity in him and through him ; he is the essence of themselves, and loyalty and obedience to him are therefore not slavery or submission to a tyrant but loyalty and obedience to themselves. Hegel started this train of thought when he declared the State to be " the divine idea " embracing and absorbing all its members ; the Nazi theorists carry it a step farther and discover the divine idea incarnated in one man. " Heil Hitler " is no mere salute to an eminent man : it is an invocation of the soul of the race incarnate in him.

On one side the doctrine resembles Tibetan Lamaism, on another it is pure British Hobbes. Let me revert to the famous passage from the *Leviathan* quoted in a previous chapter :

By this authority given him by every particular man in the Commonwealth he hath the use of so much power and strength conferred on him, that by terror thereof he is enabled to form the wills of them all, to peace at home and mutual aid against their enemies abroad. And in him consisteth the essence of the Commonwealth which (to define it) is One person, of whose acts a multitude, by mutual covenants one with another, have made themselves every one the author, to the end that he may use the strength and means of them all, as he shall think expedient, for their peace and common defence.

And he that carrieth this Person is called Sovereign, and said to have Sovereign power ; and everyone besides his subject.[1]

---

[1] See *supra*, p. 247.

Substitute "*Volk*" for "Commonwealth" in this passage, and we have exactly the Nazi doctrine of the Führer. In him consisteth the essence of the *Volk*. To him by authority of the *Volk* has been given so much power and strength that by "terror thereof he is enabled to form the will of them all." Just as the supposed contract between the multitude and Hobbes's Sovereign is irrevocable, when once made, so is the contract between Volk and Führer. If the people were to repent and depose him by plebiscite, the leader could override their repentance and continue in office. He defends, if need be, "the objective idea of the nation against the subjective arbitrary will of mistaken popular opinion." He may hold an election, but if so, the object is only to give him a vote of confidence and strengthen his hands in foreign affairs.[1] If the people should go against him he would not be bound by the result. He could carry out a measure which they condemned and override a measure which they approved. He is "the supreme Judge of the German people," and judges are of necessity subject to his will, since it "expresses the supreme law of justice."[2] The rights of individuals as laid down in the Liberal Weimar Constitution are, therefore, not, as the supreme Court appears to have assumed in the early days of the new regime, merely suspended for the time being, but abolished for all time, since they are not compatible with the new national philosophy. It follows that the individual's right to liberty in his relation to the State was extinguished

---

[1] All these ideas will be found elaborately set out by Prof. Huber in his book *Verfassung*, which ranks as an authoritative exposition of Nazi doctrine. According to Huber (*Verfassung: p. 95*) elections take place in Nazi Germany only to show the unity "zwischen dem im Führer verkörperten objectiven Volkswillen und der in den Volksangehörigen lebendigen subjectiven Volksüberzeugung" (between the objective people's will embodied in the Führer and the living subjective race-conviction belonging to the people).

[2] This idea of a new kind of justice called "revolutionary justice," which was not to secure justice for the individual or to protect him from wrong, but to promote the interests of the "revolutionary State," was first heard of during the notorious Russian trials. In the Nazi literature it is definitely laid down as the new principle of German law. Thus in virtue of his supremacy over law and his guardianship of the National Socialist idea, the Führer was exercising a power belonging to him when he confined Pastor Niemöller in a Concentration Camp after his acquittal by a jury.

with the triumph of National Socialism, for " all such liberties are irreconcilable with the principles of the national (völkisch) Reich." Nazi lawyers are agreed that there is no individual freedom which the State is bound to respect. The individual, they lay down, " has no rights apart from his function as part of the State." In the Nazi State " there are no isolated individuals, only community members who are organic parts of the whole, who are included in the totality of the political nation and united in its common operations as parts of the whole." [1] Similarly the individual cannot be permitted to go his own wilful way in art, literature or science. All activity in any of these spheres must conform to the Nazi philosophy of life as interpreted by the leader. The German writers ransack the language to find words which will express their sense of the leader's power. It is exclusive, original, universal, irresistible, independent, inalienable and unrestricted.

The idea of an infallible Sovereign for whom law is superfluous, which Plato broached in the *Politicus* but abandoned in the *Laws*, here comes to life and obtains an even wider extension than any contemplated by exponents of the Divine right of Kings in Tudor, Stuart or Restoration England.

7

Difficult as it may be for an Englishman to understand this doctrine he would regard it as concerning only the Germany people and its ruler, if it were not for a certain vagueness about the boundaries within which it is supposed to operate. Apparently it is an integral part of the German theory that all Germans, wherever they are domiciled, owe an allegiance to something variously described as the German *Volk* or the " greater Germany," expressions which may be expanded to take in almost any " Nordic " race. But if so, Germans living abroad would be playing precisely the part that the German himself attributes to the Jews—they would form a nation within other nations, and, in virtue of the loyalty which they owed to their *Volk*, be under

---

[1] *Verfassung, p.* 213. *See also* on this subject, Carl Schmitt, *Staat, Bewegung, Volk* ; Heinz Brauweiler, *Sozialverwaltung.* For critical examinations of Nazi philosophy, *Unto Cæsar* by F. A. Voigt, and Aurel Kolnai's, *The War Against the West* are invaluable studies.

an obligation to work for its interests, when these clashed with or were hostile to those of their adopted country. It would be grossly unfair to suppose that all Germans living in foreign countries are infected with this idea, but enough have proclaimed themselves ardent converts to it to produce unrest over a wide area.

There could hardly be a greater complication than this of the already difficult minority problems of Europe, for it inevitably makes other Governments reluctant to cede the autonomy or self-determination which would otherwise be the natural solution for all racial blocs.

To this I think it must be added that the adoption of absolutism by any member of the family of nations is a matter of concern to its neighbours. An Englishman with his history and traditions behind him, finds it extremely difficult to realise that a great modern nation can place itself absolutely at the mercy of one man, and strip itself bare of all the guarantees against tyranny and misgovernment, all the correctives to human infirmity and failure of judgment, which other nations have evolved through centuries of experience. But this again he would say was a matter for the German people to decide, if it were not that in all questions of international policy they were exposing their neighbours to the same hazards as themselves. History shows nothing quite like the spectacle of all Europe hanging on the lips of Herr Hitler and waiting in suspense while he decides the question of war and peace for them all. A new and incalculable element seems suddenly to have entered into the affairs of nations when not even his own officials and emissaries are able to predict the mind of the "leader."

As one reads on into the literature of both Marxism and Nazism the suspicion grows that much of it represents a combination of philosophers who know nothing about politics and politicians who know less about philosophy. There are times when mystagogue and demagogue seem to be engaged in a deliberate conspiracy to cover obvious facts and purposes with a cloud of murky speculation in which right and wrong, good and evil, generous ideals, and overreaching ambitions, are all dissolved into a nebulous gas. It seems to me probable that when posterity comes to judge the events of these times it will make short work of this mystification, and return to simple judgments based on the ordinary motives of human action.

8

In the year 1936 a traveller who had visited Moscow, Berlin and Rome in successive weeks returned saying that the three Dictatorships were being carried in each country on the shoulders of two million enthusiastic young people, and that this enthusiasm waned rapidly as they advanced in years. It is in any case a fact that the secret of the dictatorships has consisted largely in their appeal to the young. Beyond doubt in all three countries the ideologies have inspired young people with a zeal for service and sacrifice which in itself is altogether admirable and worthy of imitation in the free countries. How far this will survive when the mystical aura with which the new doctrines have been surrounded by skilful propaganda fades into the light of common day, and how far any of the dictators are in a position to found permanent dynasties or to put their institutions on a basis which will dispense with terrorism as the foundation of government are questions which only the future can answer.

But in the meantime these ideologies have closed the door on most of the questions discussed in this book. Whether there is a social contract, whether men have rights, whether there is a law of nature, a law of God, a law of conscience does not concern those who profess these faiths. They proclaim simply that they are a law unto themselves.

CHAPTER XXXVII

RETROSPECT AND PROSPECT

I

AN endless adventure, trial and error all the way, unceasing experiments with intractable material ; liberty and authority, cruelty and humanity, idealism and expediency, reason and emotion, prose and poetry in eternal conflict ; prophecy perpetually baffled by the unexpected and the unpredictable—this, at the end of it all, is the appearance which history presents.

The visibility is bad ; the lights flicker in gloom and fog. But lights there are, and by degrees we become aware of principles struggling to find expression, moral judgments fighting against cynical conclusions, the prophetic soul of the wide world dreaming of things to come. What we are reading is, according to our moods, the march of history, the pageant of great events, the martyrdom of man, the ascent of man, a tale told by an idiot, a tragedy, a comedy, even a farce. It is, above all, unfinished.

Here is one of the principal difficulties of historic judgments. Being without a time-scale we have no idea of a whole against which to measure the significance of any part. Yet the same events must assume quite different proportions according as we consider them to be a large part or only an infinitesimal fraction of the life of man on this planet. Is civilization very old or very young ? Is its recent history the record of an infantile stage, a mature stage, or a decrepit stage ? Are its ups and downs, the rise and fall of its dynasties and empires, just phases of childish disorders, or are they periodic movements in a fore-ordained cycle of growth and decay approaching its conclusion ?

A hundred years ago it was generally believed that the human story began with the creation of Adam and Eve, which was placed about 4000 B.C., and would end at no very remote date with the Second Coming of Christ. We now have reason to suppose that some human or sub-human species was in existence a million years ago ; and if the neolithic age may be regarded as the beginning of organized community life, that may be traced back some twenty or thirty thousand years. Looking into the future, astronomers encourage us to think that the earth will in some fashion be habitable for millions of years.

At this point the chief doubt is whether ice-ages will recur, and if so, whether they will again break the continuity of human life on earth, as they are supposed to have done in the past. One estimate places the present epoch about mid-way between two ice-ages, with fifteen thousand years on either side. This is pure speculation, but if another ice-age comes, the means which science has provided of making tropical regions habitable and the greater mobility ensured by aircraft and modern ocean transport will probably enable human beings to divide their time between different climates, and make far greater spaces available for habitation. If the ice-cap came down on Europe, the centre of civilization would probably shift to Africa or Asia, but with the means we now have of transmitting the records of the past, there would be no such breach between past and present as was caused by the previous ice-ages. Short of some astronomical cataclysm, such as collisions with stars from the outer universe, a sudden increase in solar combustion, or the like, we may think of human existence continuing in some sort into the depths of astronomical time.

Whatever limit we place on it, the extension of time in the thought of the present generation is enormous, and one of its effects is or ought to be to make us take modest views about what are called the teachings of history. The recorded history of civilized man, if in that we include what can be pieced together from the earliest inscriptions or remains of city life in Mesopotamia, Egypt, or elsewhere, covers at most some 7000 years. Almost everywhere the digger strikes the Stone age in the seventh millennium backward from the present time. A hundred men living seventy years each, one after another, would stretch over the whole period of civilized life. The backward limit may be extended a little by further exploration, but that would be of small importance. Whether the period is seven thousand, eight thousand, or ten thousand years, it is but a drop in the ocean of time which science contemplates as awaiting the evolution of mankind on the earth. If we bear this thought in mind, we shall take a cool estimate of the claims of all theorists to have discovered from this brief experience laws or cycles determining the fate of man and the future course of his history. Judged as veridical predictions, they are worth about as much as the horoscopes of mediæval astrologers.

2

But while keeping this sobering thought in mind, can we also resist the discouraging idea that human effort goes to waste in some gulf of eternity? Each generation appears to have thought of its own period as in some sense a culminating point in existence, and to have regarded its past as immemorial antiquity. Yet, looking back, we see all the periods and all the antiquities in a historical perspective which diminishes the spaces between them as they approach their vanishing-point on the horizon. It is natural to ask, are we too in our generation to pass into this dwindling perspective and so to our vanishing-point on the horizon? Somehow the historian has to keep the balance between the conceit which tempts him to suppose that he can deduce the laws of all time and all existence from a survey of the relatively brief past, and the pessimism which concludes that human endeavour in the brief space of mortal life can be of no avail against the immensities and eternities.

I think we are helped in this respect if we try to restore the spaces of the vanishing perspective and see them in their relation to one another—see them, so to speak, in the flat, as on a map. Looking at such a map we see that the whole Christian era occupies not much more than half the space occupied by the history of ancient Egypt. We understand what is meant when it is said that to Moses and the Israelites in Egypt the Pyramids were as much ancient monuments as the Parthenon is to us. Similarly, the people of Crete lived a vivid and highly civilized life—of which we know nothing except what the spade of the digger has revealed to us—for a longer period than from the Norman Conquest to the present time. Again, in our own history-books the Roman occupation of Britain passes in a flash, yet on our map it fills as large a space as from the accession of James I to the present time. A British-Roman living in the middle of the fourth century A.D., and enjoying the settled life of town, villa, or village as it was at that time could not have conceived of the country having any future except as a Roman dominion. He would have measured past and present by events which have utterly vanished from our ken. Many of the older villas would have been as venerable to him as Elizabethan manors are to us ; temples and public buildings would have been grey and weather-worn ; towns would have had their history and local traditions, their rolls of honour and public service going back over centuries. It would not have occurred to him that all this was presently to be swept away by a returning tide of barbarism, still less that his little capital by the Thames was one day to be the greatest city in the world, and the centre of an Empire on which the sun never set.

A few chance measurements of this kind help to give us an idea both of duration and of transience as measured in history. In the backward view whole generations, even centuries seem to be swept past like straws on the rolling stream ; but each thinks of itself as steering a stately course in a great ship. There is no inconsistency between the two thoughts. Our share in the great movement may be undiscoverable, but for us it has intrinsic value which is not diminished by the immensity of the whole. Science and religion join hands in teaching that life has an end outside itself and beyond the conscious thought of any living generation, whether of individuals or States. But this does not prevent us from holding that each has a value in itself and for itself which may fitly be called eternal. Are not two sparrows sold for a farthing ? and one of them shall not fall on the ground without your Father.

3

Is there any reality in the idea of progress ? Students, like the late Professor Bury, have traced it back to political theorists and found it in the works of French writers—Bodin, Le Roy, Fontenelle, the Abbé de Saint-Pierre, Condorcet, etc.—and so come to the conclusion that it is mainly a legacy from French writers who handed it on to the English Utilitarians. I cannot think that the truth on this matter is to be found within the covers of any books. The denial of progress is not so much cynical as irrational. If, with all its imperfections, life as it is now is not in some intelligible sense better than the life of cave men, the words "better" and "worse" have no meaning. To make pessimism about progress even plausible we have to blot out all that human ingenuity has added to the conveniences and amenities of life, all that science has achieved in the conquest of nature, all that imagination has created in art and literature, all that thinking has contributed to the enlargement of men's minds and their ideas of God and the universe. There is no doubt about the advance from savagery to the present relative state of civilization and no ground for doubting that the same process will continue. Each age has its characteristic virtues and vices, its special forms of reaction and relapse. As the possibilities of good are enlarged so are the possibilities of evil, but over any long space of time the stream of tendency is towards what we understand by progress.

The essence of the idea of progress is that there should be some standard of comparison by which an existing age judges its own achievements and shortcomings. This is scarcely ever wanting in the records of the past. As we look back there seems to have been almost no time when the greater societies did not compare themselves with some ideal outside themselves, something to which they could attain, or from which they might fall away, but which, in either case, served as a lamp to their feet like the explicit modern idea of progress. The Jew thinks of the coming of the Messiah, the Greek of the ideal republic, the Roman of the reign of Saturn, the Christian of the Civitas Dei and the Holy Roman Empire, each in his own way seeking the "pattern laid up in heaven" to which an imperfect humanity can only aspire. So long as a community keeps before itself the vision of a more perfect State it matters little whether it conceives it as something to be attained in the future or something from which it has fallen away and may with effort recover. In either case, there is the same dynamic element that we find in the modern idea of progress.[1]

History only becomes intelligible if we think of human kind as being driven forward by some such inner impulse. But the forward movement, as we are often told, is a zig-zag and the oscillations accom-

---

[1] See on this subject the author's *Public Life*, II, pp. 203-4.

panying it are at times so severe as to threaten an almost complete severance of the links with the past. In the last 150 years science has made a greater breach with the past than is recorded in any previous period of the world's history. In certain respects we are farther removed from the eighteenth century than that century was from Greek and Roman times. There are no analogies in history to the great industrialised nations of modern times. There has never been anything like the power of destroying and intimidating now in the hands of the great Governments.

Romantics are heard sighing for an idealized past, yet, if they were actually faced with it, very few would deliberately choose to go back to the " quiet " life before the machine age and cut themselves off from the new things and the new thoughts—the varied and exciting jostle of conveniences, nuisances, pleasures, pains, and deformities—with which science and inventiveness have enriched and defaced the life of men in the subsequent years. With all the trouble and anxiety of these times, it is still true to say that for immense numbers life has been happier and more varied and interesting than ever before in the world's history. Not that they have lived too late, but that they have lived too soon is, I rather think, the complaint of the keener spirits in these days. They are conscious that they have fallen upon a period which like no other in the history of the world has been swept by an avalanche of new things which it has not had time to assimilate and digest.

Such an age asks more urgently than any other, Is there anything it can learn from the so-different past, any analogy between the great modern industrial nations and the little city-states on which the Greek philosophers, supposed to be the masters of political science, based their theories? Between the Hebrew belief that righteousness exalteth a nation and the modern dictator's conviction that physical force is the measure of national greatness ? Or is the breach with the past such that we must build again from the beginning—invert all the values and virtues, as our forbears had learnt to regard them, conceive the object of the State to be not the good life in peace, but the dangerous and aggressive life in war, not the reconciliation of different classes and interests, but the extermination of one class by another, not the sober, godly, and righteous life of the Christian gospels, but the struggling of noble savages in a resuscitated paganism ? In some countries we seem to see civilization suddenly turning upon itself, or what it had supposed to be itself, and throwing on the scrap-heap everything that history had regarded as its achievements.

4

We shall not argue our way out of the present confusion. If a prediction may be hazarded, it is that the present phase will be short as history counts duration. So feverish a departure from the normal life as we are witnessing in these times cannot be greatly prolonged, whether it ends by eruption or exhaustion. In the meantime we may usefully ask ourselves what is happening to certain things that we greatly value, and by what dangers they are chiefly threatened.

Liberty, for example, which from the age of the Greeks till now nearly all mankind had agreed to be one of the chief ingredients of happiness. In past times men of all political opinions have joined in the praise of liberty. Hear Cicero :

Other nations may submit to slavery. Liberty is the inalienable possession of the Roman people.

Hear Bolingbroke :

Now the greatest good of a people is their liberty . . . liberty is to the collective body what health is to every individual body. Without health no pleasure can be tasted by man ; without liberty no happiness can be enjoyed by society.

So also said Dante :

Through freedom we have our happiness here as men, through it our happiness elsewhere as gods.

So also Rousseau :

To renounce liberty is to renounce being a man, to surrender the rights of humanity and even its duties.

It is not the intellectual or theoretical attacks on liberty which are the principal danger. These will only avail among nations which have never enjoyed liberty. What has to be feared by others is the impulse of events which may drive the free nations out of their course in the search for security and efficiency in a world living in fear of war.

Abraham Lincoln said, on the eve of the American Civil War, that the United States could not be " half slave and half free." Whether that condition is possible in Europe is one of the questions which confronts us to-day. Can there be the open discussion of policy, as the free States demand, if diplomacy is manœuvring for position in the next war, and Governments rely on the element of surprise to take their opponents at a disadvantage ? Can party politics and a free press revealing all the internal differences and difficulties in the free countries continue unchecked if an absolute unity is imposed by discipline on the unfree ? Can the concentration of wealth and human effort upon preparations for war continue without destroying all efforts to develop the free life of peace and converting nations into armed camps with the appropriate military discipline ? Is there any economic system, by whatever name it is called, which will stand the strain ? Then finally, can any great war take place under modern conditions that would not end in an anarchy in which freedom would perish in the necessity of keeping order ?

In the meantime we see freedom threatened simultaneously on a different but converging line. That is by Socialists and others who, with the benevolent intention of promoting social well-being, advocate the ordering of life in all its principal activities by Governments instead of by individuals in competition with one another. The word " planning " is now in favour with all parties in Great Britain, but not much thought has yet been given to the changes in the political structure which it implies. In the extreme form in which it is prac- tised in the totalitarian States, whether Communist or Fascist, it is necessarily fatal to liberty. All these States have extinguished the liberties of the proletariat at the same time that they have brought the bourgeois and capitalist under their control. The free workman with his independent trade union passes from the scene at the same moment as the private employer. The motive of private profit having been eliminated, discipline and terrorism take its place.

Socialism and militarism more and more join hands as this situation develops. The plans advocated by one party for military purposes are almost identical with the plans advocated by another for social purposes. The militarized State and the socialized State are in the end one and the same, and both are " totalitarian."

Ultimately the same question may present itself in world politics. Can the world be half free and half despotic ? Can free and loose federations, such as the British Commonwealth, in which each unit cherishes its own sovereignty and is free to take its own course in foreign policy and in war, stand up against the despotically controlled empires in which the word of command comes from one centre ?

To answer these questions is beyond the scope of this book. I will only say briefly that in my view civilisation in any worthy sense of the word is unthinkable without liberty, but that there are certain respects in which the free countries may have to modify the technique of their governments in order to place themselves on even terms with the unfree. No distaste for Communist or Fascist ideologies should prevent us from profiting by what is admirable in their example of self-dedication to ideals. Some part of it might with advantage be adapted to willing service in the free States.

By gradual adjustments, a state of society may be reached in which the conflict between the two principles of liberty and authority will disappear and the freedom of individual enterprise be reconciled with the provision of a good standard of life for all citizens. The social services and the various forms of insurance now adopted by the free countries point the way in this direction. Eventually the economic structure may take on new forms which cannot be predicted at the present time, but beside which our present beginnings may seem as obsolete as mediæval feudalism does to us. Industrialism is a recent growth ; from its beginnings till now it has been in an unceasing condition of change and experiment ; science is perpetually offering it new problems for which it has to find solutions. No limit need be placed on speculation about its possible developments, but in the light of history it is impossible to think of progress if liberty is extinguished.

The question of liberty comprehends all the other questions commonly raised about the structure of government. Democracy and parliamentary government are based on freedom ; they are the instruments of a free people, and have no use or function in the States in which liberty has been extinguished.

5

As we look out on the world to-day, the importance of the emotional and psychological factors is more and more brought home to us. In the totalitarian States the appeal of the leaders is deliberately to feeling and not to reflection. The citizen is to " think with his blood " and not with his brain, which means that he is not to think at all, as the free citizen counts thinking. By incessant propaganda, physical drill, military spectacles, and free entertainments, the emotional pitch is raised to the point at which there is the least temptation to employ the intellect in thinking. Vast audiences listen in a " semi-hypnotic " state to rhetoric which would be thought insane if addressed to a similar number of free people. One of the chief difficulties of conducting foreign policy between the dictatorships and the democracies is that one side is using the language of emotion and the other appealing or endeavouring to appeal to reason.

Similarly most of the questions called economic are in large part emotional. All economic analysis and experience is proving that material progress can only be achieved by increase of production, and that, even if it were possible, the redistribution of any existing wealth would add very little to the average of incomes. The unequal distribution of this existing wealth is, nevertheless, a great evil, since it creates a sense of injustice which immensely increases the difficulty of government. If it has no other existence, the class-war rages furiously in the brains of keen and ambitious young men who see their way blocked by poverty and unemployment, while the sons of the favoured few are wasting wealth on sport and pleasure. They are a minority no doubt, but the kind of minority which counts, and it is a serious loss that they should be absorbed in bitter and destructive thoughts instead of being enlisted in a positive forward movement. The cry of frustrated youth for leadership—leadership in any direction, even into the abyss—is one of the great facts in the world to-day ; and, so far, the success of the dictatorships, whether Communist or Fascist, has lain largely in their emotional response to it. One of the problems before the Free States is whether they can be equally successful in appealing to reason.

The same intangible psychological factor meets us at every turn when we come to the question of war and conquest. It can be proved to demonstration that war must be destructive even to the victors ; that conquests are liabilities rather than assets ; that colonies are of no economic value to the Powers possessing them ; but all this makes no impression upon the militant spirit. Merely to be uppermost, whatever the material profit or loss, is still the consuming desire of immense numbers. The satisfaction of pride in winning and the hurt to pride in losing a war, the loss of prestige in lowering a flag or losing a colony, the defiant doctrine of race and blood, the desire for revenge —these are motives which override all homespun arguments about economic loss or gain. The peace movement for the time being has been reduced to the hope that the piling up of destructive armaments may deter any peace-breaker from making the terrible experiment of putting them to use. It is, I believe, certain that, whether with or without such an experiment, war will one day pass into desuetude through a renewal of the humanitarian spirit which will place it outside the code of tolerable human behaviour. But at a time when militarists sing the praises of war and pacifists declare it to be disgraceful not to fight for peace, it must be admitted that the prospect is overcast.

On any purely rational principles, it would seem that the preservation of life was the supreme object of individuals and governments. If that were sincerely believed and acted upon, the business of government would be immensely simplified. There would be few crimes and no wars ; armies would be unnecessary and police a luxury. But there is apparently nothing about which mankind or its rulers are less convinced. Contempt for death is still the most heroic and the most dangerous of human qualities. Men kill without mercy when their blood is up ; they risk their lives without a thought for a flag, or a ribbon, a lost cause, to rescue the drowning, to fetch a child from a burning house, or a comrade from a fiery pit, to scale a mountain, to break a record.

Any theory which assumes man to be a rational, self-regarding animal fails to reckon with that part of him which is mystical, romantic, chivalrous, cruel, and savage. When all has been said that ought to be about the material and economic factors that enter into the lives of nations it is still the dominance of ideas that is indelibly printed on their history.

6

It would be strange if, after a century and a half in which life has been revolutionized in all its outward aspects, the religious and moral foundations remained unshaken. The evidence, I think, is conclusive that when all allowance is made for the immemorial complaint of the old about the behaviour of the young, the present generation is witnessing a change of opinion about religion and morals which has been more rapid and is more subversive than any of which we have records in recent history.

This is commonly ascribed to the upheaval caused by the war, but the ground had been prepared long before the war. All through the nineteenth century science had progressively undermined what till then had been accepted without question as religious truth except by a small minority of sceptics. Even those who count themselves orthodox have " restated " their doctrine in a form in which it would have been rejected as dangerous free-thought by the orthodox of a hundred years ago. The most rigid Churchman can no longer accept the articles of religion in the sense in which they were everywhere accepted by adherents of the Church up to about seventy years ago.

The nineteenth century continued to live on the thoughts and traditions which it had inherited from the piety of previous generations, and it was only by degrees that it became aware that the foundations were slipping. But the orthodox who predicted that, if the religious structure gave way, the moral would be in danger, were undoubtedly right. Then, accompanying or following the moral upheaval, came physical and mechanical changes without parallel in former times, immense increases of population, the greatest of all wars, and following it an unceasing struggle between those who were temporarily victors and those who were temporarily vanquished, the one to maintain their position and the other to retrieve their losses. In the war and its aftermath all the passions have been unloosed. Arrogance on the part of the victors, desire for vengeance on the part of the vanquished, well-justified fears in all countries have overridden the counsels of wisdom and justice and frustrated the hope of a new order through the League of Nations. In this struggle most of the old lights have been extinguished, and men are heard passionately asserting that all methods are lawful which will enable them to get back on an enemy or assert their strength over the weak. Strength and justice seem to be in a perpetual opposition. The weak cannot obtain justice while they are weak or do justice when they become strong.

The consequences are plain to see, and though we keep our eye upon the distant lights we have to look the present facts full in the face. In a large part of the world we are faced with a denial not merely of religious dogmas but of the whole body of human experience and its judgments of what is right and what is wrong. Methods of tyranny which the Greeks thought hateful and which have been condemned by civilized people in all ages are now said to be the necessary methods of what is called the " new civilization." The defence of political dogmas is said to justify the worst excesses of mediæval religious intolerance. The growth of a sense of humanity, which the nineteenth century regarded as one of the principal signs of progress, is condemned as unworthy of a virile people. War instead of peace, both the class-war and the international war, is proclaimed as the goal and object of virtuous endeavour. Violence and intimidation practised without distinction on belligerents and civilians and without mercy for women and children is the special feature of modern war ; modern governments deride Montesquieu's suggestion that they should do as little harm as possible to those whom they conquer.

All this is true and no facile optimism can make light of it. And yet—*Deus dabit his quoque finem.* Torrents of new wine have been poured into the old bottles and " the wine runneth out and the bottles perish." But—let us read on—" they put new wine into new bottles and both are preserved." Our present experience will count hereafter as a stage in the education of mankind leading on to new discoveries in the art of government. This is not speculation, it is certainty. There is a historic spirit, not, like Hegel's, justifying cruelty and wickedness if practised by blond beasts or self-appointed heroes, but warning that all these things will be brought into judgment. For all that the German philosopher may have said, " the litany of private virtues— modesty, humility, philanthropy, and forbearance " will unceasingly be raised against Governments and political leaders claiming to be exempt from the moral judgments universally acknowledged by men in their dealings with one another. The great experience of all ages and all lands which has led man to form these judgments and given them the sanction of religion and conscience will not be extinguished in one generation. Religion may change its forms and dogmas become outworn, but a destructive criticism will not prevail against the instincts of the whole human race about the conduct which distinguishes it from the brutes.

A chief part of the process of civilization has been a struggle to bring the public morality into conformity with what men hold to be right and just in their dealings with one another, or, if religious language may be used, in conformity with the golden rule and the law of love. So it will continue. We may admit that the judgment of one age upon historic wrong and right has often been reversed by another, and that in the imperfect conditions of human life it often seems impossible to do right to one class or one nation without doing injustice to another. The quest of justice is beset by endless pitfalls. But if we infer from this that there are no standards of right and wrong, no reality to which the human effort corresponds, we are in literal truth in the state which the Apostle described as " without God in the world."

Three-fourths of all history is the story of the entanglement of religion and politics. In the beginning king and priest are identical and government is charged with the administration of temples and religious rites. Like the Pharaohs before him, the Roman Emperor is both divinity and high-priest ; the test of orthodoxy in politics and in religion is willingness to burn incense at his shrine. In the next stage government and religion are in a partnership in which each tries to master the other and neither succeeds. The struggle continues in our own modern and scientific age. One State derides God ; another seeks to remake God in its own image ; a third invents a scientific formula and proposes it as a substitute for God. Lenin said that every revolution needed a theory ; it is not less true that every State has needed and still needs a religion. To abolish, to annex, or to transform religion has been the effort of all the advanced Governments of our own time. None can keep God out of its account.

The Communist who abolishes the religious heaven finds himself under the necessity of deifying his leaders and inventing a proletariat millennium which is more mythical than any religious myth.

All who write about the State or reflect upon the art of government are under the same necessity. To make sense of their story, they must discover some thread of purpose running through it. However stained with crime and folly it may be, it is the story of the ascent of man from savage beginnings to an imperfect civilization. Through all backslidings we see man clinging to the belief that right and wrong, truth and falsehood are realities which correspond to the divine nature of things. Why alone of the animals he has this belief, what impulse set him on a road so different from that followed by other living creatures, whence comes the inner prompting which he calls conscience or his unquenchable instinct for admiring, hoping, loving—these are mysteries which, when science and philosophy have said their last word, can only be penetrated by the eye of faith. It is impossible to believe that any Government or system of government which, on the plea of public necessity, sets itself against the great human judgments of what is right and wrong between men and men will be of long duration.

INDEX

373